Getting Sauced

Praise for
GETTING SAUCED

Getting Sauced is one big heaping dish of deliciousness. Reading it was like sitting down to dinner with Karen. You know there's going to be some crazy story about her family, you know you're going to laugh, you know at some point she's going to say something that touches you deep in your soul, and of course, you know you can't end the night without discussing where you're going to eat next.

—EMERIL LAGASSE, chef, restaurateur, author, and TV host

Getting Sauced is an extremely entertaining account of food television's explosive coming of age, written from the perspective of one of the era's key behind-the-scenes players. And bonus! There's a tasty recipe at the end of every chapter.

—SARA MOULTON, host "Sara's Weeknight Meals"
on public television

Wow! *Getting Sauced* reminds me how crazy those early days were at Food Network. It's a wonderful glimpse of where all the magic began as we simply rolled cameras and just were cooks doing what we do. It shows you our lives back then.

—SUSAN FENIGER, James Beard award-winning chef,
restaurateur, and cookbook author

If you want to know what it was like to be on the ground floor when Food Network began … stay tuned! Karen Katz was a creator, innovator and culinary magician with Emeril and other FN chefs. *Getting Sauced* is one very satisfying dish.

—MARC SUMMERS, TV host, executive producer, performer

Getting Sauced takes readers on an unforgettable culinary adventure, sprinkled with behind-the-scenes tales and seasoned with a dash of love and enthusiasm, making it a must-read for Food Network fans and food lovers too!

—GEORGE DURAN, chef, author, TV Host

What fun it is to go with Karen Katz behind the scenes of the iconic *Emeril Live*! (And I was there!) Karen, the consummate professional gives the reader a peek into her super strengths as a leader, genius creator, fab collaborator, and exec producer extraordinaire. And by the way, she's a blast as a work partner, road warrior companion, and eating and drinking buddy. And her paella slaps!

—HEIDI DIAMOND, executive, board member, board advisor, Angel Investor

Reading *Getting Sauced* is akin to settling in for a long, G&T-fuelled chit-chat with KK in person. I can hear her giggle-laced New York accent describe each TV & travel adventure with glee. And I can literally taste the cocktails & meals she so vividly recollects. From a woman with two kitchens: one dedicated solely to making desserts, this book is a delicious cackle of a journey. I loved it!

—LOUISE ROE, founder & creative director, Sharland England

When Karen Katz joined the Food Network in 1998, she produced shows from a soon-to-be legendary generation of culinary celebrities. In *Getting Sauced*, Karen shares how the network's earliest hits came to be and set a standard for culinary television for decades. I loved the trip down memory lane, the family stories and the recipes.

—CHRISTINA GRDOVIC, former publisher *Food & Wine*

GETTING SAUCED

How I Learned Everything I Know
about Food from Working in TV

KAREN S. KATZ

NEW YORK

LONDON • NASHVILLE • MELBOURNE • VANCOUVER

GETTING SAUCED

How I Learned Everything I Know About Food from Working in TV

Published in New York, New York, by Morgan James Publishing. Morgan James is a trademark of Morgan James, LLC. www.MorganJamesPublishing.com

Proudly distributed by Publishers Group West®

A **FREE** ebook edition is available for you
or a friend with the purchase of this print book.

CLEARLY SIGN YOUR NAME ABOVE

Instructions to claim your free ebook edition:
1. Visit MorganJamesBOGO.com
2. Sign your name CLEARLY in the space above
3. Complete the form and submit a photo of this entire page
4. You or your friend can download the ebook to your preferred device

ISBN 9781636983103 paperback
ISBN 9781636983110 ebook
Library of Congress Control Number:
2023944803

Cover Design by:
Debbie Berne
debbiebernedesign.com

Interior Design by:
Chris Treccani
www.3dogcreative.net

Morgan James is a proud partner of Habitat for Humanity Peninsula and Greater Williamsburg. Partners in building since 2006.

Get involved today! Visit: www.morgan-james-publishing.com/giving-back

For Daniel, who taught me how to savor each bite.

"*After a good dinner one can forgive anybody, even one's own relatives.*"
—Oscar Wilde, *A Woman of No Importance*

"*It seems to me that our three basic needs, for food and security and love, are so mixed and mingled and entwined that we cannot straightly think of one without the others. So it happens that when I write of hunger, I am really writing about love and the hunger for it, and warmth and the love of it and the hunger for it … and then the warmth and richness and fine reality of hunger satisfied … and it is all one.*"
—M.F.K. Fisher, *The Art of Eating*

Table of Contents

Preface

It's 5:30 a.m., and I'm standing over a burning hot *imu* pit, an underground steamer being prepped to hold a 250-pound pig. Two Hawaiian workers, the size of sumo wrestlers, are stoking hot lava rocks in preparation for a big luau, just as their ancestors have done for generations. The sun is just rising over the Pacific, soft flicks of morning light dance over the water. I can taste the salt coming in with the ocean breeze. I breathe deeply, suspecting that this will be my only moment of peace in paradise.

Breaking my reverie, one of the burly men taps my shoulder and says, "It's time."

My blood pressure starts to rise and my jaw clenches as I scan the area anxiously wondering, "Where on earth is everyone?"

Just at that moment, the production truck sputters into the parking lot with my crew in tow. They know they are late and they know I won't be happy. They burst out of the van filled with excuses, coffee cups in hand.

"Listen. 5:30 means 5:30—not 6:00! You've already missed the lava rocks going in and now they need to lay down the *ti* leaves. The whole point of coming to Hawaii was to capture this luau. You think this is supposed to be a vacation?!" I shriek.

As my shamed Keystone Cop-crew scrambles to set up this shoot, tossing their video cases and cables out of the back of the van, I realize that for all the fun I'm having, I might as well be in Newark.

It sure sounds glamorous from the outside looking in: an all-expenses-paid trip to Hawaii with America's most popular chef, eating and cooking our way across the islands. But here's the catch—and there's always a catch—I have to shoot three broadcast hours of mouth-watering, hunger-provoking food porn on three different islands at fifteen locations in six days. And just to make matters worse, both my crew and my star resent that we're here in Hawaii and that I am actually making them work.

There have been days like this. There have been many. And there have been some good ones too. It's the good days that sustain me. I've been a television producer my entire career. I've seen actors behave as if they were reliving their terrible twos. I have nearly had a live show shut down by a bribe-seeking union foreman. I've run up Sixth Avenue in the middle of gridlocked traffic from 14th Street to 34th Street, the final show master in my hand, with only four minutes left before it's supposed to hit the air. The stress and chaos are the only things consistent about the work I do. The rush comes from being assigned an impossible task and making it possible.

That was before the Food Network called asking me to be the executive producer for a hot new chef out of New Orleans. His name is Emeril Lagasse. I think to myself, "Why not? Cooking has got to be better than this. I'll give it a shot for six months."

Those six months turned into thirteen years and over 1,500 hours of food television. Eyewitness to the scrappy early days of the fledgling TV Food Network, I was one of the many that worked on the transformation of cooking shows from sleepy on-air instructional manuals to glitzy must-watch TV. And during that time, I came to understand why the food we eat is so much more than just something to fuel our bodies. It's about love and comfort and pleasure. Whether it's searching the local farmer's market for the sweetest heirloom tomatoes with just the right amount of acidity or learning how to cook *à la minute*, almost everything I know about food, I learned from TV.

I've had the pleasure—and sometimes trauma—of witnessing some of the country's top chefs in action from a front-row seat. It has made for some vivid storytelling at parties (and perversely made me a popular guest). Some of these culinary stars may not remember me, but I remember them. I remember their precise insight into the perfect ingredients, their ability to share their passion to the point of contagion, and most importantly, their generosity of spirit—give or take an egomaniacal tantrum or two. All of them, in their own way, have taught me not only how to cook, but how to cook with love and enthusiasm.

But as much as they may have influenced my personal culinary techniques, I have to give credit to the family and friends early in my life who truly inspired my zeal for food. From learning how to make my Nana's apple pie to realizing there's no point in ever making my mother's Lipton Onion Soup semi-homemade glazed brisket, most of my strongest memories have food as my co-star. It has shaped me, in more ways than one.

My home today has two kitchens. No, not one for milk and one for meat like some of my ancestors, but one for sweets and one for savory foods. I have a thermostat-controlled wine cooler, and a culinary library with over 500 books. My next-door neighbor and I have been trying to perfect all five mother sauces by cross-referencing my copy of Julia Child's *Mastering the Art of French Cooking* with his copy of The Culinary Institute of America's *The Professional Chef*. We're up to velouté. The tomato and espagnole were big hits, but we still have to conquer hollandaise and béchamel. My husband and I have gotten so much praise for our own cooking that we are no longer invited to our friends' dinner parties for their fear of disappointing us. (My specialty is grilled white pizza with a mélange of mushrooms, shallots, garlic and pancetta beneath a bed of taleggio cheese finished with a drizzle of truffle oil.) When I go into a restaurant "announced," the red carpet is rolled out, and after lunch or dinner I roll out with a sated smile, extended stomach, and Tums standing by in my purse. It's been a long journey from a childhood sponsored by

Kraft and Mrs. Paul's to three-star Michelin dinners. I can honestly say that I've lived a good life very much thanks to food. If only I could dig an *imu* pit in Brooklyn, I could die a happy woman.

My culinary awakening is forever entangled with the evolution of food television becoming our national comfort pastime. I like to think we grew up together, learning from our mistakes and trying to push the boundaries of how we think about food and cooking. At times my story might seem a little half-baked, sometimes a bit overdone, but at its heart, it's one deep dish of a delicious journey.

Chapter One

WHAT DO I KNOW ABOUT FOOD?

What do you mean, there are no messages?" I shout. "We've been away for three weeks!"

"I don't know," replies my husband, Dan. "Susan must have done something to the machine."

We had asked our friend to keep an eye on our place while we were away for our tenth anniversary trip. What we forgot is that Susan has this knack of sabotaging pretty much any piece of technical equipment just by looking at it. I think her kinetic energy sends out negative impulses to all things electronic. For two people who are freelancers like Dan and me, dependent upon the kindness of contacts, this is a very bad thing. We reset the machine and hope whoever might have called, will call back.

"Why didn't you answer my calls?" Eileen asks. "I've been trying to reach you for days. I almost gave up."

"I'm so sorry, I've been out of town and my machine wasn't working," I apologize. "How are you?"

"All good. It's been a long time," she says. "I wasn't sure you'd remember me."

Remember her? Of course I remember her. I'm only surprised that she remembers me. Eileen Opatut is now the head of programming for a new channel, the TV Food Network. We met about fifteen years ago, when she was a development executive at Nickelodeon. Back then, my boss was trying to pitch her a show idea that she had no interest in. I was along for the meeting as his "development person," a title that was a tad inflated, considering I was really just his secretary.

Over the years I've been re-introduced to her many, many times at industry events and other professional occasions. She's hard to miss with her big round glasses, untamable brown hair, infectious laugh, and round physique. The interesting thing about Eileen is that you can bump into her twenty times before it actually registers in her mind. I used to think that she was looking down her nose at me, but in fact, as I came to know her, I realized that she wasn't looking at all. Eileen is all smarts with genius running around screaming in her head. She has a nose for talent and for putting the right people together. She just has trouble remembering them.

"I was watching the *Big Help* on Nickelodeon with my daughter, and I saw your name go by in the credits, and then I realized you'd be perfect."

"Perfect for what?"

"Have you heard of the chef, Emeril Lagasse?"

"Emerald?"

"No *Emeril*. He's from New Orleans and he's been on our network for a couple of years. He's got sort of a cult following."

"Oh yes, yes," I lie. "I've seen him."

"Well, we've started doing a show with him in front of a studio audience, but we've been having a lot of problems getting our team up to speed. Most of our staff comes from the world of food magazines and cookbooks and they don't have a ton of TV experience."

"But I'm just a home cook. I don't really know anything about serious food, although I am a professional eater."

"That's OK," she laughs. "We've got plenty of culinary people here. I need someone like you who can be creative, knows TV, and manage a team. We need a strong executive producer."

As she's talking, I'm thinking, who is this guy Emeril?

"Well, I'd be happy to meet with him," I say.

"Great, I'll set something up."

As I hang up the phone, I wonder if a cooking show might be the kiss of death for my career. Julia Child and Graham Kerr have been the most popular cooking shows for years and aren't exactly popular with anyone under fifty. With shows like *Three Dog Bakery* and *How to Boil Water*, Food Network is just a little disrupter cable network with shows that look more like infomercials or *Saturday Night Live* parodies than they do real TV. I don't even know if they have the budgets to make them look like they have any production value. I really have to think about this. Why would they want someone who knows practically nothing about food?

I grew up in a home where my mother's idea of spaghetti and meatballs was rounding some unseasoned chop meat into balls and dumping them into a pot of store-bought sauce, bringing them up to boil, and then ladling them over pasta that hadn't been completely drained of water. That wasn't how Mrs. Minchillo, my friend Desi's mom did it. She was born in Italy and brought all of her family recipes with her. She seasoned the meat, fried the meatballs in oil, and used her homegrown tomatoes and basil, allowing the sauce to simmer for hours on her stove. She even made her own pasta on an old wooden board that her mother had used and her mother before her.

But in our house, my mom was too busy being an abstract painter. She was totally obsessed with her artwork. She barely slept, getting up in the middle of the night, awakened by ideas and rushing down to her studio to execute them on canvas. She poured every ounce of her energy into her artwork, which meant not a lot of pouring was going on in the kitchen.

Except for concrete. It was handy that Dad was a contractor because he blew out the back wall of the house to enlarge the kitchen and added an extra room that became Mom's studio.

I once overheard Mom on the phone with one of her artsy friends say, "I don't think Bernie has a clue, but it's like I'm in a tug-of-war between these two rooms. I'm drawn into the studio as if there's a magnet pulling me, while at the same time it's like the family has hogtied me and is trying to pull me back out. I don't know what I'd do if I couldn't paint. I think it's saving my soul."

I didn't realize her soul needed saving, but I guess growing up in a middle-class Brooklyn family in the nineteen forties didn't offer her a ton of opportunities besides getting married and having babies. And so she did. By the time she was twenty-seven, she had a responsible husband, three kids and a split-level house in the suburbs. It was supposed to have been ideal. In reality, it was stifling. June Cleaver was never her true destiny.

My dad instinctively understood that supporting what she wanted to do was important. Not that he was a particularly sensitive guy, but he adored her and knew better than to try to break her will. I think he wished she could be happy being "just" a wife and mother but realized early on that it was a lost cause. He was a tough, street-smart, first-generation kid from Brooklyn who worked hard for everything he had. Nothing was ever given to him. No one ever asked if HE was happy. However, dinner was always on the table when he came home. Asking for it to be tasty was pushing things.

I think my mom managed to slog through 365 days of meals by getting incredibly regimented so that she could go on autopilot. After all, if her creative energy was being spent in her studio, why waste any of it on cooking? So she created a system that was responsible and simple and predictable. She set a weekly menu for herself—and for the rest of us. As pathetic as it sounds, this was the foundation of my culinary experiences:

Monday—Tuna Noodle Casserole. Ah, there's nothing like this good old-fashioned American classic with a little help from Kraft Mac & Cheese, Campbell's Mushroom Soup, Bumble Bee tuna, and Jolly Green Giant peas. What could possibly be better? True, you have to open the cans, boil some water to make the noodles, dump, stir, and bake. It was a dream recipe for a busy mom. Not that my brothers and I complained. We *loved* it. What made it even more special was how Mom managed to burn the edges ever so slightly. Some of my friends' moms made it just from the box and didn't "tunafy" it. The "tunafying" took out a lot of the orange color and made the casserole turn a lovely shade of beige.

Tuesday—Mrs. Paul's Fish Sticks. Mrs. Paul's had become such a regular at our table that we should really have called her by her first name. My brothers and I usually stacked the fish sticks on top of each other to make little huts. That's where we hid the canned peas that none of us wanted to eat.

"Stop playing with your food!" Mom would shout out from the studio.

How she could see us from there, I'll never know. I'm convinced she had X-Ray vision. This was absolutely the only way Mom could get us to eat fish, except for canned tuna, but that wasn't saying much. The directions were simple: open the box, lay the crunchy covered cod cakes on a pan, and bake. True, it was fake fry, but I doubt my mother made it because she was concerned about our cholesterol. Mom never fried food. It was a mess to clean up, and it stank up the house. When not in the studio, she was impressively fastidious. People always said, "You can eat off her floor." Not that you would have wanted to. Her food would not have tasted any better down there. There was not a crumb to be found anywhere in the house. She would have had to actually bake something to make a crumb.

Wednesday—Steak Night. Dad was a real meat-and-potatoes guy. Eating steak every night was his idea of heaven. Mom always served his steak well done, even though that's not how he liked it. When Mom was in the kitchen, the concept of medium or medium rare was unfortunately not an option. She was far from chintzy when it came to Dad's steaks. She went to a well-known local butcher and restaurant—Manero's Steakhouse on Jericho Turnpike—to buy him beautifully marbled sirloins. Then she returned home and broiled them until they were charred and leathery. It was her form of rebellion.

Thinking he might be able to salvage his steaks, Dad installed a natural gas grill in the backyard. Oddly enough, Mom decided to use that grill all-year-round. Even in the dead of winter, she was out there with her boots, gloves and winter coat, cooking the crap out of those poor steaks.

"Barbara. You've been out there for twenty minutes. You're gonna pulverize that poor steak. What did it ever do to you?" Dad shouted out the back door.

"If you don't like it, then cook your own freakin' steak next time."

Thursday—Roast Chicken. To this day, Mom thinks she makes a good roast chicken. Truthfully, it's not awful, but she does have this thing about well-done meats. First, she seasons the bird with a smattering of salt, pepper and paprika—the only three spices in her cabinet—then she places small pats of margarine around the bird, and roasts it at 375 degrees F—for hours.

"Now here's my secret sauce," she would instruct me. "Take one package of Lipton's Onion Soup Mix and one can of frozen orange juice. Heat it up so that the juice melts and pour it over the bird, basting every twenty minutes until the skin gets good and brown."

When it came out, little pieces of burnt onion adhered to the sides like barnacles on a sailboat. As kids, we all argued over who would get the dark meat. No one wanted the breast. The dark meat was so much more forgiving.

Friday—Spaghetti and Meatballs. I don't know what it is about Jewish mothers and Italian cooking, but the two just don't seem to mix. In our house, we were destined for watery sauce and mushy spaghetti. It was the only Italian dish Mom could make and she would never vary the pasta selection. Even back then, Ronzoni made a dozen different types of pasta noodles in all kinds of shapes. Would it have been a crime to have ziti one night instead of spaghetti #8? It's not that Mom preferred one type of pasta to another. I truly believe the thought had never occurred to her to choose a different one, because *thinking while shopping slows things down.* She hated waiting for anything, so she went to the market when it opened to avoid the lines. Mom knew the local Waldbaum's aisle by aisle. She made her shopping list accordingly, and could be in and out of the store in less than fifteen minutes. Her motto, "Why waste time?"

Saturday—Swanson's TV Dinner. When I was about seven, Dad's contracting company had started to do very well. He could now afford to take Mom to dinner *and* a movie. He also got a bargain because he didn't need to pay for a babysitter because my brother Paul was old enough to keep an eye on my other brother, Barry, and me. And that meant Swanson's for all! I loved how the steam practically burnt my hand as I pulled off the foil cover to reveal the crispy fried chicken inside. The chicken was so hot that I burned the roof of my mouth with the first bite, which was a small price to pay for that crunchy skin and moist chicken meat. And who could forget those mashed potatoes with butter? They must have been beaten to a pulp in a factory somewhere, but to me, they were heaven. And I loved the little triangle of apple pie, minus the crust, for dessert. It was sweet, but not too sweet. For a major treat, Dad set up the snack tables so my brothers and I could eat our dinner in front of the TV. Tell me, who got the better of the Saturday night deal?

Sunday—Chinese Takeout. What Jewish family doesn't have a near-sacred relationship with Chinese food takeout on Sunday? We ordered the same thing every week: Wonton Soup with "extra crunchies," (aka fried noodles), Shrimp in Lobster Sauce, Moo Goo Gai Pan, Spare Ribs, Egg Rolls, Fried Rice, and Roast Pork. Needless to say, we didn't keep kosher.

One of us always went with Dad to pick up the food. It was a short drive down South Oyster Bay Road to China View. I never minded going with him as long as we didn't have to actually sit down and eat. Eating at a Chinese restaurant is still a rather traumatic affair for me. One might wonder what hidden horrors existed at the local Chinese restaurant to cause such drama. You'd be surprised.

One night my parents decided to take us all out to dinner for the first time. I must have been about four years old. Mom wanted us all to have good manners, so she taught us how to tuck our napkins in our laps, how to use the right utensils for the right job, and encouraged us to keep our screaming to a minimum. I was a real people-pleaser, so I wanted to do the right thing. I learned how to tuck my napkin in my lap, use the right utensils, and not scream in public.

That night at Dragon Sky, the fancy Chinese restaurant on top of a short hill in Plainview, we were in the middle of our Moo Goo Gai Pan when I realized I really had to go pee. I politely rose from the table and tried to dash off to the Ladies Room. What followed me, to my surprise and horror, was the Wonton Soup, Shrimp in Lobster Sauce, Moo Goo Gai Pan, Spare Ribs, Egg Rolls, Fried Rice, and Roast Pork. I had tucked the tablecloth, not my napkin, into my favorite striped Capri pants. Unlike a magician who could yank the tablecloth out from underneath every plate, I took it all with me.

Catastrophe! Two waiters rushed over and started picking up the shattered plates. My brothers broke into hysterics, and I made a beeline for the bathroom and proceeded to cry for what seemed like an eternity. My cheeks felt like they were on fire from embarrassment. Mom tried to comfort me, but I could sense she was fighting back her own laughter. This story became part of our too-oft repeated family lore. My brothers couldn't wait to share it with all the neighborhood kids so that my humiliation extended beyond the family circle. To this day, I have a lot of issues with napkins.

And that's what we ate, day after day, week after week, and year after year—interrupted by the occasional brisket. How can you wreck brisket?

Mom just had a knack. Her brisket was so dry, the sauce pooled up around the meat, never sticking to it. It was almost as if she sprayed a secret sealant on it before it went in the pot so that the liquid just beaded up on the meat rather than integrating through the braising process. There was no falling off the bone tenderness that one might hope for—not even close.

The quality of the food was not the only challenge at our house. First of all, no one got along with anyone. My brothers fought with each other, I fought with my brothers, and when my parents were not yelling at each other, they'd yell at us for fighting at the table. Not a meal went by where someone didn't choke on his food, not because it was *that* bad, but because it was really difficult to yell and eat at the same time. We have all become speed eaters. It's a tough habit to break.

After each meal, I escaped to my "ivory tower," as Dad called it. It was my eight-foot by eight-foot oasis, my bedroom. The focal point of the room was a hand-me-down 10-inch Panasonic black-and-white TV. It had two knobs on the right-hand side—one that controlled Channels 2 through 13 with an extra "U" for UHF. The other knob carried the UHF channels, none of which ever came in well. The *TV Guide* was my bible and my life revolved around its schedule. In this little room, I watched reruns of *Father Knows Best,* imagining what it would be like to live in a family where the veins on the father's neck didn't pop out every time you did something wrong. I saw families that stuck together and clearly loved each other, even if they were a little odd, like the Addams Family or the Munsters. I saw our country at war as Paul fretted about whether his number would come up in the lottery. I watched a president go down because of his lies and corruption. A world different from my own came to me in that little room, and it was the drama inside that little black-and-white altar that I chose to worship over the drama downstairs.

Every Saturday night I stayed home to watch *The Mary Tyler Moore Show.* I had a bucket of Dunkin' Munchkins, which I snuck into my room and stashed in my closet so that I didn't have to go downstairs to get anything. I really liked Rhoda and thought about getting some scarves to wear around my head like she did. It made me think that it might be fun to be a window dresser like her or, even better, maybe a TV producer like Mary. Yeah, a producer. *That* sounded cool.

TUNA NOODLE CASSEROLE FROM SCRATCH

No one really wants to admit that some of those 1970s semi-homemade dishes our busy moms fed us were actually tasty on occasion. In truth, there is some comfort to them, if you can just get past the guilt of opening cans, dumping the contents and then heating. I have trouble with that, but in times of stress, I need this dish. So, here's my take on it, using fresh ingredients. You'll note that I have substituted edamame for peas. I hate peas.

Serves 4

INGREDIENTS

1 stick butter, divided, and softened
1 pound elbow macaroni
½ medium onion, finely chopped
1 clove garlic, minced
1 cup sliced cremini mushrooms
¼ cup all-purpose flour
2 cups milk
Salt and pepper to taste
1 large can tuna, drained and flaked
½ cup edamame
½ cup shredded cheddar cheese
½ cup shredded Gruyere cheese
4 tablespoons breadcrumbs

DIRECTIONS

Preheat the oven to 375 degrees F.

Using 1 tablespoon of butter, grease a large Pyrex or ceramic baking dish.

Fill a large pot with salted water. Don't be shy; I use 2 tablespoons of salt. Bring to a boil on high heat. Cook the pasta as per boxed instructions until al dente. Drain and set aside. Do not rinse the pasta.

Melt 1 tablespoon of butter in a medium skillet over medium heat. Add the onion and sauté until translucent, about 4 minutes. Add the garlic, and cook for 1 minute. Add the mushrooms and cook 4 minutes, stirring occasionally, until the mushrooms have softened. Remove from heat and set aside.

In a medium saucepan over medium-low heat, melt 4 tablespoons butter. Whisk in the flour until smooth. Slowly whisk in the milk, and cook 5 minutes, or until the sauce slightly thickens. Season with salt and pepper to taste.

With the saucepan on low heat, add the tuna, edamame, the mushroom mixture, the cooked pasta, and the cheddar and Gruyere cheese, and stir to combine just until the cheese begins to melt. Pour into the buttered baking dish.

In a small bowl, combine the breadcrumbs with the remaining 2 tablespoons melted butter and mix well. Sprinkle evenly on top.

Bake 25 minutes, or until the breadcrumbs are lightly browned. Let the casserole sit at room temperature for a few minutes before serving.

Chapter Two

HAVE YOU SEEN MY HIPS?

It's a bitingly cold and windy December day. All bundled up, I look like the Michelin man as I walk into The Mark Hotel in New York City for a power breakfast. I try to reassemble myself as I take off my coat and scarf, shocking myself with a sparkly sizzle of static electricity. Depending upon the weather, my hair has a way of making its own statement and I just never know if I'm going to look like Andie MacDowell or Phyllis Diller. I make a quick trip to the Ladies' Room to check my lipstick and smooth down my flyaways. I take a deep breath and make my way to the table.

I'm always terrified during interviews. I'm not great at small talk or selling myself, so I overcompensate by trying to be witty. My scorecard is fifty-fifty hit and miss.

"Ah, there she is," Eileen announces. "Chef, this is Karen Katz, the woman I was telling you about."

Emeril stands up and offers his hand.

"Nice to meet you," I say.

"I've heard a lot about you," Emeril remarks. "This is Felicia, my culinary assistant."

"Thanks for coming to meet with us," she adds.

"Man, it's cold outside," I say, pretending to be relaxed and natural.

"It's 80 degrees in New Orleans," Felicia replies. "We can't wait to get home."

"Already? I haven't said anything yet," I joke.

Emeril is just studying me. He doesn't laugh or say a word. *Oh no, kill me now.*

There's lots of food on the table, but no one is eating. I'm starving, but I don't want to eat if they're not eating. It would be bad manners. A chocolate croissant with my name on it next to a cup of espresso with the perfect amount of crema is tempting me. I just hope no one can hear my stomach growling. I have to force myself to make eye contact with the people sitting across from me, rather than the croissant. This is more difficult than it sounds. I find out that I am last on a short list of producers to take breakfast with them that day. They've already eaten, multiple times.

"So Karen, tell Emeril about some of the work you've done," Eileen urges.

I hate that question. How do I sum up twenty years of working my butt off—from when I started out delivering coffee for D-list celebrities to supervising over ninety people on multi-camera TV events?

"Well, I've been producing now for over ten years. I actually started in the business as an editor but worked my way up doing everything from children's programming, documentaries, and talk shows to a comedy special for the Playboy Channel. I was actually so embarrassed by that one that I changed my name for the credits to *Bubbles Katz*."

That's my icebreaker story. I had to throw that one in. Out of the corner of my eye, I can see Emeril let out a tiny laugh. He's actually not a bad-looking guy with his stocky frame and wavy slicked-back black hair. He's dressed all in black, except for a white T-shirt under his blazer.

"Have you ever produced a food show?" Felicia asks.

I was waiting for this question. I was worried that my lack of culinary experience would put the kibosh on any chance of landing this job. But I came prepared.

"Funny you should ask. I did produce a pilot for a children's cooking show once, but it was challenging because the sponsors wouldn't let the kids use knives."

Felicia laughs. She's a zaftig, attractive southern woman with long sandy blond hair and a hearty laugh. She's got a big personality and is taking the lead on this interview. On our call, Eileen made it seem like the job was mine if I wanted it. Clearly, that's not the case. I'm realizing I'm going to have to work for this and make a good impression. I have done my homework and have watched some of Emeril's shows. He is quite charismatic on TV—a regular Joe having a great time kicking things up a notch or two. There is such a joy and playfulness about him on TV that I am surprised to see a very quiet, thoughtful, and serious man sitting at the table.

The meeting goes on for over an hour. I get asked all kinds of questions by Eileen and Felicia, most of them hoping I have ways to solve their backstage dysfunction. Thankfully, there are very few food questions. Emeril just sits and studies me through it all.

"So, we've got a bit of drama going on behind the scenes," Felicia divulges. "Everything takes forever, and it's too chaotic. Emeril is used to discipline in his kitchens and he expects that on set."

"Well, I like to run a show the same way," I state. "There's no reason things should be disorganized. I just have to set up the right systems and everyone needs to know what's expected of them."

"Right, exactly," Felicia agrees. "So let me ask you something else." She pauses, making this seem like a well-thought-out question. "Do you think this is a cooking show with entertainment or an entertainment show with cooking?"

I take a beat to think about that. It feels like a trick question. Emeril, who has been practically silent the entire time, shifts in his seat, waiting for my response. This TV thing is relatively new to him. He's been sweating away in kitchens since he was a kid but must know enough to realize how TV can raise his profile and his business prospects if he stays true to himself.

"It's a cooking show with entertainment," I answer.

I can see Emeril relax. I didn't just tell him what he wanted to hear. I believe it too.

He looks me straight in the eyes, as if to reach into my soul, and finally asks me one and only one question. "Do you like food?"

I shift in my seat and meet his gaze. "Have you seen my hips?"

He smiles ever so slightly, leans back, and quietly chuckles to himself.

By the time I get home, there's a message on my machine: I got the job.

I call Mom to tell her the good news.

"You're going to be the executive producer on a cooking show? Oh, Dad would have loved that," Mom declares. "You know, he was so proud of you. Let me know when it's on, and I'll try to watch."

"Well, it will be in a couple of months," I estimate. "I need to start prepping everything, but I'll let you know."

"Honey, I've been meaning to ask you. What does an executive producer actually do?" Mom asks.

"Well, basically, I'm responsible for the creative content and managing the production team, the crew, and the talent."

"You're the boss of all those people? That sounds like a big job. Who's the star?"

"Well, he's a chef, actually. His name is Emeril Lagasse."

"What kind of name is Emeril?"

"It's either French or Portuguese—I'm not really sure."

"I just realized, will you have time to make Thanksgiving this year?" Mom asks.

"Of course. I doubt we'll shoot on holidays."

"Ooh, maybe you can make something new? Let's shake things up this year."

Thanksgiving is a big deal in our family. It's the only holiday my family celebrates together, and it is sacrilege to miss it. Since Dad passed away a few years back, Mom moved out of their house into one of those fifty-five-plus townhouse communities a few towns away. Although she tries to put up a good front, she just can't deal with the family traditions anymore, so the mantel has fallen to me, which is a blessing in disguise, considering Mom's disdain for cooking. But my mom's mom was the true source of the tradition. Unlike Mom, Nana loved to feed us. It's probably been over fifty years, but I can still smell her apple pie coming out of the oven.

"Faster! Go faster!" I squealed.

Riding in a rusty shopping cart that Granddad permanently borrowed from the local A&P, I whizzed by Nana's oversized panties hanging on the drying rack, as my brother Barry pushed me through the creaky swinging door and straight into the laundry room. Within seconds, Nana's freshly folded towels fell into a massive heap as we gunned our imaginary engines en route to Granddad's "Temple of Torture," a room where all his carpentry tools dangled from the ceiling. The acrid smell of turpentine almost overpowered the mouthwatering aroma of Nana's turkey happily resting upstairs on the white enamel stove, its juices glistening over its browned skin. The sweet smell of baking apples and raisins from Nana's noodle pudding urged us on to the feast awaiting us. We were neck-and-neck as we reached for the photo finish.

Heading toward us at lightning speed with a maniacal look on her face, my cousin Sue was at the helm of another shopping cart. Her little brother Dave was in the basket, giggling with pure delight. We crashed head-on and lurched forward, just missing each other's heads, as my knee bashed against the front of the cart.

"And there's a pileup on the field! Any injuries?" Paul bellowed.

"OWWWWWWWW!" I screamed.

"Uh-oh. Barry, you're gonna get it now." Paul snarked.

"There's no blood. It's just a little scratch. Stop being such a baby," Barry yelled, as he punched me in the arm.

"I'm not a baby!" I shrieked, pushing back at him, barely suppressing my tears.

I could hear the click, click, click of my mother's gray-suede high heels running down the stairs.

"What on earth is going on down here?" She was really mad, her voice so loud it made the cling peach cans in Nana's pantry vibrate.

"If you kids can't behave, you can spend Thanksgiving dinner down here!"

"MOMMMMMMMY!" I shrieked full-throated, tears instantly pouring down my chubby cheeks.

"Barry pushed the cart and …" I couldn't get the words out as my hysteria accelerated my breathing.

"She's such a faker. She wasn't crying a minute ago."

"Barry, how many times have I told you those shopping carts are not your personal bumper cars? You should know better than to let her ride in one."

My brother's face was beet red, and he shot me a dirty look. I stood behind Mom and I stuck my tongue out at him. She turned to me and asked, "And you, missy. Did you just tear your brand-new tights?"

I looked down and saw a rip straight across my knee. I was in trouble.

"You march upstairs and see if Nana can fix it. And the rest of you, clean up down here and get ready for dinner. I don't want to hear another peep out of you for the rest of the night!"

Mom shot us all a threatening glance and click, click, clicked back upstairs. As I followed, Barry tried to get in one more jab, luckily missing me. The kitchen door opened, and I ran into Nana's arms. She looked up at Mom.

"Chariot races again," Mom explained to Nana, holding back a tiny smile as she picked up some dinner plates and left the room.

Nana looked me over, not finding any serious injuries, except for my torn tights.

"Well, I don't see any boo-boos, do you?"

Still gasping for air, but calming down, I whined, "No-oh."

"OK then, let's sew this up lickety-split before anyone else sees it."

Always at the ready with a needle and thread, Nana started to stitch up the tear as I buried my head into her neck and my heaving subsided. She was wearing a slightly stained white full-bodied apron with blue embroidered edges over her holiday best. All day she had been busy prepping the one, good old-fashioned, made-almost-from-scratch meal of the year—Thanksgiving.

The bird was huge that year. Nana said it was an 18-pounder. Savory and sweet aromas perfumed the room as the stuffing's pungent onions and chicken livers collided with sugary baked sweet potatoes topped with small melted marshmallows. On the counter, an empty can of Campbell's Mushroom Soup sat next to the string bean casserole. The cranberry jelly mold was already jiggling on a beautiful hand-painted green and yellow floral ceramic plate she had brought back from a trip she took to Spain with her sister Helen. There was no better place to be at that moment than in Nana's kitchen. It was the warmest room in the house, as her love was baked into every bite our lucky bellies were about to enjoy.

Nana and Granddad lived just twenty minutes away from our house in Bethpage, not far off the Long Island Expressway in New Hyde Park. Their house was a two-bedroom ranch on a quiet street with manicured lawns and newly planted birch trees lining the road. They moved out to Long Island from East 34th Street in Brooklyn because *everyone* was moving out to Long Island from Brooklyn. On a normal day, it had the familiar scents of Old Bond Medicated Foot Powder and Borax emanating from the bathroom at the end of the hall. Outside on cold nights, the smell of freshly baked bread from the local bakery froze me in my tracks.

Nana pulled the needle through one last stitch, made a knot, and cut the end of the thread with the cutest little scissors.

"There you go, good as new." She spun me around. "Look at you—you look so nice today."

I was wearing my favorite brown suede jumper with a long-sleeved white Healthtex turtleneck underneath. I only wore jumpers. I hated frilly dresses.

"How would you like to help me finish the pie?"

She tied a matching little white apron around me and pushed over a small wooden stool so I could reach the yellow and white speckled Formica counter. She handed me a big wooden spoon, and I slowly tried to spoon out all the apples without having any fall on the counter. I missed a few, but Nana never minded if you messed things up—not like Mom.

Next, she put her brown spotted hands over mine as we held the rolling pin to place the top crust over the apples. She took a knife and trimmed the edges so that the crust looked nice and round and even.

"I know what to do next!" I squealed.

I took a fork and pressed the two crusts together, going all the way around the frame of the pie, and then I poked an *N* for Nana into the top so the pie could breathe.

Bounding up the stairs as if they were cartoon characters lifted by animated aromas under their noses, my brothers and cousins were lured by the familiar scent of juicy apples baking.

"What's for dinner?"

"You know the rules, look on the door," Nana reminded them.

A small, white, four-by-six-inch piece of notepaper was posted on the door with her handwritten menu.

THANKSGIVING DINNER

APPETIZER

Fruit Cocktail

ENTRÉES

Roast Turkey Au Jus with Chicken Liver and Herb Stuffing

SIDES

Sweet Potatoes with Baked Marshmallows
String Bean Casserole
Noodle Pudding
Cranberry Mold with Apples and Walnuts

DESSERT

Nana's Apple Pie à la mode

It was as if this meal was engraved in stone, brought down from Mount Sinai by Moses with the first commandment, *Thou shalt not veer from this menu.*

Dad walked in, inhaling the feast to come, and put his arm around Nana.

"Mom, you are the queen of Thanksgiving. All hail."

And she was. She deserved her own crown made with as much love as she stuffed into every turkey carcass and baked into every pie. Her noodle pudding alone, with its sweet melted raisins and apples wrapped in perfectly cooked egg noodles, could silence any argument. She managed to keep us all together with every slice of turkey, schmear of cranberry sauce, and bite of stuffing we gladly devoured.

If it weren't for Nana, I might never have had any early appreciation for food or how it could make someone feel loved. Thankfully, I stored that somewhere deep within my psyche, not knowing how much I would come to treasure it in the years to come.

NANA'S APPLE PIE À LA MODE

When my Nana passed away, there were only two things my brother Paul and I wanted of hers; her rolling pin and the stained and faded apple pie recipe that she had kept in the top kitchen drawer next to some dried-out rubber bands she had saved for years. Paul has the recipe framed in his kitchen, and I have the rolling pin. By now, I have committed the recipe to memory.

Although Paul would say it is sacrilege, over the years I have taken some liberties with Nana's recipe. It is all here in its purest form, but I have come up with a few improvements.

1. This is a classic Crisco shortening crust recipe. If shortening freaks you out, you can make a butter crust. Personally, I prefer butter crusts, but if you want to stay true to Nana's version, you have to pull out the Crisco.
2. You shouldn't use a Cuisinart because they weren't invented when Nana started making pies. But I won't tell if you won't.
3. Nana used one teaspoon of cinnamon, which, personally, I feel is one teaspoon too much. I'm not a huge cinnamon fan. Don't tell anyone, but I only use a ¼ teaspoon. But hey, if you like cinnamon, go for it—just don't say I didn't warn you.
4. Nana used Rome baking apples, but I prefer Granny Smiths. You can really use any firm apple you like, just avoid the mushy ones.
5. When you prick the top of the pie with the tines of the fork, you should form the letter **N** for Nana. You may use another letter, but it might break my heart.

Serves 8

INGREDIENTS

For the Crust

2 cups all-purpose flour, sifted
½ teaspoon salt
¾ cup shortening (12 tablespoons)

4 tablespoons ice water

For the Pie Filling

1 cup sugar
1 teaspoon cinnamon (or less, if you prefer)
1 heaping tablespoon all-purpose flour
1 dash salt
½ teaspoon vanilla extract
6 apples (or 7 cups), peeled, cored, and thinly sliced
1 tablespoon butter
½ cup raisins, or walnuts (optional)
1 teaspoon lemon juice
1 egg yolk
1 tablespoon coarse raw sugar
Vanilla ice cream, your favorite brand (optional)

DIRECTIONS

CRUST

Whisk together the salt and flour in a big bowl. Using a pastry blender, add in the shortening, working it into the salt/flour mixture until it resembles little pebbles.

Drizzle 4 tablespoons ice water, 1 tablespoon at a time, over the flour mixture, tossing lightly with a fork. The pastry should be moist, not sticky. If it's still too dry, you can add up to 2 more tablespoons of ice water, as necessary.

Bring the dough together into a ball, being careful not to overwork it, and cut in half, making one half slightly larger than the other.

Shape each half into a ball again, then flatten it like a hamburger patty, wrap in clear plastic wrap, and refrigerate for at least 30 minutes. (Dough can also be made the day ahead and refrigerated or frozen.)

Cut a piece of wax paper larger than your pie plate. Place the pie plate upside down on the paper, and draw a circle around the pie plate in pencil, then flip the wax paper over (because no one likes pencil-flavored dough). Roll out the larger dough half, using the penciled circle as your template. Roll the dough ½ inch beyond the circle.

Repeat all of the above for the other dough half, but without rolling the dough much beyond the penciled circle. Cover with wax paper or plastic wrap and refrigerate both crusts again for 30 minutes.

APPLE PIE FILLING

Preheat oven to 425 degrees F.

In a small bowl, combine the sugar, cinnamon, flour, and salt and mix well.

Add the sliced apples to the sugar mixture and toss lightly. Add the vanilla and toss once more. If you like raisins, chopped nuts, or other add-ins, now is the time to toss in ½ cup of your preference.

Take the larger dough out of the fridge and flip it over onto the pie plate. Gently peel off the wax paper and flatten the dough to fit the pie plate. Allow the extra dough to flop over the lip for now. Feel free to trim any excess odd pieces so you have a nice round shape.

Gently pour the apple mixture onto the bottom crust, spreading out the apples so they are at an even height throughout. Dot the apples with pieces of 1 tablespoon butter. Sprinkle the lemon juice over the mixture.

Remove the other dough half from the fridge and flip it to cover the apples. Make sure it's centered before gently removing the wax paper.

Fold the top edge of the crust over the bottom edge so that you have a nice seal around the lip. (Or, if the bottom crust has more excess, fold the bottom over the top.) The goal is to have the two crusts meet and look even around the edge. For a good seal, crimp the crusts together with a fork around the lip of the pie plate.

Prick the top of the pie with the tines of the fork so that you form the letter *N*.

Beat an egg yolk with one tablespoon of water and brush over the crust. Sprinkle coarse raw sugar on top.

Bake for 45 to 50 minutes, or until the crust is golden brown. Remove from the oven and let cool for twenty minutes. Serve warm with vanilla ice cream.

If you can figure out how, bottle the smell in your kitchen.

Chapter Three

CULINARY IN A HURRY

I have to admit, I never really watched cooking shows, but I'm giving myself a crash course so I can see what I'm up against with my new job. I'm nervous about working with all these chefs and culinary professionals. I know they're going to see through me in two minutes. What they don't realize is that producers are rarely experts in the topics of their shows. Although not an MD, I've produced medical shows about beta-blockers. I've worked with Pfizer on their anti-depressant drugs, never having taken them or proclaiming to be a psychiatrist. I'm tone-deaf and can't carry a tune, yet I've worked on concerts for PBS. Still, I keep asking myself, why do I feel that I'm supposed to be a gourmet cook?

The Food Network is still pretty green, just coming out of its infancy phase. Their programming has been on the air for only four years and it's basically a collection of what has become known in the business as "dump-and-stir shows," where the chef just stands behind a counter and cooks to the camera. Originally, the concept for the network was to be the CNN of cooking shows with programs cycling through the day, as disposable as yesterday's news. Their production values look like tacky infomercials, costing a mere fraction of what competitive programming on other networks spend.

"We're so glad you're here," Erica says on my first day at work. "We're really at a crucial juncture. We've got to compete with the other cable networks and the look and quality level of our shows need a big facelift. I'm relying on you to do your magic, within budget of course."

Erica is the president of the network and also an old friend and colleague I had met earlier in my career when I worked at Lifetime. I have a feeling she may be the reason I'm actually here. She's put a lot of chips on the table in terms of bringing Emeril in front of an audience. It's my job not to screw it up.

"Well, let me get my feet wet and see what we're up against," I tell her.

On my first tour of the studio, I can't help but think this is the modern-day version of an old Mickey Rooney and Judy Garland movie, where you put up some flats, get a bunch of kids together, and put on a show. In one 5,000-square-foot studio, there are four different small sets crammed into each corner. In the center of the space are four cameras. The cameras simply move in front of each set when it is time to shoot. As rinky-dink as it is, I must say, at least it is efficient.

"In the west corner, we have David Rosengarten's set for *Taste*. To the east is Sara Moulton's *Cooking Live* set. As you can see, we're moving *Three Dog Bakery* from the north side to make way for Mario Batali's new show, *Molto Mario*, and south of us is the *Two Hot Tamales* set," Eileen points out, walking me around. "But now that we've got an audience for *Emeril Live*, we have to shoot out-of-house because there's not enough room here. Right now, we're using a stage over on Ninth Avenue. You'll be working with the team over there once production starts. But for now, while you're prepping, we've made some room for you here."

I don't know how this happens, but for some reason, the higher up the professional ladder I go, the smaller my office gets. Actually, I don't even have one here. I'm the executive producer of the network's most important show and I have been put in a cubicle with my desk facing the show's pro-duction assistant, Sandy. She's a young, skinny little know-it-all with all the bravado of someone who doesn't know what she doesn't know. In the course of my first hour here, she manages to trash everyone on the show, making it seem that nothing would get done if it were not for her.

"Seriously, the producers on this show don't have a clue," whispers Sandy. "I have to arrange everything—from how many plates we'll need on set to setting up Emeril's dressing room."

"Uh-huh. You do all of that yourself?" I ask sarcastically. "So, really, the producers don't do anything?"

"I suppose they do something. But if I took a sick day, the whole thing would fall apart."

Throwing people under the bus becomes an ongoing theme as I meet separately with the staff. It doesn't take me long to realize why Eileen and Felicia were so concerned about backstage issues. The entire team spends most of their time competing with and backstabbing each other as if they were still in high school. I know I'll need to do some house cleaning, but I try to reserve judgment and not overreact based on my first impressions.

"Hi, I'm Wendy. I'm sooooo excited you're here," gushes a woman dressed in a fuzzy, oversized black sweater with flecks of paint she may or may not know are running down her back. "I'm the art director. We're going to have lots of fun together."

I notice that she's not wearing matching shoes and the dark circles under her eyes belie the joyful, kidlike, bordering on insane, glee that comes from her smile. She peeks out from the corner of her cubicle, one that I can barely see because every inch is covered by some kitchen prop or artifact. After the first week, I notice that when I come in each morning, she's already working and when I leave each night, she's still at it. I begin to wonder if she ever goes home, or even has one.

First, I need to get up to speed with how the food itself gets produced. I've got the TV part down, but prepping food for television is a show within itself. And from the looks of it, there's a lot to learn. Susan, the earth mother in charge of the kitchen staff, is warm and welcoming. She is probably mid-forties, with shoulder-length straight blond hair and a play-ful smile. She seems comfortable in her own skin and there's a kindness behind her light blue eyes. Dressed in her denim Food Network chef's coat, she hovers over her team of cooks and culinary school graduates, offering solutions to any and all problems. She emanates a calm sense of competence that permeates this room filled with pots, pans, cooktops, ovens, and every imaginable gadget.

"We're prepping for Sara Moulton's *Cooking Live* show right now. Let me walk you through it," Susan says.

Steam rises from pasta pots as the whir of a blender makes a pesto, the basil releasing the scent of a warm summer's day. The clanking of dishes and pots being washed sound almost syncopated adding to the rhythm that seems to flow in one big choreographed culinary dance. It's the kitchen staff's job to prep the food for this show and every show, and Susan has created a system that is streamlined, efficient, and practical.

"Let's say you're making a turkey. Well, in the real world, it takes about four hours, right?" Susan explains, more than happy to show me the ropes.

"Right, uh-huh," I nod, clueless.

"But in TV land, you can't wait around with your crew while some-thing takes that long to roast, so you've got to do things in stages."

"Makes sense."

"That means you need three to four turkeys to get the job done so you can shoot it quickly. We call them 'swap outs.' The first one is raw so that the chef can show you how to prep and season it. The second one might be cooked halfway so you can show how to baste or turn the bird if you want. The third is a completed bird the chef pulls from the oven, ready to slice to show the moisture content of the bird or even the technique of how to carve it. And the fourth and final bird is placed on a dressed platter, pristine and ready for its close-up or what we like to call its *beauty shot.*"

"I get it. Of course," I say, hanging on every word. "Do you do some of those tricks they do in commercials like subbing out ice cream with mashed potatoes?"

"Actually no, we really try to use all the true ingredients whenever possible. We might do a little glycerin spritz when we do a beauty shot, but that's about it."

"Very cool."

"The entire process is documented in what we call a "recipe breakdown" before we even get near the set. The chefs provide a standard recipe and send it to the culinary producers who break it down on paper, step-by-step for television so that the kitchen team knows what to shop for, how far to cook things, and in how many stages."

As she continues in detail, I start to hyperventilate. I'm getting worried that this might be more than I can handle.

"Each show has its own culinary producer, right?" I ask anxiously.

"Right. But between you and me, some are better than others."

"Yeah, I've been getting the lay of the land."

Susan laughs, "I'm sure you'll figure it out soon enough.

"Where do the ingredients come from?"

"We have two shoppers that buy all of the ingredients, allowing for enough time if things need to be prepped a day or two before. On shoot days, my team preps a cart with all of the pre-chopped ingredients broken out per commercial break. Next, we put the *mise en place* on the set."

"A what?" I ask.

"Oh sorry, that's a culinary term. It means *putting everything in its place* so the chef has all the ingredients at his or her fingertips. We just line them up in the order they need to be used. That's what all these ramekins are for."

"Oh, I see."

"Someone like Emeril hates doing retakes. He really likes to blast through things, so we really need to be on our game. Once we have everything laid out, he'll come on set, review everything with my team, and then off he goes. You'd better be ready to roll those cameras. He waits for no one."

What does that mean? Is she saying he's a tyrant? I've been so busy prepping with the team that I haven't thought about what it would be like to work alongside him. *What is she not saying? Suppose he's a complete jerk?*

"Huh. Waits for no one," I say. "I'll remember that. Thanks for the tip."

Susan looks at me thoughtfully, putting her hand on my shoulder.

"Don't worry. You're gonna do just fine."

Is my panic that obvious? I'm a little overwhelmed by this whole kitchen process and hope that by the time Emeril comes to shoot in a few weeks, I'll be fully up to speed. Learning so much about food prep and presentation so quickly makes me feel as if I've enrolled in a crash course at the Culinary Institute.

For the first few days, I'm basically trying to fake it until I make it. I try to keep my eyes from glazing over as my team starts debating the merits of baking soda versus baking powder. But after a few weeks, I do start to get a handle on how to manage this beast. The kitchen staff is more than eager to help me because it makes their job that much easier if I know what I'm doing.

"I made a little more than we need for the show, would you like some?" Marie offers with a smile.

Marie, one of the backstage cooks, hands me a hunk of citrus gravlax that has been curing for the past three days. She cuts a slice so I can taste it.

"Oh wow, that's delicious! I expected it to taste like lox, but it's a lot more delicate."

"Well, lox is smoked. This is cured with lemon, orange, and lime zest. I garnished it with some dill. Take it home. It will keep for a week or so."

"Really? I can do that?"

"Honey, you're the boss. You can do whatever you want." Many of the crew and staff have been a bit distant as they size me up. I'm used to that. It comes with the territory. But Marie is different. She's one of the cooks on Susan's staff, and she's a genuinely warm person with a homespun sense of humor that just wants everyone to play nice. She's probably fortyish, around my age, with short dark brown hair and eyes. But there's an inno-cence about her that makes her seem younger than her years.

"Listen, all of us in the kitchen think you're doing a great job getting this place organized," says Marie. "How has Emeril been?"

"I think he's happy so far. It's hard to tell."

"Believe me, if he weren't, you'd know," she says. "Just watch your back. There are a lot of people here that try to get into Emeril's ear and stir the pot."

"Thanks for the warning," I say.

I'm not terribly surprised to hear it. I could tell from day one that this place thrives on gossip with a pinch of backstabbing. At this point, there's not much I can do about it, and I don't really have time to think about it. I've got fifteen rundowns to prep, a meeting with our director, and some last-minute recipe changes Emeril's camp wants to make. We start shoot-ing on Monday, and I was hoping to rest up this weekend before we start our first week of taping, but I've got to take Mom up to Rhode Island to see my Uncle Allen, who we now affectionately call by his initials, A.G. He's sick—really, really sick. I've been pushing this trip off for weeks, hop-ing that the news would change, but it hasn't.

Trapped in a car for four hours, Mom lets loose. "I don't know how much more I can take. First, it was Nana, then your father, and now my brother. Soon I'll have nobody," Mom whines.

"What about us?" I ask.

"You know what I mean."

"Sort of."

"Both Bernie and Allen were so young. It doesn't make sense. Why can't your father come back, just for a little while?"

Oy, here we go again.

"Mom. You know he's not coming back."

"I know, I know. But if only …"

"Mom, please."

When we finally get there, we're both shocked to see my uncle's frail body, now forty pounds lighter than his norm.

"I hear the doctors want you to eat. You need to keep up your strength," Mom says.

"Can you imagine?" he shrugs. "For once in my life I can eat whatever I want, but I just don't have an appetite. Go figure."

This is another one of cancer's cruel ironies. A.G. has stage-four lung cancer, and it has ravaged his body in just four short months. And what's most heartbreaking is that he has lost his wonderful, zestful, voracious appetite. A.G. is my eating buddy. If there's a chocolate parfait or a decadent soufflé to be eaten, he's the first one to pass the fork around the table. He's always on the hunt for a great meal, and it is this delightful, knowledgeable, and adventurous man who first taught me about the joys of tasting everything and anything put in front of me.

ROAST TURKEY IN THIRTY MINUTES

Roast turkey in just thirty minutes? Yes, it can be done, but the first thing you need is your own cooking show with a staff that includes one shopper, two sous chefs, one food stylist, two production assistants, and a culinary producer. Oh yeah, and you'll need double ovens as well.

INGREDIENTS

4 turkeys, cleaned, turkey necks and giblets removed
4 sticks of butter, divided
4 onions, quartered, and divided
4 lemons, zested and halved, divided
4 heads garlic, halved, and divided
4 sprigs rosemary
4 sprigs thyme
12 sage leaves
Salt and pepper

DIRECTIONS

Preheat the bottom oven to 350 degrees F.

Melt one stick of butter in a small saucepan. Stir in the zest and juice of one lemon and set aside.

Clean and place one raw turkey, (bird #1), in a large roasting pan. Generously season the inside of the cavity with salt and pepper. Stuff the cavity with the 2 lemon halves, 1 sprig each of rosemary and thyme, 3 sage leaves, 1 quartered onion, and 1 head of garlic.

Brush the bird with the melted butter mixture, and season the skin with salt and pepper. Using butcher's twine, tie the legs together. Place the bird in the bottom oven—never to be seen again.

Open the top oven and remove the bird that has been cooking for two hours, (bird #2). Show everyone how to baste it using the juices that have now drained into the bottom of the roasting pan. Place the turkey back in the top oven, and go to commercial break.

Stand back as the two production assistants swoop in to clean up your cooking area, remove both birds from the ovens, and replace a fully cooked turkey in your top oven, (bird #3).

Welcome back your audience. Pull the perfectly roasted bird out of the top oven. Wait a moment as your cameraman comes in for a close-up of the bird. Explain how normally you'd let the bird rest before carving, but you want to show everyone how to properly carve it.

Using your best technique, fan out pieces of the breast onto a beautiful serving tray. Wish everyone a happy Thanksgiving and continue plating until the stage manager says, "All clear."

Stand back as another perfectly roasted bird, (bird #4), flies out from backstage and is set up on a Lazy Susan for its beauty shot. Go back to your dressing room.

Chapter Four

A PALETTE IS BORN

My uncle A.G. outdid himself the year we found ourselves arriving in the adorable Tyrolean village of Zermatt for our annual family ski trip. It was the winter of 1972 and my very first trip to Europe. Knowing our family's priorities, the first thing he did was make a reservation at a fancy restaurant down a dark side street, where the shadows looked like monsters, and I was convinced Dr. Frankenstein's lab couldn't be far away.

"Good evening. I vant to suck your blood," A.G. teased, hovering over me.

Everyone laughed, even though I was a bit spooked by the surroundings. The cobblestones beneath my feet made my ankles turn, and more than once I caught myself just before a fall. Looking as if straight out of the pages of *Hansel and Gretel,* the quaint A-frame wood-and-stone cottages featured heavy beams crisscrossing the white-painted crooked exteriors. I half expected an elf or gnome to pop out of a window. I could already tell this was going to be a wild, fun trip. It didn't matter that it took us twenty-four hours of travel time; we hadn't slept at all, and Dad was worried that the hotel was going to misplace our skis.

Another perk of the trip was that Mom and Aunt Toby, A.G.'s wife, had stayed back, neither of them being skiers. It was a win-win for everyone—the fathers and kids relishing a break from the moms. And vice versa. The inmates had escaped, with nobody but Dad and A.G. in charge. And that meant letting the good times roll. It was a once-a-year respite where we were all free from arguments, restrictions, and rules—like those fake snakes in a can, just waiting to spring out when the lid is pulled off.

We followed our noses as the aroma of wood-burning meat guided our way. As we turned a corner, we finally arrived at our destination. We pushed through an enormous arched wooden door and were welcomed by the warmth of a gigantic pig slowly spinning around an open fireplace that went all the way from the floor to the ceiling. There was a big metal stick that ran through the pig's mouth and out its butt, its eyes glazed and open, as if frozen from shock. I could see its little legs and tail going around and around as its skin crackled and turned a crispy dark brown. I was both grossed out and fascinated at the same time.

"Whoa!" I whispered to Paul. "We're supposed to eat that?"

"Shush. Be polite. It must be a Swiss thing. It's a wild boar. It smells pretty good, doesn't it?"

I had to admit, it did. The pork fat dripping onto the beech wood smelled like a cross between roasted marshmallows and thick-cut grilled steaks.

As he moved toward the maitre d', A.G. muttered to Dad, "Oh Jeez, would you look at the size of that poor thing."

"Don't look," Dad joked. "Just inhale."

A waiter wearing a formal starched white shirt with a matching black vest, tie, and pants escorted us to our table. Once we were seated, he walked around the table laying our napkins in our laps, snapping each napkin open and placing it down in one smooth gesture. I wondered if he thought we didn't know we were supposed to put our napkins in our laps, but we knew—even if we were Americans.

The scrumptious-looking menu offered various cuts of the beast we saw on our way in: Braised Wild Boar Shanks, Wild Boar Ragu over Spaetzle, Wild Boar Rack with Potato Gratin, and Wild Boar Ribs with a Fig Sauce. For appetizers, they didn't waste a thing, using the ground bits to make wild boar salami and sausages for their charcuterie platter. If the dead boar could have seen this menu, even he might have been impressed. If it was going to be eaten by a bunch of people from Long Island, hey, at least it could be in a fig sauce.

Sharing this pig feast, we each ordered something different, knowing that our ancestors would forbid every bite. Somehow, that made these dishes tastier and more decadent. The fat had done its job, oozing out from every piece, making each bite tender and juicy. The sauces were thick and buttery, leaving a shine on the meat as it was poured. I thought it might taste like chicken or maybe spare ribs, but it didn't. It tasted like funky brisket.

"What wine would you recommend?" Dad asked our waiter.

"Dole is our local red wine. It's a blend of gamay and pinot noir grapes. It's light and fruity and our chef recommends it for many of his dishes."

"Sounds perfect."

"How many glasses shall I bring, sir?"

Dad looked around the table and smiled. "Six please."

My cousin Dave, my brothers, and I all started to quietly snicker, knowing there was no way our mothers would ever let us drink. Our ages ranged from twelve to twenty, but there was no age limit on drinking in Europe, so our dads let us all imbibe. And imbibe we did, giggling and turning bright red as the plates kept coming.

Smiling at me, Dad nudged A.G. "Look at her, she's almost fourteen and she's already a lush."

"I beg your pardon, sir. I'll have you know that I can ... *hiccup* ... hold my liquor just fine."

Everyone laughed. A.G., still working his way through the meal, said, "Hey, if there's any more of that ragu left, send it down my way."

A.G. had a great appetite and I've never known anyone who loved food more. I've yet to see a morsel left on any plate when he was around. Since I was a little girl, we'd always bonded over desserts, especially chocolate ones, like blackout cake and mud pie. It was our thing. We usually shared something, but that night in Zermatt, it was every man, woman, and child for herself because this freakin' fabulous restaurant had profiteroles!

Those adorable vanilla ice cream-filled pastry balls arrived at our table as our waiter hovered over us with a big silver teapot. He was about to tip it over as I wondered why he would be pouring tea on the ice cream, but then a thick stream of chocolate sauce poured out, covering the pastry puffs in a smooth sweet blanket. I would not have minded being covered in that. As we spooned into it, the chocolate melted the ice cream and it quickly became a messy mix of sweet and bitter, creamy and cold. One thing I knew for sure, if I had been alone, I would have licked the plate.

As we left the restaurant and headed out into the cold, frigid air, we all said in unison, "Thannnnk yooooou." It was our family tradition after a meal out. The blood rushed to my stomach, my body chilled and my teeth started to chatter. We were all shivering but didn't mind paying the price after such an extraordinary meal. Dad put his arm around me to keep me warm, as A.G., true to form asked, "That was a great appetizer. Now what's for dinner?"

The next day, we were all anxious to hit the trails. Making sure to fully carb load on croissants and baguettes, we made our way up the mountain in a rickety old train called a *funicular*. As it went higher and higher, the trees disappeared, leaving an expanse of untouched, glistening white snow that seemed to drape the mountains like Cinderella's gown. I couldn't wait to make some fresh tracks and dance through the snow as if I were on the way to the ball.

When we finally got to the top, we were so high up that we could almost see the curvature of the earth. The sky was blindingly blue, with only wisps of high clouds on the horizon. And in front of us was a sea of snow in all directions. Speaking of directions, which way should we go? All of the signs were in German, but fortunately, A.G. remembered some of the language from his time in the war. We followed the sign for Cervinia, an Italian village on the far side of the mountain, seven winding miles down from where we were standing. We were actually going to cross a border to have lunch. How cool was that?

The trail seemed endless as it snaked down valleys and wrapped around the mountainsides. I really had to gun it down the steep part so I didn't get stuck on the approaching uphill stretch. The conditions were perfect, and the only thing ruining the moment was the gurgle coming from my empty stomach. I was starving, which meant cranky was not far behind.

"Are we there yet?" I whined.

"A.G., do you know where you're going?" Dad asked, irritated.

"Bernie, my good man, down is the direction I'd go. Remember, gravity is on your side," A.G. teased confidently.

"Hey look. There's the village!" Barry shouted a few minutes later.

In the distance, we could see coils of smoke rising from the chimneys of little gingerbread-like houses. As we got closer, we noticed decks on some of the wood-framed lodges filled with people eating outside on picnic tables. It was so warm most people were sitting outside without their ski jackets. We found a spot with a table big enough for our group, overlooking the trail we had just taken. We could not believe that we had just skied right into Italy without a passport.

"This is glorious," sighed A.G., as he inhaled the fresh air. "Hmm, something smells good. Pass that menu over, please."

Usually when we went skiing in the US, where the mountains are foothills compared to these Alps, we just grabbed a quick sandwich or a bowl of chili and got back on the mountain as soon as possible. We didn't like to miss a minute of ski time. But on this day, lunch would not be rushed. We were sitting at the foot of the Swiss/Italian Alps on a spectacular sunny day, starving for this new adventure. Back home I knew Nana was making her millionth pie and Mom was deciding which shade of blue would blend best with sea green, but I was here in the Alps and we were about to do some serious eating. I could see in A.G.'s eyes that we were going to take our time and thoroughly enjoy this meal. He called the waiter over and ordered a bunch of different things.

"We'll also have a couple of bottles of Dole wine and glasses for everyone."

Oh boy, drinking at lunch. This was a first. He turned to us and warned, "Let's share everything, but you guys better go easy on the wine. We do have to ski back, you know."

Three waiters came over, each with two plates, and they placed them down in unison in front of us, around the two baskets of semolina bread, two bowls of grated Parmesan cheese, and a bottle of olive oil and balsamic vinegar that were in the center of the table.

As he dug into some spaghetti with Bolognese sauce, A.G. joked, "This will make a good appetizer."

We all took turns passing the plates and tasting every dish. I think this might have been the first meal without one cross word from anyone. Ravioli served with sausages in a pink vodka sauce, tagliatelle in a creamy alfredo sauce, clams in a white wine sauce over angel hair pasta, spaghetti with Bolognese sauce, eggplant Parmigiana, and spaghetti with shrimp in a squid ink sauce. I memorized this meal as if it were the Pledge of Allegiance. Every whiff, every bite, every crumb made my eyes roll back in my head. It was all a very far cry from Chef Boyardee. Up until this point, I only had pasta out of a box or a can, but the waiter said each one was made fresh every morning, and they tasted different because they actually had a taste. Some of the pastas were a little firm, not mushy like how Mom made it. We couldn't stop eating. The sauces were all so rich, but each so different. Some didn't even have tomatoes in them. I had never had a pasta sauce that wasn't a tomato sauce. Once we got past the pasta, we used the bread to mop up every last drop.

"They won't need to wash the dishes with this crew." Dad joked, as the waiters came by and cleared our completely empty plates. He looked at A.G. who had just been handed the menu by the waiter.

"Now, let's get down to some serious business. What's for dessert?"

We spent the rest of the week stuffing our faces and attempting to work it off on the slopes. As was family tradition, at the end of the very last run of the very last day, we all gathered at the base of the mountain, fell down, and put our skis in the air, saying in unison, "What a trip!"

That marvelous trip triggered a wanderlust in me that I have to this day. I figured the further away from my mother's cooking I could get, the better the food would be. My fantasy was to just show up at an airport, look up at the departure board, pick a place to go, buy a ticket, and take off. Of course, not being an heiress, my options were limited, particularly when I became a college student. My big plan was to study abroad for a semester and travel through Europe for a few months before classes began. I had saved up enough money to stay in youth hostels, but I totally miscalculated the cost of everything else.

As I arrived in Paris, I realized I had to quickly become savvy in the ways of a young woman traveling alone. Most of the hostels closed during the day, so I was forced to roam about, regardless of the weather or how badly I would have loved to sleep in. Even on a dreary day, Paris was beautiful, particularly in the early mornings before the heat rose and hazed everything over. I promised myself I would return someday when I had more cash in hand so that I could actually go inside some of the places I drooled past. I practically trailed the waiters at outdoor cafes with hopes that something might fall off their trays. Steaming pots of mussels, boards of charcuterie, baskets of pastries, and bottles of wine were shared by lovers, friends, and families. At one café, I spied two older women who could have been the long-lost twin sisters of Nana and her sister, Helen. While they kibitzed in French, they sipped on tea and enjoyed some divine-looking miniature raspberry tarts. It felt like a scene straight out of *Gigi*. All they needed was some champagne and a saucy gentleman like Maurice Chevalier to escort them home.

My hunger rose with my loneliness. With only $10 to spend each day, there was a limit to what I could do. I hadn't had a sit-down meal since I got off the plane, living only on bread, cheese, yogurt, and fruit. Not that that was so bad. The stinky cheeses were enough to sustain me, but I wanted to get to a place where my dollars would buy more. Maybe Italy.

I booked an overnight train from Paris to Venice with my Europass, fully aware that I had no place to stay once I arrived.

"*Scusi, dov'è l'ostello?*"

"It's okay, my English pretty good."

"Oh, great. I'm looking for a hostel for the night."

"Me too," a young woman said, tapping me on my shoulder. I could immediately tell she was another member of the Single-College-Girl-Tak-ing-A-Semester-Abroad-Traveling-By-Herself-And-Realizing-It-Might-Not-Have-Been-A-Great-Idea-Club. We quickly introduced ourselves and decided to travel together. Phyllis had heard about a convent that took in travelers, and off we went in search of it.

We made our way out of the station and were immediately struck by how much we felt like we were on a movie set. The aging buildings seemed to be standing only because they were so cramped together they supported each other. If I looked behind them, I would not have been surprised to find two-by-fours holding the facades up like scenery flats. Gondolas full of tourists were leisurely making their way up and down the canals, floating by windows of local Venetians hanging laundry and yelling at each other. The paddles created tiny wakes that reflected the sun, making the murky water seem almost inviting as little sparkles of light danced on the surface.

We arrived at the convent and were welcomed by Sister Maddalena, a tiny, wrinkled woman with kind brown eyes. She spoke no English but pointed a lot. She handed us a sheet of paper with various international icons that made clear no food, no booze, no cigarettes, and no men were allowed. It was an immaculate old convent that had made some rooms available for female travelers. It was a bit medieval in feel and I noticed a musty old book smell as we were escorted past the chapel with rows of empty hard wooden pews. The stained-glass windows allowed colored patterns of light to mark the floor, leading like a runway to an alabaster statue of Jesus. Sister Maddalena motioned that we were welcome to pray there, and I whispered to Phyllis, "I wonder if I'll be converted by morning."

She led us to our room where we quickly dumped our bags and collapsed on the beds.

"You hungry?" Phyllis asked.

"Starved."

"Let's go look around. I could go for a plate of pasta."

It was lunchtime and tourists were walking up and over the tiny bridges, peeking into little restaurants, trying to translate the menus to decide where to eat.

"How much is 4,000 lire in US?" I asked, turning to Phyllis.

"About five dollars I think."

"We can afford to eat here!" I squealed, a little too enthusiastically.

An older gentleman wearing the uniform of a professional waiter—black pants, white shirt, black vest, and tie—led us through the main room, out into a tiny, peaceful garden in the back. A trellis of grapevines shaded us from the sun and offered a cool break from the midday heat.

"You think the food is any good? There's no one here," Phyllis wondered.

"This is Italy—how bad can it be?"

We looked through the menus, suddenly realizing that not everything was as inexpensive as we had hoped, but the vegetable dishes were in our range. We ordered a pasta dish to share, *Linguine con Broccoli Aglio e Olio*, and a bottle of red wine. The waiter looked a bit disappointed at our limited choices.

"*Signorina*, no fish, no meat for you?"

"I wish we could, but we're students on a small budget," I admitted.

"*Ah, capisco.* You no worry. Giancarlo will take care of you. I have a daughter your age. She never eats enough."

He tipped his head toward us in a charming little bow and walked back into the kitchen. A moment later, he returned with a full basket of focaccia and two plates of antipasti.

"*Signore, mille grazie, mille grazie*," I enthused.

"I think he's taking pity on us," Phyllis whispered to me.

"Oh, I hope so."

We devoured the focaccia within minutes. The bread was warm and soft on the inside with some grilled onions and sea salt on top. The olive oil was flavored with hot red pepper flakes and a couple of drops of aged balsamic vinegar, giving it a nice sharp kick. We closed our eyes as we took each bite, thanking someone's good Lord for what we were in the midst of eating. I could see Giancarlo, the waiter, looking our way, smiling like a protective uncle. He refilled our breadbasket as soon as it was empty. He opened our wine and poured us both a full glass.

"This wine comes from Piedmont, in the north. My brother Marco has a small vineyard there, and this is one of his favorite wines. I hope it becomes one of yours. *Saluti*," he offered with a sweet smile.

"*Grazie.*"

I raised my glass for a toast and said, "To new adventures, new friends, long lunches, and Marco's winery."

"Amen, sister."

The antipasti platter had slices of fresh mozzarella, grilled red peppers and eggplant, a big hunk of Parmesan, pitted green olives, and some caramelized onions. We took turns trying each one, luxuriating over every bite.

"Oh my, this is heaven," I gushed. "I haven't eaten a full meal since I left New York."

We could smell the garlic emanating from the kitchen a moment before Giancarlo brought out an enormous platter of linguini. He offered us some Parmesan, and we gladly accepted. I could see the imprint on the chunk he was holding as he grated it on top of the perfectly blanched green broccoli florets, making the platter look as if it had just been lightly dusted with snow. I was never a huge broccoli fan, but this dish changed my mind. The broccoli was drowning in garlic and oil—in a good way— with a light dusting of breadcrumbs absorbing the Parmesan as it mingled with the florets.

We just sat there slowly eating, talking about our travels, enjoying our wine, and relaxing. After Giancarlo snuck us a piece of tiramisu to share, we looked at the clock and realized we had been there for four hours. We wobbled a bit as we stood up to thank him. He kissed our hands and said, "It was my pleasure. Safe travels and remember Italy is to be enjoyed. *Ciao bellas.*"

After a couple of days, Phyllis and I went our separate ways, and I spent the next two weeks on my own, making my way South through Italy. And then—disaster.

"What do you mean that's the last ferry for tonight?" I shrieked at the ticket clerk in front of the Brindisi launch. "There's supposed to be one at 6:30."

"*Sì Signorina*, but boat have engine trouble, we cancel it."

I was supposed to meet my college roommate, Sarah, in Athens the next day at noon, and I was freaking out because I was stuck in Brindisi, a small town on the southeastern side of the heel of the boot—the armpit of Italy.

"Is there someplace I can send a telegram? I need to send a telegram."

"There is a post office, but it's a few miles away. You'd better hurry because it closes at 6:00."

Crap. I was tired; I was hungry, I was dirty, and the only good meal I had eaten in the last two weeks was with Phyllis. I was so done with Italy. I rented a motorbike and strapped all of my stuff to it, hoping to make it to the Post office in time. I got there just as they were about to close the doors, but thankfully they let me in. I quickly wrote out my telegram: *Sarah—so sorry for delay. Will meet you at American Express office in Athens Wednesday at noon. KK.*

I knew she would be worried. We had become as close as sisters. This was our backup plan just in case something went south. And things had gone south, way south. Giancarlo might have been the only decent man in Italy. Everywhere else, waiters and shopkeepers couldn't be bothered with a budget-conscious student, and to make matters worse, men harassed me everywhere I went.

"*Americano*? You sleep with me, yes?"

Leer, pinch, touch, and repeat.

"*Bella*, you want a piece of this?"

Expose, thrust, point, and repeat.

My fantasy of a Latin lover quickly dissolved when a squat middle-aged man, seated next to me at a café, smelling of cigars and B.O. with challenging dental hygiene, grabbed my butt and suggested, "*Signorina*, you marry me. We make babies all night long, heh, heh."

I could barely swallow the delicious pasta fagioli I was trying to eat. I was now officially a target. In Italy, the image of an American woman alone was loose, sex-crazed, and easy to bed. It didn't matter if you were short, tall, thin, fat, pretty, plain, or disinterested. It was as if we all had a sign on our back—*Take me hard*. Over those last few weeks, I had gotten pretty good at dodging gropes. I even resorted to spitting when necessary. It was very effective.

I hopped back on the motorbike I rented to make my way back toward the ferry. I was on an old country road with occasional barns and houses dotting the landscape. It was actually quite bucolic as the setting sun backlit the wheat fields and the sky shimmered orange to red. As I enjoyed the view, I didn't notice the gas tank was nearing empty until I heard the putt, putt, putt of its last breath.

"Oh no … no, no, no, NO!"

Tears welled up as I got off the bike and I started walking, and walking. I moved through the long shadows of the cypress trees, listening to the gossip of the sparrows. The only sound that interrupted their conversation was the growl from my empty stomach. Now both tanks were on empty. Finally, after about twenty minutes, a man on a similar motorbike approached and stopped next to me.

"*Hai bisogno di aiuto?*"

"*Non parlo Italiano.*"

We started to play a game of charades as we tried to communicate through hand motions. I pointed to the empty gauge, and he nodded understanding. I gestured that he should go back to town and bring back some gas. He shook his head no, offering a better idea. He pointed to a nearby barn where we could store my bike and then he would bring me back to town for gas. That seemed dumb to me, so I tried again.

He insisted on his plan. Realizing I didn't have much choice, I relented. We both walked into the barn and I parked my bike against one of the horse stalls. There was a bed of hay behind me, and the smell of horse manure hovered over us. Just as I turned around, I saw he was blocking the entrance. He stood there trying to look sexy like Marcello Mastroianni, as he put his hands up suggesting, "What's the rush?"

In a split second, I understood his intent, and I summoned all the rage I had endured from every pinch and leer and exposed uncircumcised dick I had seen in the past few weeks. I clasped my hands together as if I was a human bat and I took a huge swing at him, knocking him out of my way as I ran outside.

"You get your mangy butt out of here, now, you freakin' scumbag!"

"*Aspettare!*"

"GO, MOVE, *USCIRE!*"

I continued to rant and swear like a crazy woman in both English and broken Italian until he took off. I think I scared him more than he scared me. He got on his bike only to realize his back tire was flat. Crap. Double crap.

"I don't care. GET MOVING!" I continued to scream.

He got on his bike and motored off, the bike swerving every now and then from the flat. He didn't notice the small bag that fell off the back of his bike. As soon as he was out of sight, my adrenaline started to calm down and I burst into tears. I began to play the various scenarios about what could have happened in my mind. I made a note to my future daughter—*No, you can't travel to Europe by yourself. Ever!*

When I was sure he was long gone, I picked up the small bag. Inside were a loaf of semolina bread, a small container of mozzarella balls, and a bag of pignoli nut cookies. Jackpot! I took a moment to collect myself and enjoy my winnings. The bread was actually still warm and the mozzarella balls were mixed with some olive oil and roasted red peppers. A few stray tears added a nice touch of salt. The cookies were thick and spongy on the outside and soft on the inside with a hint of almond flavoring. *Delicioso.* The shadows were quickly disappearing, and I had to get back, so I decided to save the rest for later and continued my trudge along that lonely road, hoping that creep's bread wouldn't get too stale before I got back to town.

LINGUINE CON BROCCOLI AGLIO E OLIO

Sometimes the simplest dishes can be the most satisfying. This is one of my go-to dishes when I need to get something on the table quickly. The aroma of the garlic always brings me right back to that backyard garden in Venice.

Serves 4

INGREDIENTS

1 lb linguini
1 large head of broccoli, cut into florets
3 tablespoons olive oil
6 cloves garlic, minced
½ teaspoon red pepper flakes
Salt and freshly ground black pepper
¼ cup freshly grated Parmesan cheese

DIRECTIONS

In a large pot, bring 4 quarts of water and 2 tablespoons of salt to a boil. Cook pasta as per boxed instructions.

Add the broccoli florets to a lidded pot, or a vegetable steamer, filling the bottom quarter of the pot with water, and steam the florets for about 5 minutes until they are bright green.

In a large sauté pan, heat the olive oil over medium heat. Add the garlic and sauté for 1 minute, or until fragrant. Stir in the red pepper flakes and cook for another minute. Add in the broccoli and cook for 4 minutes. Season with salt and pepper to taste, and set aside over low heat.

Drain the pasta, setting aside some of the pasta water, and add pasta to the sauté pan. Stir to combine the ingredients and, if dish looks too dry, add in ½ cup pasta water.

Pour out onto large serving platter and garnish with Parmesan cheese.

Chapter Five

DON'T BE MESSIN' WITH MY BOLOGNA

As I drive Mom back home from visiting A.G. at the hospital, she stares off into space as if watching the movie of her life passing by. She is silent—something I have rarely experienced. It's a bit unnerving. I've been quiet too, lost in my thoughts about losing my favorite uncle and feeling guilty about needing to focus on work and my first staff lunch with Emeril tomorrow.

"Mom, are you going to be OK? Do you want to stay with me and Dan for a few days?"

"I'll be all right. I want to be in my own bed. Besides, why do you want your poor old mother underfoot?

In truth, I really don't, but it feels callous to just drop her off. It's been over three years since Dad died and she's nowhere near recovered from that. None of us are. Now I'm worried that the loss of her brother will really set her back.

"Honey, call me when you get home so I know you got there safely," Mom says as she gathers her things."

"I will. I will."

I watch her rummage through her purse for her keys. It is as if she has aged ten years before my eyes. I manage to hold back my tears until she's in the house and then I sob most of the way home.

Eventually, my thoughts focus back on work. I've really got to be alert and on top of things tomorrow. This is the first time I'll be face-to-face with Emeril since I landed the job. I'm not sure what he's all about. It's been tough to get a read on him over the phone. I don't think he trusts easily, not that I blame him. I don't either.

"Ah, Chef Emeril, so good to see you," says the owner of Sant Ambroeus, one of Emeril's go-to places when he's in town. "We have your table ready; please come this way."

Like Moses parting the Red Sea, Emeril and I walk in with my whole production team in tow. Almost saluting, the waiters line up as we pass. Although it's the middle of the day, the room is dark and windowless. White draped curtains balloon out from the walls as if we're walking inside an oversized coffin. For a fleeting moment, I feel as if I'm in a funeral home.

As soon as we're seated, the maitre d' comes over. "Welcome back, Chef, welcome back. May I start you all off with some antipasti for the table with our compliments?"

"Thank you, that would be great. Any food allergies?" Emeril asks. We all shake our heads no. Pointing to the wine menu he continues, "Okay, let's start off with this bottle of the Sangiovese Bianco and a bottle of the Barolo."

"Excellent choices," the maitre d' responds, trying to take the wine menu from Emeril.

"No, let's leave it here," Emeril says, holding on to it.

"Certainly, Chef."

Within minutes, the maitre d' returns and opens the wines. It's a really warm June day and the Sangiovese Bianco is refreshingly crisp with a nice citrus nose and the taste of apples and pears on the tongue. More importantly, it goes down very easily. As soon as I take a few sips, it seems that there's a waiter at the ready to refill my glass. Eventually, three waiters place two platters each on the table, all in unison. The maitre d' goes clockwise around the table explaining each dish.

"Here you have our Caprese—buffalo mozzarella, Kumato tomatoes, and fresh basil, with a drizzle of twenty-five-year-old aged balsamic vinegar from Modena. This is our Melanzane alla Parmigiana—crispy layers of eggplant in a tomato sauce topped with provolone. Next, my favorite, Vitello Tonnato—a slow-roasted veal tenderloin with a yellowfin tuna sauce and pickled capers."

"Veal with tuna sauce? That's interesting," says Emeril.

"I know, but you must try it. This is our Insalata di Aragosta—Roman-style artichokes and lobster served with orange segments. We also have a platter of Prosciutto San Daniele with Mozzarella di Bufala, and, last but not least, our Asparagi Freddi—steamed asparagus, tomato, hard-boiled egg, and rainbow micro greens. *Buon Appetito.*"

Just as the maitre d' leaves, two baskets of freshly baked focaccia fly in with plates of olive oil for dipping.

I lean over to Emeril and whisper, "I could get used to this."

"Welcome to my world," he says, clinking his glass against mine.

Chills of anticipation raise goose bumps on my arm. I can't believe I get to eat all of these scrumptious dishes. But by the time the antipasti are done, so are the two bottles of wine, plus another two. Emeril and I seem to have done most of the heavy lifting on those wine bottles, because the room is suddenly swishing from left to right and back again, like a canoe after a motorboat has raced by. I don't know if it's the heat of the day, worrying about A.G., or drinking wine on an empty stomach, but somewhere between the Tagliatelle alla Bolognese and the Scaloppine ai Funghi, I realize I'm hammered. This is not what I wanted for my first full meal with Emeril Lagasse, not to mention my whole staff. This is not good.

"She went one-for-one with him. Bad mistake. Ooh, she's gonna feel that tomorrow," I overhear someone whisper from across the table.

Trying to seem nonchalant, I attempt to stand up without falling down. Barely successful, I make my way to the bathroom just in time to hurl out each and every mouthful of antipasti and sip of wine, making the kid from *The Exorcist* seem like a lightweight. After my third uncontrolled purge, I splash some water on my face and make the mistake of looking in the mirror. My face is all red and blotchy, my eyes are teary and practically crossing, and there's a little dribble of vomit on my shirt. I'm mortified. I've spent the past few months trying to gain the respect of my team and Emeril, and now I'm about to blow it.

I do everything I can to put myself back together. I wipe off the mascara that has formed streaks under my eyes, I carefully remove the vomit, trying not to leave too big a water stain, then I take about five Altoids from my purse, crush them in my mouth, and palm some water to swish out what must be the worst breath on earth. I gather all the strength I can muster, which isn't too much, and hobble back to the table. Thankfully, everyone is pretending not to notice and politely ignoring the fact that I've been gone for about fifteen minutes, or they're just as drunk as I am.

Emeril is sitting back enjoying some espresso and a snifter of Grand Marnier as the rest of the team destroys a platter of Italian pastries. He is perfectly in control, not a slur to his speech or even the slightest droop in his eyes.

He leans in towards me and quietly says, "So, did you have a date with the porcelain bowl?"

My cheeks feel on fire as they instantly blush. I am totally busted.

"Uh, well, yes, unfortunately."

He laughs, "Don't worry, you'll learn to keep up."

"If it doesn't kill me first."

"It's part of the job," he says. "Welcome to the team."

Did I just get hazed? I can see some of my staff trying not to laugh.

"Don't worry about it," Marie whispers. "After my first meal with the team, I was out for two days. You'll get used to it. My advice: drink lots of water. Lots."

I have no choice but to laugh at my own stupidity.

The next day, with my head still pounding from one of the worst hangovers of my life, I pull myself together for my first show in the studio.

"Coming to the Countdown."

"The animation will be on D."

"This is the slate, twenty seconds to the open."

"Stand by on D."

"Stand by music."

"Ten seconds to the open."

"Ready black."

"Tracking A."

"Six to the open, five, four, three, two, …"

"Music, dissolve one, cue Emeril."

Sitting in the control room, I can feel my heart rate spike as those last few seconds of the countdown run out. This is the moment when all the hard prep work comes together and explodes out from behind the curtain with Emeril as the cork to our champagne bottle.

"How you all doing tonight? You ready to kick it up a notch?"

The audience goes nuts. He's like an evangelical preacher, but instead of embracing God, he embraces garlic. I can't believe what I am seeing, what I am a part of. People have come from all over the country to see this guy cook. They love his man-on-the-street style, his playfulness, and his genuine passion for food that comes through as hard as a meat mallet tenderizing a veal steak for schnitzel.

"Hey, pork fat rules, you know what I mean?" he'll say while waiting for his bacon strips to render.

The first time we set up a call-in number for audience tickets, the phone lines crashed. You'd think the Beatles were getting back together. But where else can you get dinner and a show for free? Dan always asks me what his food is like, but I rarely get to sample it because we actually serve it all to the audience. On occasion, Emeril will call me behind the counter and offer me a morsel.

It is the last day of my first week of taping. I am exhausted. We have completed three shows a day for the last five days, which by any standard is insane. Most of us are punchy, including Emeril. It's one of the last commercial breaks and the kitchen staff comes out with their cart as usual, placing a two-foot by five-inch wide phallic-looking bologna on his cutting board.

"You've got to be kidding me," I hear him say over my headset. "What am I supposed to do with this thing?"

The earnest sous chef goes through the recipe with him and Emeril shakes his head. "Yeah, yeah, yeah. I got it, I got it."

Just as the band starts to play and we bump in from commercial, I see a little twinkle in Emeril's eye and I know we're in trouble. Emeril leers at the bologna, teasing the audience as if he's not sure what to do with it. Little laughs start to wave across the room. He picks it up and holds it, making sure we all admire its size and girth, then stands it up erect on a cutting board.

"Basically, what you want to do with your bologna is you want to peel back this outer skin, if you will."

The audience cracks up. He looks over at a woman who is just shrieking with laughter.

"Lady, don't go there, please."

He continues peeling back the skin and then tries to fit it on his baking sheet.

"You see this bologna is so big, it won't even fit on this pan."

He playfully tries to maneuver it, purposely failing.

"What you want to do … ladies, you all right over there?"

More laughs, as he reaches for some oil and slowly rubs the bologna up and down and up and down.

"What you want to do is rub it all down nice, like this with some oil and spices, and then put it in the oven."

As all of this is happening, I realize it is my job to decide whether he's going too far or not. My instincts tell me to let him ride along the edge, praying he doesn't go over it. If I shut him down, he'll be pissy and we'll never get the momentum back. If I let him go long, then I'll always be able to edit something out if necessary and he'll never need to know. The latter option is by far the better bet.

Because the bologna is bigger than the baking sheet, it doesn't fit into the oven. I can barely hear him over the audience's laughter, not to mention the hysterics from the gang in the control room.

He tries and tries to make it work and then finally says, "Sometimes you just gotta say, hey, don't be messing with my bologna," as he forcibly shoves it into the oven, slamming the door shut.

He milks the moment, proving that his instincts are spot on. Without any formal training, he knows exactly how to play the audience. He rarely makes a joke that doesn't work or has a moment that seems insincere. Working with him is like riding a bucking bronco, holding on for dear life. I can let him out of the pen so he can go wild for a while, but at some point, he might need to be brought under control.

During the break, I go down and give him my best schoolmarm glare. He knows he was naughty, and he doesn't want to get the teacher mad.

"You're gonna keep that, right?" he asks. "I don't have to do it again, do I?"

"You came pretty close, but no, you don't have to do it again."

He gives me a devilish smile, slices a piece of bologna for me, and says, "Here, try my bologna."

I take a bite. Not being much of a bologna lover, I am surprised by how spicy and tasty it is, even if a little too salty.

"Not bad, right?"

"Not bad."

"I'll be good, you'll see. I promise."

Although I'm still not sure what he may pull next, we are starting to develop a trust, and I realize my job is to create an atmosphere where he is comfortable to be himself. Once, in an interview for a behind-the-scenes show, I asked Emeril what excites him about doing the show.

"My goal from day one has always been, if I could influence one person, to get them just a little bit more excited about food or wine, or about cooking or eating, then I could sleep well at night."

For the record, I am imagining Emeril sleeps very well indeed.

After a few months, the show gets into a steady rhythm. As Emeril would say, "We're cookin' on all burners." He can't walk down the street without someone screaming out, "Bam!" By the end of the second season, his face isn't just on TV; it is on spices and pasta sauces. His trademarked signature is etched onto everything from pots and pans to blenders and knives. He's a walking merchandising conglomerate and he's been opening restaurants in Miami and Orlando and Las Vegas, not to mention a third one in his adopted home of New Orleans. Life is sweet, and no one wants to stop eating dessert.

The ratings have been consistently strong, and the network wants us to break as much new ground as possible. Traditionally, most of the shows on the network have been dump and stir shows. *Emeril Live* has taken this a step further with the addition of an audience and a band, but it's still the same principle. But now the network executives are giving us the latitude to try new things and Emeril and I are more than game.

"I think we need to get you out of the studio," I say.

"What do you mean?" Emeril asks.

"Well, you should meet other people in the food biz—butchers, cheesemongers, other chefs," I say. "We can shoot these on the down low, without the entourage, edit them, and then roll them into the show. You should also interact with regular people, your fans."

"What do you want me to do? Sell crap out of a hot dog cart?" he jokes.

"Actually, why not?" I respond. "That's a great idea."

And that's how Emeril's alter ego, *M the Street Guy*, was born.

Wendy, our ever-eager art director, rents a hotdog cart and the kitchen staff trick it out with all his *mise en place* and three to four of his favorite New Orleans dishes. It's now the dead of winter, so Wendy scours some vintage stores and finds him an oversized army surplus jacket and an Elmer Fudd-style hat as his character costume. Before our show starts taping, we have to shoot these short segments early in the morning, so I make sure he comes to the location unshaven and grumpy, knowing full well that he's not a morning guy. Then we put him behind the cart, roll the cameras, and let him loose on the streets of Manhattan.

"Crepes Suzanne with Marchand de Vin Sauce, Bananas Foster, Shrimp and Grits—hey lady, don't touch the merchandise. No free samples."

People start lining up, not believing that Emeril is actually there serving food. In the midst of it all, a cab driver pulls over and screams out his window, "Hey Emeril, kick it up a notch for me."

"The name's 'M'. Whaddya want? I got some boudin blanc here with your name on it, buddy. You want mustard with that?"

"I'll take the works."

Emeril preps the sausage and delivers it to the cab driver.

"Bam," the driver says, laughing.

"What, no tip?"

The driver pulls away. Emeril looks at the camera and says, "What a cheapskate."

The crew and I do everything not to crack up so we don't wreck the scene. Emeril LOVES this, and he doesn't stop until his cart is completely empty.

We roll these pre-taped pieces out during the show taping so we can get some reactions from the audience, and they eat it up. His character is easily accepted because Emeril is truly a man of the people. He has gotten truck drivers talking about *beurre blanc* sauces, and school kids asking what they can make *à la minute*. And the press is taking notice.

"Check this out," Felicia says, handing me a copy of this week's *People* magazine.

"They named him one of the twenty-five most intriguing people of the year? Holy crap!"

In the blink of an eye, he's everywhere. His ability to excite the average Joe about food is becoming a national phenomenon. He's made it cool for manly men to cook, and he is making people realize that good food is not just for the elite. For the crew and me, there's nothing like riding on the wings of a jet as it takes off. Here's hoping we can keep our altitude high because it feels as if the sky truly is the limit.

I realize that I've drunk the Kool-Aid too, and it's been spiked. Working side-by-side with Emeril has jacked up my own gastronomic enthusiasm so high that I begin obsessing about food. He has that effect on people. Breakfast is no longer just a bagel with a schmear, it's a free-range, two-egg omelet with sautéed spinach, oyster mushrooms, chevre, and fresh herbs from Citarella's, served with a lightly buttered, fresh brioche. My VISA bills are getting so out of control, I have no choice but to cook more at home.

I always thought of myself as a decent cook, but now that I have gotten a glimpse of what goes on in the professional world, I realize I have no clue what I'm doing in the kitchen. I don't read recipes all the way through, my knife skills are abysmal, and my repertoire, although occasionally successful, is painfully limited. Just being better than my mother does not automatically make me a good cook.

I have never made a roux or stirred a risotto, or reduced a port wine sauce. But with every recipe I read and every show I produce, I'm learning. This is cooking school for me; I'm getting a free culinary education and loving every minute of it. Along the way, I have become fearless in the kitchen. When something in particular strikes my fancy, like Emeril's delicious rack of lamb, I can't wait to try it at home for myself.

"I'd like a rack of lamb, please," I request.

"Would you like me to trim the fat?" the butcher asks.

"That would be great, thanks."

"That will be sixteen dollars, please," the butcher says, handing me the wrapped rack.

Hmm. That's surprising. I thought it would be smaller, and cost more. Maybe he gave me the Food Network discount.

The butcher shop is one of the many small food shops at Chelsea Market, a new food hall on the ground floor of Food Network's new home. Originally, it was the site of the old National Biscuit Company, aka Nabisco, where supposedly the Oreo cookie was invented. The funky, arched brick hallway boasts shops on either side, featuring everything from Amy's Bread and the Chelsea Wine Vault to Sarabeth's Bakery. Just walking in each morning to the smell of freshly baked bread is enough to make me realize that I have one of the best jobs in the world, even if the fresh mozzarella from Buon'Italia is helping me put on a few too many pounds. Bowery Kitchen is at the end of the hall by the elevators to our offices. It has every type of kitchen tool I could ever want: paella pans, fish tweezers, crab crackers, cupcake stands, and everything else I didn't know I needed. Every day, as I make my way home, I can't help picking up yummy treats and new gadgets.

"What time should I tell Mary to come?" Dan asks.

"How about seven o'clock? I think we'll be ready by then," I answer.

It's Friday night during one of our dark weeks, so Dan and I are making dinner for our neighbors, Mary and Troy, who are always enthusiastic and willing to go with the food flow, no matter what food emergency we might have. And we've had many these past few months. These include the chocolate soufflés we attempted for the first time. Chef Roy Yamaguchi was a guest on the show and he gave out soufflé kits to everyone in the audience. I was lucky enough to snag one. Basically, it's just a kit with good-quality chocolate and a recipe. As I pulled them out of the oven, they were perfect, just like the picture. But we had eight of them, and soufflés wait for no one. They have to be eaten at once.

"We're having a food emergency; come over quick and bring the kids!" I shouted into the phone.

And they did, helping us devour every last spoonful. Not only are Mary and Troy neighbors we can count on, but they even help with the dishes.

For tonight's dinner, I need to get busy. I have begun to cook *Emer-ilistically*, so I know the importance of the Seven Ps: *Proper planning and preparation prevent piss poor performance*. This job is seeping into my brain. I read through the recipe, not once, but three times, making sure I understand what's needed. I prep all of the ingredients and then carefully begin, seasoning the meat, then searing it with the fat side down, first for two minutes, and then flipping it for another two minutes. After allowing the rack to cool for a few minutes, I brush it with mustard and then dredge it in an herb-crumb mixture. Next, off it goes into the 400-degree oven. Dan sets the table and Mary arrives with my favorite—Patricia Well's Cheesemaker Salad. The dressing is so simple, yet so delicious. It is basically red wine vinegar marinated shallots and heavy cream. The vinegar sort of curdles the cream, hence the name. It sounds gross, but it's divine. We pop a bottle of Petite Syrah and then wait for the timer to go off.

One glass down and I pull out the rack. It's practically still raw. I check the oven. No, the temperature is right, it seems fine. I put it back in for another twenty minutes, figuring maybe the cooking time was wrong.

Twenty minutes later, still nowhere near done.

Another twenty minutes and the internal temperature is only 100 degrees. By now, we've finished the first bottle of wine and we are moving on to the next. In total, by the time it's done, dinner is over an hour late, but at least it smells good. And it was almost worth the wait.

"Yum. This is delicious. It's not gamey at all," I say, patting myself on the back.

Mary takes a bite, not knowing quite how to put it. "Um, I hate to say this, but I think it's not gamey because it's not lamb. It's pork. And that's why it took so long to cook."

"Ohhhhh …" I say.

"But you're right. It still is delicious," she says.

Major blush. I am humbled. Here I am, the executive producer of the country's most popular cooking show and I can't tell the difference between pork and lamb. Pathetic. Just when I think I've pulled it all together, I realize I'm just as lame as I've ever been.

Another confession—the last time I made a Thanksgiving turkey, I left the plastic package of giblets inside the bird. Idiot. I have got to work on my game.

I have to get up extra early the next morning because we're doing a pre-tape at The Lobster Place, the fish store on the ground floor of Chelsea Market.

"Hey guys, watch the electrical wires. The floor is wet," Emeril says to the crew. "No electrocutions today, please."

Emeril and I are sitting on two milk crates at the back of the store, waiting for the crew to finish lighting the room for a quick remote shoot. The floor is wet from the ice that the workers schlepp out of the freezer to fill the seafood cases. Red snapper, cod, trout, squid, tuna, swordfish, clams, mussels, and shrimp of various sizes are all beautifully laid out like chorus girls waiting for the curtain to go up. In the back storeroom, there's an enormous tank of lobsters taking their last swim.

"So, what are you making for dinner tonight?" Emeril asks.

"I'm not sure yet," I say. "Any suggestions?"

"You want to blow Dan's socks off?"

It's not surprising that he's thinking about dinner. The man lives, breathes, and dreams about food. Not just what he's going to eat, but what everybody else is going to eat too.

"You're going to make him lobster risotto," he says.

"I am?" I ask.

"Yeah, this is what you need to do. Ask the dude in the back for four lobster bodies. Don't let him charge you for it 'cause he's just gonna throw them out anyway after he's picked them clean of meat. Then you're gonna make a stock with onions, celery, carrot, bay leaf, salt, and pepper and throw those puppies in a pot with water just covering them, bring 'em up to a boil, and then down to a simmer for about an hour-and-a-half.

If you want, buy a whole lobster and throw that one in once the water is boiling. Take out the whole lobster when done and let it cool. You'll use the meat later."

I start furiously writing, my hand barely keeping up as he spits out the recipe.

"Once the stock is done, taste it and make sure you've got enough salt. It's okay if it's a little too salty because the rice is going to absorb it. Once you've got it all nice-nice, strain it through some cheesecloth. Now you're ready to make the risotto."

"Hold on, hold on, let me catch up," I say.

He waits for five seconds, then says, "You ready? Okay, next, pick that whole lobster clean of all the meat. Pull out the tail intact and slice it into eight pieces. Chop up the claw and knuckle meat and set aside. Are you getting all this?"

"Yeah, yeah … hold on … okay, keep going," I say.

"I like to sauté some onions and garlic in a little olive oil for a few minutes, then add the rice. Make sure it's Arborio rice, not that Uncle-who-ever crap. Toss it around to coat the rice and let it just start to brown. Then add in a ladle of the stock. You've got to constantly stir it. Don't be putting the top on and doin' your nails, you got me?"

"I gotcha, I gotcha." I laugh.

"When the rice sucks it all up, add in another ladle and keep stirring. Keep an eye on it, and keep adding stock when the liquid gets absorbed. It should take about twenty minutes or so. Right before it looks done, add in a ¼-cup of grated Parmesan and the chopped-up lobster meat. Keep stirring another minute or so. Don't overdo it and let it get mushy. Taste it. It should be slightly al dente. To plate it, scoop some into a bowl, place the sliced tailpieces on top, garnish it with more cheese and some chives, and drizzle on some truffle oil. You're done."

"Oh, that's all?" I ask.

"No. Go buy yourself a nice Viognier and a loaf of crusty bread at Amy's. You can thank me in the morning," he says, and then turns to the crew. "Hey, can we get this show on the road? This ain't the Oscars. Let's do this already."

Emeril's impatience reminds me of my father. If it wasn't so un-PC, I'm sure he'd call my crew "a bunch of morons" while they dither with their cables and clamps. He hates wasting time because he's got five million other things on his plate to deal with when he's done with us—opening his new restaurant in Orlando, finalizing the recipes for his latest cookbook, partnering with Wusthoff on some knives, hiring a new GM for his restaurant NOLA, talking to a reporter from the *Times Picayune*—and it's only Monday.

"Okay, guys, we've only got ten minutes to shoot this before I have to get him into makeup for the show," I say. "Stevie, is Emeril's mic hot? He's ready to roll."

"Emeril," Steve nods to Emeril for a mic check.

"Testing, one, two … hey, Steve, did you hear my recipe for risotto?"

"Every word," Steve says. "Making it tonight."

"Hey, and I thought that was just for me," I tease.

"Gotta share the love baby," Emeril says.

And that's what food is to Emeril: love. He's not a touchy-feely guy and often has difficulty expressing his emotions, so his best way of communicating is through food. He loves to turn people on to tastes and flavors and new ways of approaching old standbys, whether you're a VIP from our most important sponsor or our show dishwasher.

"Steve, I told Karen to pick up a Viognier to pair with it. Sauvignon Blanc would be good too."

"Thanks, Em," says Steve.

The entire crew is now obsessed with food and cooking. It's hard not to be. Emeril's passion is contagious. He shares his love of food with everyone and that has earned him the loyalty of all of us who spin in his orbit. He respects people for their hard work, regardless of where they are in life. He once was that dishwasher, and that guy peeling potatoes, and that woman on the line trying to keep up with orders. He doesn't take for granted where he is, and he certainly doesn't forget where he started, so he knows the value of committed workers. And you'll know if he likes you if he calls you by a nickname. When he's in a good mood, I even get one—*KK*, my initials.

The fishmonger nervously stands in his place. Emeril chats him up to relax him. We roll cameras and Emeril greets him as if they're old poker buddies.

"Hey, Joe, how's it going? What's looking good today?"

Within minutes we've learned how to pick out a fresh fish, how to scale and fillet it, and the best way to cook it.

"Thanks, Joe. Listen, next time I'm here, save me some of those porgies, will ya?"

"You got it Emeril."

"And cut. Nice job, guys. Okay Em, you're good to go," I say, turning to our cameraman.

"Hugh, can you pick up some B-roll for me? I need shots of all the fish they talked about and some more close-ups of Joe filleting the snapper."

"Got it," Hugh says.

"KK, I'll see you upstairs. You think we'll start on time?" Emeril asks.

"Yeah, the team is already loading the audience. I'll be up in a few," I say.

"Hey, aren't Dan and your mom coming today?" Emeril adds.

"Oh yeah, they sure are," I say.

"Well, I hope they come hungry."

"Don't worry. They can eat," I say. "It's a family trait."

PERFECTED RACK OF LAMB

Once I figured out the difference between pork and lamb, I was able to actually perfect this dish after a few more tries. Rack of lamb can be expensive, so try your local Costco. I promise—I'm not getting a kickback from them. Their lamb is grass-fed from New Zealand, and it won't break the bank. It has a little more fat than some of the racks you might find at your fancy butcher shop, but it's worth doing your own trimming to save a few bucks.

Serves 4

INGREDIENTS

2 racks of lamb (about 14–16 chops)
¼ cup olive oil, plus 3 tablespoons olive oil
1 cup panko (or breadcrumbs)
Salt and pepper
1 cup finely grated Parmesan
2 cloves garlic, minced
1 cup Dijon mustard

DIRECTIONS

Preheat the oven to 400 degrees F.

Trim as much fat off the lamb as possible. Cutting between the bones and joints, slice the racks of lamb into individual chops. Liberally season all sides of the chops with salt and pepper.

In a large skillet, heat ¼ cup olive oil over medium-high heat. Add 5 or 6 chops at a time, being careful not to crowd the pan. Sear the lamb for two minutes on each side, until lightly browned. Drain on paper towels. Repeat the process for the rest of the chops, adding more olive oil as needed.

Pour the panko into a shallow bowl. Season the panko with ½ teaspoon each of salt and pepper. Stir in the Parmesan and garlic until combined. Drizzle 3 tablespoons olive oil on the panko mixture and stir again to combine.

Brush all sides of each chop with mustard. Dredge the chops in the panko mixture, covering the entire chop, and shaking off any excess panko.

Place the chops on ovenproof grill pan, and roast for 16 minutes. Let rest for five minutes before serving.

Chapter Six

THE WAY TO A MAN'S HEART ...

... is indeed through his stomach. It's a cliché, but in my case, it's a pizza that clinched the deal with Dan. We met by chance on a street corner in the late 1980s. He was walking uptown with a mutual friend as I was walking downtown to meet her for dinner. She introduced us and I was charmed by his smile. Little did I know then that fate had shown its hand and given me a life partner who loves food maybe even more than I do.

"How can you say deep dish Chicago-style pizza is better than New York pizza? There's no contest." I demanded, dismissing his opinion.

We're sitting knee-to-knee on our very first date at La Bonne Soupe, a cute bistro in Midtown. Our fondue forks are dancing around each other as we each dip cubes of bread into a piping hot pot of Gruyere.

"Well, because it just is. There's so much more going on with it. First of all, you have the cornmeal crust, that's way better than your floppy New York crust," he insisted, not willing to give an inch. Being born just north of Chicago, he was making his loyalty crystal clear.

"Floppy? Where have you been getting your pizza? Our crusts are crunchy with just enough give to fold if you're that kind of pizza eater. Don't tell me you're a folder?"

He laughed. "Sometimes I fold, but not all the time. That's beside the point. New York pizza doesn't have nearly the amount of toppings that Chicago style does. You have to eat a whole pie here just to get what one slice of deep dish gives you."

Even though he didn't know what he was talking about, I liked that he stood his ground. The waiter arrived with our chocolate fondue for dessert, and our conversation moved to the world of sweets where chocolate is king and there is no argument.

"Ooh, this is delicious!" I said, dipping a banana into the chocolate. "But my favorite dessert is profiteroles."

"I'm more of a brownie kind of guy. I actually bake these incredible Hello Dolly cookies."

He bakes? This is promising. "Hello Dolly?"

"Yeah, they're like normal brownies but they have a layer of condensed milk and some coconut added in. I'll make them for you sometime."

He'll make them for me sometime? That's a future-thinking thing. Guys don't do that. We finished the meal, and he offered to walk me home.

"But I live way down in the Village. Isn't that out of your way?"

"It's a nice night. Let's walk."

I had heels on and it was a good fifty blocks to my place, but I was game. It was the week before Christmas and New York was magical with holiday lights hanging over the avenues like strings of shimmering diamond necklaces. Storefront windows along Fifth Avenue displayed mannequins dressed as Santa's helpers and ornaments hung from the reindeers' antlers. People were loaded down with shopping bags and scurried about, waiting for the dazzling light show projected against the walls at Saks. We nudged our way past the rushing masses and found a spot at the southwest corner of Rockefeller Center to admire the magnificent seventy-five-foot Norway spruce Christmas tree. With its thousands of twinkling lights, it was more magnificent in person than any NBC-TV special could ever show. He reached for my hand and I swear an orchestra swelled in my head. The smoky aroma of chestnuts roasting on the coals of the nearby street carts wafted past us as we watched the skaters slide and fall, our fingers trying to find that comfortable spot where everything seemed to fit just right.

I don't think we let go of each other's hand the whole way home. We walked right past Penn Station, his last chance to jump on the Express train back to his place in Queens. We made our way down through Chelsea and then into the village, walking past the big spruce tree in Washington Square Park, as the Christmas lights cast colorful patterns on the arch. Like a gentleman, he walked me to my door and gave me a sweet, long kiss goodnight. Soft lips. Yum.

"I'll call you," he said, looking deep into my eyes.

"Are you just saying you'll call me, or will you really call?"

He laughed, "I'll really call."

I watched him walk off and then he turned, smiled, and waved. I didn't even notice that I couldn't feel my feet anymore.

For the next month, I needed to travel for work, so I didn't have a chance to see Dan, although we spoke almost every day. It turned out he was a composer and wrote a lot of underscoring for TV. Although he was in a related business, his work rarely pulled him away from his computer, and I was often on the road. My lack of availability turned out to be a good thing because, without trying, I had become a worldly, mysterious woman, at least in his eyes. When I finally got back to New York, I called to invite him for dinner.

"Come hungry," I teased.

I actually had a pretty cool surprise for him. For once, I had met a man who actually seemed to want to see me as much as I wanted to see him.

Garlic permeated the apartment as my oven warmed the room. I had scattered some candles about, put on some smooth jazz, and set the table with new placemats and linens I bought on sale from the Third Street Bazaar. Tingles ran up my spine when the doorbell rang. He didn't arrive empty-handed. He brought a sweet bouquet of irises and a bottle of Mouton Cadet, the same wine I had in my rack. We were both a little nervous as we caught up on the past month.

"How was your shoot? What was it for again, a tennis magazine or something?"

"Good memory. Yeah, it was one of those subscription commercials. It was cool shooting in Key West. It's a funky, party town. Great conch fritters, though."

The oven timer went off and I excused myself and sauntered into my tiny kitchen, trying not to reveal the big surprise too soon. I opened the oven and inhaled. It was perfect.

"Ta-da!" I proudly announced as I brought out our main course on a big round platter.

He took one look at it and then he looked up at me as if he had just seen his first Mustang Convertible. He took the plate from my hands and then gathered me in his arms for a big appreciative kiss that made my knees weak.

"How did you get this?"

"One of my flights connected in Chicago and I passed a neon sign, *Sky Pies to Go.* I couldn't resist."

Who knew you could buy Chicago Deep Dish Pizza on dry ice to go, with four different toppings, no less? I opted for the sausage, a good choice, it turned out. He kissed me again, just long enough that I was left a little breathless. And then we got down to the good part—the pizza. I had to admit, there was something about this deep-dish style that had its charms. The crust was crunchy, the cheese was oozing and the sausage had a sweet and spicy kick to it. I just prayed the garlic didn't get in the way of our budding romance.

"This is so good, so good," he moaned, enjoying every bite. "I haven't been home for a while and this brings back some great memories, big time."

"I'm so glad. I have to admit, it's not bad."

"Not bad? Chicago deep dish is the best."

"I'm still not totally won over."

"It's getting to you, isn't it? Admit it."

"Yeah, it's getting to me. It's getting to me."

We smiled, devoured almost the whole pie, and then moved on to each other. Best dessert ever.

Within months, I knew he was the one. But two years into our relationship he hadn't quite figured that out, so I came up with a brilliant plan—a ten-day trip starting in Paris, making a loop down through the Rhone Valley and up through the Loire to celebrate the second anniversary of our first date. I made reservations at bed and breakfasts, private inns, and even one castle. I was hoping that with our two-year anniversary fast approaching, he might pop the question. In my mind, I knew we were going to be together forever. I knew he knew it too, but men really can take a while to put it all together. I was sure that this trip would do the trick.

Each day the sun rose into a crisp blue sky. We traveled the side roads through quaint villages and countryside, dotted with the brilliant colors of autumn. We stopped in local markets and made picnics of Saint-Marcellin, a farmhouse cheese, and paired it with a Saumur Champigny, a lovely burgundy wine given to us by one of our innkeepers. We even listened to Edith Piaf as we drove from one breathtaking vista to the next. Then, with the scene set and Van Gogh's afternoon light draping over us like a warm blanket, I waited for those four simple words, "Will you marry me?" Nothing. Day after day, one Hollywood set-up after the next, I didn't hear a peep from him.

When I closed my eyes, I could still see the blazing foliage coming toward me at warp speed. Burgundy, crimson, amber, and mustard-colored leaves blurred together as we zoomed past the backlit trees. We were on hour six of our drive from Avignon to the small town of Le Blanc in the Loire Valley, and I was drunk on flora overload, like a sailor finding his balance on land after a month at sea. I was ready to stop for the night, but we still had a few hours to go.

"How are you holding up? Do we need to stop to feed you?" teased Dan.

Not finding any humor in his questions, I responded, "Very funny. No, let's have dinner in town when we get there. I'm sure there will be a bistro or café open. But could you step on it? You're driving like an old lady."

Our rented red Citroen gallantly sped through the kaleidoscopic forests, down into the verdant green valleys of wine country. The lines of perfectly placed vines looked animated as we raced past vineyard after vineyard. The sun's rays sparkled off the dew settling on the engorged grapes, hinting at the harvest soon to come. And that made me think of wine, which made me think of food, which coincided with my blood sugar dipping below a safe level, whereupon I turned into a venom-spewing psychopath. Hunger and I did not get along. Dan bore the burden of my tirades, as nothing would make me human until I was fed. Like a caged animal, my claws and fangs came out just ready to pounce on any unsuspecting passersby.

Sensing my mood shift, Dan suggested, "Maybe we should stop somewhere, just for a quick snack."

"You think?!" I spit back at him.

"You know how you get," he rebutted, trying to sound reasonable.

"No, how do I get?!" I bit back.

He knew better than to engage with me at this point, and we drove on silently, in search of any place, for a morsel of anything. But we were deep in farm country and unless we pulled over and slaughtered a cow, there was nothing and nowhere to eat. The sun was setting, the sky was going from indigo to black, and if there was a full moon, I suspected the hair on my knuckles would have sprouted from my skin.

Just past 9:30, we arrived in Le Blanc, only to find that every restaurant was closed for the night. I could feel the rush of panic rising up, forcing the first few tears down my cheeks. We arrived at our B&B, and although I tried to keep it together, my voice quivered as I asked the owner in my high school French, "*Y a-t-il un endroit ouvert pour le dîner?* Is there any place open for dinner?"

Looking at me with a combination of disdain and pity, Madame Martin answered, "Zere iz nowhere. All cloze at nine."

She hesitated for a bit, sensing I might burst into sobs, and grudgingly continued, "Maybe I can bring some cheese, some wine. Zat be good?"

I was so overcome I could not speak. Dan stepped in and said, "That would be perfect. *Merci Madame, Merci.*"

As we opened the door to our room, we were welcomed by a light breeze floating in from the floor-to-ceiling windows that led out to a veranda. The silk drapes undulated like a dancer performing in *Madame Butterfly*. We could smell eucalyptus and pine mixing with the distant scent of *Gitanes* wafting up from Madame's kitchen. Dan came up behind me and pulled me close. For a fleeting moment, I was overwhelmed by the romance of the moment only to be shocked back to reality as my stomach continued to growl. Knowing all too well that I was close to the point of no return, Dan whispered, "Just hang on a few more minutes."

"I'm fine!" I snapped.

Moments later, Madame entered our room with a tray of Mother Nature's best gifts—a luscious chunk of Curé Nantais, one of the valley's best raw cow's milk cheeses, a slice of country paté with cornichons and Dijon mustard on the side, a cluster of local purple grapes, a bowl of fresh raspberries, a classic French baguette, and a bottle of Sancerre. Like a prisoner being given her first meal after freedom, Madame could see the gratitude on my face. She smiled, half-laughing to herself as she said, *"Bon Appétit,"* and left us to feast.

Tears of joy streamed down my cheeks. I never had a meal that was simpler or more satisfying. As we popped the last grapes in our mouths, I exhaled in relief, finally sated. Dan quietly asked, "Are we better now?" I smiled lovingly, shook my head "yes," and then licked the last morsel of paté off the knife as I curled up next to him, hoping against hope that he would see that this was another perfect moment to propose. But he still hadn't read the memo.

By the time we got back to Paris, I was so frustrated I could barely speak to him. We had time for some breakfast before we made our way back to the airport. I know he knew I was pissed. As we walked towards the café, there was dust everywhere from the jackhammers tearing apart the street. People jostled and pushed past us on their way to work. A taxi driver cursed us as we accidentally walked in front of his moving car. In the midst of all that, Dan turned to me and announced, "Maybe it's time we get married."

"What? I can't hear you over the jackhammers."

He raised his voice, spitting out the words one at a time, "I said, I … think … it's … time … we … get … married."

"Really?! Really?!"

"Yes, really."

Soot was mixing with my tears of joy as I jumped into his arms. It wasn't quite like I had pictured it. As a matter of fact, it was nothing like I had pictured it. There was no bending down on one knee, no well-thought-out elaborate ruse to surprise me, no extravagant romantic gesture. No violins. But it still was pretty sweet. As he justified it later, "I just wanted to cheer you up."

CHICAGO DEEP-DISH PIZZA

As a New Yorker, I think I have some type of block when it comes to making Chicago deep-dish pizza. I've bought the pans and I've scoured the internet for recipes but, quite frankly, nothing I've made has come close to the real deal. So, here's a different option, if you want your pizza to taste authentic.

Step 1. Buy a round-trip ticket to Chicago. While you're there, take in the sights and go to Lou Malnati's and order the deep-dish pizza called The Lou—a spinach, garlic, basil, and onion mix with mushrooms and sliced Roma tomatoes covered with three cheeses on their trademark garlic butter crust. You won't be sorry.

Well, you might be if you eat too much. Take your favorite antacids with you, just in case.

Step 2. While you're waiting for your flight home from O'Hare, look for a small kiosk called Sky Pie to Go. They will sell you a pizza on dry ice. It fits perfectly in the overhead. The last time I bought one was a while ago, so just in case the kiosk no longer exists—or if you don't have time to go to Chicago—you can actually order online from Malnati's. They ship. https://www.loumalnatis.com

Chapter Seven
ONE BIG FAMILY

I'm actually a little nervous about Mom coming to the show for the first time. She's watched a few episodes and is not exactly a fan, as she made clear to me last night on the phone.

"Honey, it seems like a lot of fun, but, you know, cooking shows aren't really my cup of tea," she says. "And what's with the bamming all the time? He's so loud."

"That's just his thing Mom," I say. "People love it."

"I guess so. But his food seems so spicy. You know I don't like spice."

"Mom, listen, when you come to the show, just go with it, okay?"

"What? You think I'm going to embarrass you?"

"Yes."

"Very funny. I'll see you tomorrow. Is there parking nearby? I don't want to have to walk too far in that neighborhood."

"Mom, the neighborhood is fine. It's changed a lot since you were last here at the turn of the century. They have electric lights now."

"Ha, ha. It's not nice to make fun of your poor old mother."

"Oh yes, it is," I tease. "There's a parking lot on 17th Street between Ninth and Tenth Avenues. The studio is just one block down from there. You'll be fine."

The next day, Mom manages to find her way to the studio with no problem. As I head up to the control room, my crackerjack audience team has made sure to seat Mom near Emeril's cooktop. Dan is with her and they're both pretty camera-shy, so they don't want to sit at the bar where they would actually have to talk on TV. From the control room, I can see various members of the crew stopping by to chat Mom up. It's an unwritten rule at the show: moms are always treated like queens for the day.

"Your mom is a hoot," Marie says. "That Long Island accent is really something."

"Yeah, it's a killer isn't it?"

Marie is no longer working in the kitchen. I snatched her away, and now she's our culinary producer.

"She's gorgeous," says Mike, our director. "The camera loves her."

All the cameramen can hear Mike over their headsets; so all seven of them get various angles on Mom. Mom's face is plastered across every monitor, including the ones on the floor. Her reaction is priceless as she realizes she's on *Candid Camera*.

"Is that me?" she asks Dan, her face turning beat red, "I'm going to kill her."

"Mike, you'd better get off her or she'll flip out," I say.

"Okay, okay," says Mike. "Cameras go to your opening positions. Phil, pan a little left. Jay, you've got Emeril behind the curtain. Everyone set? Okay, I'm ready to roll."

"Okay people coming to the Countdown," says Keith, our assistant director.

"The animation will be on D," calls Mike

"This is the slate. Twenty seconds to the open," Keith continues.

At the end of the countdown, Emeril bursts out onto the set and the audience has the same reaction it always does, ecstatic bedlam along with a standing ovation. I can see on Hugh's camera that Mom isn't sure what to do. Dan nudges her up and they stand, politely applauding. As everyone continues to go nuts, Emeril makes his way around the counter to his opening position. He stops to shake Mom's hand and he gives Dan a quick bear hug before the audience cheers die down.

"How you all doin' tonight?" he says.

As the audience sits down, I can see Mom is relieved that Emeril is talking to them and not to her. He continues on with the show and I have to admit, I'm a bit relieved too—not that Emeril would ever intentionally embarrass her or anyone.

"Hi, I'm Emeril Lagasse and welcome to *Emeril Live*. Hey, you know the saying, 'Where there's smoke, there's fire?' Well tonight, I decided to turn up the heat and do some firecracker cooking. And speakin' about firecrackers, give it up for Doc Gibbs and the *Emeril Live* Band."

Applause.

"We're lighting the fuse tonight in my Red Hot Kitchen, right here on *Emeril Live*," Emeril says, pointing to the camera.

"Roll music, roll graphics," Mike says, as the opening graphics give Emeril enough time to get out of his sports jacket and wrap his apron around his waist.

"Not the best show for your Mom. It's a spicy one," Marie whispers to me.

"I know. But Dan will eat everything for her."

"Good thing I'm packing Tums," Marie says. "He's gonna need 'em."

"You think of everything," I say.

There's a wonderful camaraderie that's developed over the past year with the entire production team. We are now a well-oiled machine and everyone knows what needs to be done. We've weeded out the whiners and back-stabbers, and now have a group that actually enjoys working together. We've become our own little family and the lines have started to blur between professional and personal. Many of the crew has had their spouses and kids and parents in the audience, and Emeril goes out of his way to make everyone feel welcome and special. For as gruff as he often may appear, he's actually got a big soft spot for family.

"Dan the man, how ya doin'?" Emeril says, wiping his face with a towel as he heads toward his dressing room at the end of the taping.

"Great show today, Em," Dan says, shaking Emeril's hand.

"Emeril, this is my ..." I say.

"Ah ha, you must be Mama Katz," Emeril interrupts.

"Call me Barbara."

"Did ya have a good time?" he asks.

"Oh, it's all so exciting!" Mom enthuses, "I had no idea so much goes into making this show. There's an army here. It looks so easy on TV."

"Well, talk to your daughter about that," he says. "She's the one keeping the train on the tracks. Hey, did you get to try all the food?"

"I tried, but it was a little too spicy for me," she admits as I give her a little nudge to shut up.

"Ah, another critic," Emeril laughs. "Next time, I'll make something that doesn't set your mouth on fire."

"Ooh, I'd like that," Mom says. "Do you make shrimp scampi?"

"For you darlin', whatever you want," he says, then turning to me. "She's a pistol. Bring her around more often."

"Honey, you look tired," Mom nags at me. "You know, if you don't have time for dinner, we can skip it."

"Well, I do have to get up pretty early tomorrow. We're going up to Emeril's hometown, Fall River, Mass, to shoot a special."

"Fall River? That's where your Uncle Allen had his Ford dealership, you know."

"You mean, Garten Ford?" Emeril asks.

"Yes, Garten Ford," Mom answers surprised.

"I bought my first used car there!" Emeril says.

"Wow, you're kidding! What a small world. It must be a sign."

Okay, what are the odds of that? My uncle meeting Emeril before he was *the Emeril,* our lives brushing up against each other in a random exchange over an old Thunderbird. Emeril gives Mom a quick hug and then walks off to greet some other guests backstage.

"You see. That's Daddy and A.G.'s way of saying they're proud of you." Mom says. "Oh, he's so nice. I like him much better in person than on TV."

"Mom, you couldn't just say you liked his food?" I ask.

"He should know it's too spicy," she insists.

"Not for everyone," Dan interjects.

"Well, he didn't ask everyone, he asked me," Mom says.

I'm not sure what it is about Mom and her lack of filters. Does it come with age? Or is she just at a point in her life where she has no more time for bull? Emeril's mom, Hilda, is the same way. She tells it like it is. She's like an older Emeril in the female version. She's got dark hair, thick black eyebrows she paints on, and has the gravelly voice of a lifelong smoker. Her laugh comes from the gut and the lines on her face reveal that her life was not always an easy one. She raised her family with Emeril's dad, Mr. John, in the blue-collar town of Fall River, Massachusetts. But unlike my mom who had no interest in food, Hilda treasured her Portuguese heritage, gladly passing down many of her family recipes to a hungry and curious Emeril.

"No, don't add the kale yet," she says, during a visit to the show, slapping Emeril's hand away from a pot, as the audience laughs.

"I forgot to tell you, in the kitchen, don't mess with Miss Hilda," Emeril jokes.

It's always nice when Hilda is on the show. Like me, Emeril is a bit on edge having his mom around, never knowing what she might say. But it's easy to see how much he cares for her. It makes me curious to see where he grew up, and how the community shaped him. He often talks about another woman who was like a second mother to him, Chef Ines de Costa. Now in her seventies, she runs the kitchen in the back of an old VFW, bringing back memories of her Portuguese roots with every *bacalhau* and *caldo verde* she makes. She welcomes my crew and me as if we're beloved distant relatives.

"Come in, come in," she says, as we arrive after our long drive. "Please, put down all your heavy gear. First, you eat, then you work."

Although she's the same age as my mom, she looks ten years older, having lived the life of an immigrant, working hard since the day she arrived. Her hands are wrinkled and chapped, not accustomed to manicures. She's hunched from years of standing over pots, her skin scarred by various burns. Her gait is slow, but that doesn't stop her from working in this rundown old kitchen seven days a week, no matter how badly her knees ache or how much her family nags her to slow down. Her purpose in life is to make people happy through her food.

"I've made all of your favorites: fried belly clams, grilled mackerel and onions, sausage and beans."

"Chef Ines, you're spoiling me," Emeril says. "Let me help you. It will be like old times."

Emeril goes back into the kitchen with Chef Ines, picking up the heavy flour bag for her breading mixture. He treats her with tenderness and respect, offering to do whatever she needs. He lifts up the lid from a cauldron of caldo verde, tastes it, and then picks up the salt.

"Uh, uh, uh. No more salt," she says, taking it out of his hand. "There's enough."

Smiling to himself, Emeril obeys her orders.

I think we're ready," Chef Ines says. "Emeril, will you carry out these two platters?"

"You got it."

They lay out a feast for the crew, everyone salivating from the smell of frying fish and slow-roasted pork snaking its way into the dining area. You'd think the crew had been stranded in the woods without food for a week by the way they gulp down everything in sight.

"Hey, leave some of those belly clams for me," Emeril says, noticing the platter is almost empty.

"Don't worry, I have more in the fryer. Eat, eat," Chef Ines insists.

She hovers over us like a proud mama bear watching her cubs pick apart a salmon that got caught upstream.

"Won't you please join us?" I ask.

"I will in a minute. But there's more coming."

She waddles back into the kitchen, touching the backs of some chairs for balance.

"This is incredible," I drool.

"She's incredible," Emeril says with affection. "You know she won't sit down. She'll just keep feeding us until we can't move."

Emeril isn't wrong about that. After all of Emeril's favorites are gleefully eaten, there are still platters and platters to come: cod fish cakes, grilled sardines, braised beef and vegetable stew, grilled sausages, and *feijoada*. They are served along with *massa sovado*, a sweet Portuguese bread that we use to soak up every last drop. Then she stuffs us with Portuguese pastries—my favorite being a small egg custard tart that's similar to a crème brûlée. This meal may not be the fanciest or most "gourmet" I've ever eaten, but it rates as one of the most delicious and emotional feasts I've ever experienced. It proves to me that it is actually possible to taste love.

MY CALDO VERDE

For years I've been trying to recapture Chef Ines's magical Caldo Verde. So much of what she made had the intangible element of love on her ingredients list. Whenever I make it, I always think of her and hope that some of that love lives through my cooking, too.

I've taken some liberties with this recipe, like garnishing it with Parmesan, so I hope the Portuguese community forgives me. Serve this with some nice crusty bread and it is a meal in itself.

Serves 8

INGREDIENTS

2 tablespoons olive oil

1½ cups finely chopped Spanish onions, or you may substitute yellow onions

1 tablespoon minced garlic

2 pounds Yukon potatoes, peeled and cut into 1/2-inch cubes

8 ounces firm chorizo, or other hot smoked sausage, diced or crumbled

Salt and freshly ground black pepper, to taste

½ teaspoon red pepper flakes

7 cups turkey bone broth, or low-sodium chicken broth

8 ounces kale, large stems and ribs removed, and leaves thinly sliced

¼ cup chopped fresh parsley

¼ cup finely grated Parmesan

DIRECTIONS

In a large Dutch oven, heat the olive oil over medium-high heat, and sauté the onions for 5 minutes until translucent. Add the garlic and cook for 1 minute. Add the potatoes and sausage and sauté 2 to 4 minutes, or until the potatoes begin to brown. Season with salt and pepper, and stir in the red pepper flakes.

Add the broth, stir, cover, and bring to a boil. Reduce the heat to low and simmer about 15 minutes, or until the potatoes are fork tender.

Stir in the kale and simmer another 15 minutes. Season with salt and pepper to taste.

Ladle the soup into large bowls, and garnish with fresh parsley and Parmesan.

Chapter Eight

FEED ME YOUR FOOD OF LOVE

"It's only seven-thirty in the morning, and it's already so freakin' hot," I complain to our director, Mike.

"It's supposed to go up to ninety-five, but it's gonna feel like a hundred-and-five with the humidity," he warns. "Glad we'll be in the air-conditioned truck all day."

"Yeah, but Emeril is gonna melt."

We're standing outside our production truck, grabbing a quick cup of coffee as our crew busily lays out cables, hoists lights, and moves our cameras into position. We're in the middle of Chicago's Petrillo Music Shell in Grant Park, about to tape something that has never been done before—a cooking concert in front of a live audience of 10,000 people. It's part of the city's annual Taste of Chicago Festival, and *Emeril Live* is the main event.

We're at least 200 yards from the stage as our production assistants lay out chairs for the audience. Grant Park is huge, and I pray that there will be enough people to fill all these seats. It's just ten hours to showtime, and there are a few diehard fans lined up, but we're going to need busloads more. The sun is blinding as it ricochets off the windows of the surrounding buildings. In the distance, I can see the haze moving slowly across Lake Michigan. It's one of those miserable, sticky, hot, humid summer days that make your inner thighs chafe. Sometimes I wonder why I do what I do—so much for the glamour of TV.

"A front is on its way," Mike says. "Let's just pray it holds until we're done."

"Don't worry, I've got my mom working on it."

I've brought Mom to Chicago as our weather guarantee. For years, she has been able to predict the weather, and will it to change when needed. She calls it her "witching powers." A huge storm is supposed to move in tonight, and her job is to keep it at bay until the show is over. She makes it clear she's on it, calling me throughout the day.

"Honey, I've watched The Weather Channel, and I think you're going to be fine," Mom reports. "The storm has stalled a bit over Iowa, so I'll put in a few good words upstairs to keep it that way. You might get a few sprinkles, but if you start on time and don't mess around, you should make it. The real downpours won't start until tonight around 8:30-ish. I can't be held responsible after that."

I've bitten off a lot with this show. There are so many variables at play here that I'm nervous it will all end in disaster. What if it does pour? What if no one shows up? What if we can't finish the set in time? What if Emeril freaks out and can't hold the audience? We only have a couple of hours for rehearsal and one shot at taping it. We're going to try to do it as live as possible so the audience won't get restless. We only gained access to the stage last night, so our set design and lighting teams have already been working for hours. Just wait until the network sees the overtime bills for that.

"This is quite a production you've got going on here," Judy says. "Are you going to get everything done in time?"

"It always looks like it's impossible at this stage, but the production gods always come through," I say, faking confidence.

"Do you have a rain contingency?" Judy asks.

"Yes. We get wet."

I didn't mean to be cocky with our new network president, but it's the truth. There are no do-overs for this. Fortunately, Judy is a very level-headed executive who gives her staff a lot of leeway, provided they deliver. She's got a good fifteen years on me, but she keeps herself younger looking with a sleek, short haircut, that is never out of place. She walks as if she's got a little too much weight on her shoulders, probably from all the stress that comes with the job. So far, she seems to like what we've been doing for the network. She's tough, having come up the hard way as a leader in a business driven by men, but she's also willing to listen, taking in all sides before making her decisions. She's always the grown-up in the room. If I pull this one off, hopefully, I'll stay in her good graces and she'll allow us to keep trying new things.

"This is a great opportunity for outreach with our affiliates," Judy adds. "And if this type of thing works out, there will be a lot of requests"

This is good. Now all I have to do is not screw up.

"What do you have left to do?" she asks.

"Right now the art department is laying down risers for the band and for the on-stage VIP audience. They still need to set Emeril's cooktop and portable oven and then dress everything."

"It looks like all of the crew have already soaked through their Food Network T-shirts."

"Yeah, well, if you think it's hot standing here, it's at least 10 degrees warmer on the stage with all the lights."

"This is a big area. How many cameras do you have for coverage?"

"We've got twelve cameras which should cover the stage and the audience. I've even got a camera on top of that building across the park so we can capture the size and feel of the event."

"Impressive. Well, I can see you've got answers for everything. I'll leave you to it. What should I say, 'break a leg'?"

"I like to say 'break a lens.' Thanks."

I really went to town on this one. I even enlisted the whole family. Not only is Mom in charge of the weather, but also Dan wrote the music for two specialty songs, and I wrote the lyrics. Doc Gibbs and the band have brilliantly brought them to life, and for me, it is as thrilling as birthing a healthy newborn. I might produce hundreds of hours of television, but nothing is as exciting to me as hearing a song I wrote performed by professionals. I actually got the idea for a cooking concert based on Emeril's love of music. Had he not become a chef, he probably would have been playing drums for Van Halen or the Doobie Brothers. Our show band has always given him energy and the venue almost demands music to be played, so why not combine music with food? Seemed like a no-brainer to me, but now that I hear the roll of thunder in the distance, I'm beginning to think we didn't have to rent those timpani drums after all.

"Hey, just checking in to see how you're holding up," Heidi says. "Everyone is so psyched. The first cooking concert ever. Brilliant idea, Kar. The press is eating it up, so to speak."

"Oh great, now there's hype to live up to," I say.

"Stop worrying. It's gonna be fine."

I love Heidi. She's the head of marketing for the network and she's the one that really pulled this deal together with Taste of Chicago. She once told me that the first person that has the *cojones* to say the *F-word* in a meeting owns it. If she had balls, they would be made of steel. She's got an infectious enthusiasm that can win over any cynic. She's fortyish, lean and fit with shoulder-length blond hair, and dresses like Carrie Bradshaw. She prides herself in being the queen of takeout, especially since she removed the kitchen from her apartment in order to have more closet space.

"How's Emeril doing?" she asks.

"Good, really good. I just went over everything with him in his trailer and now he's talking to Susan about the recipes as if nothing special is going on."

"That's good. I'll be curious to see how he handles all of this."

"You and me both, sister," I say.

Little by little, things start to take shape. The art department has finished painting the flats and is moving the set pieces into place so lighting can get back in to set focus. All the cameras are on their platforms, so Mike is working with the camera team to set up shots for the food close-ups as well as some wide-sweeping cover shots of the crowds. I've already gone through the rundown with Mike and have checked all the graphic packages with newly designed logos made specifically for this special that will bump in and out of the commercial breaks. The kitchen team is on their game and now all I have to worry about is ... everything.

I don't know where the day went, but it's now five minutes to our announced 6 p.m. start time. Miraculously, every single seat is filled and the audience is chanting, "Emeril, Emeril, Emeril." We're close, but not close enough to start.

"Mike, are you ready? Those skies are looking way too angry, and the audience is totally ramped up. Uh-oh, is that a raindrop on Jay's lens?"

"I could use ten more minutes," he begs.

"Mike, I don't think we can wait. You've got to go and you've got to go *now*."

"Okay, I can tweak the rest during the breaks. Rhoda, is Emeril ready?"

"I was born ready," I hear Emeril say over Rhoda's headset.

"Copy that, Mike?" Rhoda, our stage manager, asks.

"I copy, I copy," Mike says. "Okay, everyone. Let's do this. Keith, start the countdown."

And with that, there's no turning back. My adrenaline jacks up and I'm practically shaking in anticipation.

"... five, four, three, two, fade up," Keith calls.

"Cue announcer," Mike orders.

"Ladies and Gentlemen. Food Network and the Taste of Chicago welcome you to Emeril's Big Bam Blast. It's time to kick it up a notch for the man you've all been waiting for, Chef *Emerilllllllllll Lagasseeeeeee!*"

"Cue the band. Cue Emeril," Mike shouts.

Doc and the band have already gone from zero to sixty as they play Emeril onto the stage. The crowd goes absolutely insane as every one of those 10,000 people gets to their feet, applauding and screaming. Little do they know Emeril has a surprise. He heads over to the band and nudges Teddy, our drummer, to the side, picking up his sticks and ripping into a drum solo Buddy Rich would be proud of.

"Steve, is that thunder?" I say to our audio engineer.

"No, it's the audience!" he says.

It must take at least a minute before the applause dies down after his solo.

"*Hellllloooooo Chicagoooooo!* Are you ready to kick it up a notch?" Emeril shouts.

The energy is electric and Emeril has turned on the switch full blast.

"We've been wanting to take the show on the road for a long time and we couldn't think of a better place to start than here in Chicago."

The audience cheers again.

"This is my kind of town. Now I know there's a lot of people here, so I'm gonna cook some really big food tonight! If you think I've kicked things up notches unknown to mankind before … just you wait. You ain't seen nothing yet! And if that's not enough for you, we've got Nell Carter and Charlie Musselwhite in the house to sing you some very special tunes. Not to mention Doc Gibbs and the *Emeril Live* band. Tonight we're gonna blow the roof off this town! So, let's get started."

Oh man, he is loving this. He has no sign of nerves or fear. I don't know how he does it. I would be a total drooling mess if I had to stand up in front of this crowd. Without missing a beat, he launches into his first dish—Fred Flintstone-sized, bone-in rib eye steaks cooked on an enormous grill. As he starts seasoning the steaks, we settle into familiar territory, chatting on headsets discussing plans for what's next.

"Rhoda, is Nell standing by?" Keith asks over the headsets.

"Standing by," Rhoda responds. Rhoda is our beloved stage manager in New York and on the road.

Emeril wrestles with the huge steaks and you can smell the scent of them searing on the grill all the way back here in the production truck.

I've had his steaks before and my mouth is watering just thinking about them.

"Okay, coming to the break in five, four, three, two, and fade to black. Cameras, when clear, move into position for the Nell Carter performance," Mike instructs.

The kitchen staff swarms onto the stage like ants at a picnic, removing all of Emeril's used tools and dishes. Another group sets up for the next recipe. The audio department puts Nell's microphone center stage, and the lighting team does a last-minute tweak. We're keeping our breaks tight, only giving the crew a couple of minutes to reset. I step outside to check the weather and all I see are dark, gray ominous clouds. At least they're blocking the heat of the setting sun.

"Mike, I don't know if we're going to make it to the end," I say.

"Let's just keep going," Mike says. "I have faith in your mom. We won't stop unless there's lightning."

"Stand by. Roll tape."

"Bucky, give me a sweeping shot from back to front over the crowd on the bump in," says Mike.

"Graphics coming in on D in five, four, three, ... cue music, cue graphics."

Rhoda is frantically waving her arms so the audience cheers as we come into the next act. Quite frankly, they'd be cheering whether she waved her arms or not.

"Hey, hey, hey. Welcome back," says Emeril. "We're here at the Petrillo Bandshell in the heart of Chicago!"

He waits a beat until the audience settles down.

"You know, I often talk about the importance of cooking with love. It makes everything taste so much better. Well, please give it up for a very special guest who sings with so much love, she makes everything sound better. Let's hear it for Nell Carter."

Nell saunters onto the stage, soaking in all the adoration. The piano starts out with a slow, jazzy intro as Nell steps into the spotlight.

Baby, baby, I need a good man
Who knows how to use a frying pan
I'm hungry for you, my sugar pie
Can you serve me up honey now, don't be shy

Her voice hits a husky crescendo on that last line as the piano does a glissando, launching her into the upbeat part of the song.

We can slice it up and dice it up
We'll cook through the night
Oh let's shake it and bake it
We'll make it taste right
Let's mix it up and fix it up
Please give me a bite
Of your tasty lovin' food tonight

Her backup singers step forward for the chorus.

Feed me, feed me your food of
Feed me, feed me your food of
Feed me, feed me your food of love

This is going better than I ever could have imagined. Emeril is dancing along behind his counter. The audience is going wild. She's singing our song! I can barely hold back the tears welling in my eyes. I wish Dan could be in here with me.

Please puree me, sauté me, and stir me with style
Whip it up now honey, ooh stay here a while
Got my burners on high, and I'm waiting for you
To make us a hot dish for two
Feed me, feed me your food of
Feed me, feed me your food of

Feed me, feed me your food of love

As the backup singers take over the chorus, Nell starts to ad-lib some spoken lines. "I'm starvin' honey. I can't wait much longer. Don't put me on your back burner."

And then she continues with the song.

> *When I watch you cook, I'm caught in your spell*
> *You drive me wild with all of these smells*
> *All my senses are aroused by your tasty treats*
> *Oh baby, when can I eat?*
> *Think it's 'bout time to add some spice*
> *Kick it up now honey … ummm make it nice*
> *Take a pinch and, BAM!, oh baby, that's right*
> *Gettin' hot in here tonight*

Nell adlibs against the next chorus again, shimmying closer and closer to Emeril who happily plays along, plating her a dish and following her orders.

"You got some hot sauce, honey? Oooh, I like it spicy! Oh honey, pour it on! Did I hear seconds anyone? Over here now baby. That's right, just keep dishin' it out. Now we're cooking."

Nell cradles herself inside Emeril's open arms, singing directly to him.

> *Feed me, feed me your food of*
> *Feed me, feed me your food of*
> *Feed me, feed me your food of looooovvvvveeee.*

She milks every last bit of the chorus, as the audience jumps out of their seats screaming for more.

"That … was … awesome," I say, barely able to contain myself.

Mike raises his hand in the air for a high-five with me but doesn't miss a beat as he continues to direct the show. Now I remember—*this* is why I do what I do.

"Bucky, keep panning the applause," Mike orders. "Everyone else, back to your cooking positions."

The entire team is hustling to keep the show moving. At this point, it's all up to them. There's nothing more I can do except be a cheerleader. I've prepped as much as I can and gone over every detail with the team. They know what they have to do. Act after act, Emeril still keeps the audience enthralled with every "Kick it Up a Notch" and "*Bam!*" It's now the penultimate act, and Charlie Musselwhite ambles on stage to sing the other song Dan and I wrote, *Pork Fat Blues,* adding in one of his signature harmonica solos. I get tingles throughout my body as the audience sways along when he sings:

> *Way down in Louisiana*
> *Deep in the Great Bayou*
> *Was raised by my mama*
> *Papa took off—I was two*
> *But every night at six she sat me down*
> *And fed me the best food this side of town*
> *I got them Pork Fat Blues*
> *I got them Pork Fat Blues*
>
> *When mama passed on*
> *Didn't know what to do*
> *So I took to the road*
> *Needed a life that was new*
> *But no matter where I roamed around*
> *My stomach was stuck in the lost and found*
> *I got them Pork Fat Blues*
> *I got them Pork Fat Blues*

Charlie rips into his harmonica solo, bringing the audience to their feet.

Found my way back home
Down to New Orleans
At a place called Emeril's
Could not believe what I seen
In ever' dish and bite I swear to you
That man puts Pork Fat in his shoes
He says that Pork Fat Rules
He says that Pork Fat Rules

In rehearsals, Charlie was a little hesitant to sing a new song that happened to be written by the executive producer of the show and her husband, but now I think he's surprised at the audience's reaction. Up until this point, the show has gone off without a glitch or a flub or a … wait … is that thunder? I open the door to the production truck, and I can see lightning over the lake. I start counting. It's a good ten-count before the sound of the thunder reaches us.

"Mike, the storm is close. Push the crew through this break. We only have one more act to go."

"Heads up everyone, Mother Nature waits for no one," Mike says. "Let's do this."

"Mike, let's go. It looks like Armageddon out here." I hear Emeril say over his mic.

"Okay, back in five, four, three, two … fade up," says Keith.

Emeril races through his last recipe, a banana cream pie. Within seconds, he pulls the finished swap out from under the counter, rushing to say his goodbyes and thank-yous.

"And then you just hit it with some powdered sugar. *Bam, Bam, Bam!* There you have it. Hey, I wanna thank you all for coming! This has been an incredible night! Thanks again to my guests Nell Carter, Charlie Musselwhite, and Doc Gibbs and the *Emeril Live* Band. And a special thanks to our weather goddess, Barbara, for keeping us dry. Chicago—this was a blast! See ya next time!"

As soon as the audience rises to their feet for their final applause and as we go to black, a deafening crack of thunder precedes an avalanche of rain that soaks everyone within seconds. It's as if the gods were pushing back on a dam for as long as they could before letting the floodgates open.

But we got it. We got it all and now all we have to do is turn off the power, get everyone to safety (most especially the audience), and celebrate.

"Honey, that was wonderful! And did you see? I held the rain off as long as I could," Mom says proudly.

"You did a great job, Mom. Did you hear Emeril thank you?"

"I did, I did!"

"Honey, what did you think? Did you like the songs?" I ask Dan.

"Well, it was actually hard to hear over the audience."

"Oh, no. It was so cool from the truck. I wish you could have heard it."

"Don't worry, I'll hear it when it airs," he says. "The show was great, really great. I couldn't get over how many people were here."

"I know, it's nuts," I say.

"Honey, Dan is going to take me back to the hotel," Mom says. "I'm tired. That took a lot out of me."

"Me too, to tell you the truth," I agree. "But I have to make an appearance at the wrap party."

"Okay, I'll see you in the morning. Don't stay out too late."

Now she's mothering me?

The crew is meeting at a bar near our hotel called *Man vs. Margarita*. With a name like that, I already know who is going to win. I love our crew, but whenever we are on the road away from family and responsibilities, they party like frat boys. And that puts me in the position of den mother, which I hate.

"Okay, no one is driving right?" I ask. "You're all going to walk or cab back to the hotel?"

"Yes Mom," Steve assures me. "Relax and let me buy you a drink. You deserve it."

I hang for a while, chatting with Steve and Mike. But once I see one of our production assistants doing a pole dance, I realize it's time for me to go.

"Okay, that's my cue. I can never un-see that," I shudder.

What I don't know won't hurt me. They're all supposedly adults and off the clock, so they're on their own. I just pray the cops don't show up. Besides, we all have a 7 a.m. call tomorrow because our work here in Chicago is actually just beginning. We're doing a week of *Emeril Live* shows in a local studio, so we've got some long days ahead.

The next morning as I walk into the studio, I can smell alcohol oozing out of the pores of some of the crew. They're all wearing sunglasses and I'm not even sure if they've slept.

"Hey, do you like our Blues Brothers look?" Steve asks.

"Ah, so that's what those are for? Nice try," I say. "You guys had better pull it together."

"Have we ever let you down?" he says.

Nope. They never have. But just in case, I pull a production assistant aside and tell him to go get extra strength Tylenol and a few buckets of black coffee. I feel bad for the kid, a recent college graduate with dreams of directing, but we all have to start somewhere.

"CAN'T UN-SEE THAT" MARGARITA

For better or for worse, being on the road with a production crew guarantees some wild nights. If there are things you really don't want to remember, have a few of these and you'll be just fine.

Makes 1 drink

INGREDIENTS

2 ounces tequila
1 ounce Cointreau

3 ounces freshly squeezed orange juice
1 ounce freshly squeezed lime juice
½ ounce cranberry juice
1 slice lime, for garnish
1 slice orange, for garnish

DIRECTIONS

Place six ice cubes in a cocktail shaker and add in all ingredients, except the cranberry juice and garnish. Shake vigorously. Place 4 fresh ice cubes in a margarita glass and pour in the strained contents from the shaker. Lightly pour the cranberry juice on top as a floater and for color. Garnish with 1 lime slice and 1 orange slice.

Chapter Nine

COMPANY'S COMING

"I think we should buy a whole cow. We can have it butchered, split up the pieces between us, and start cooking our way through all the parts," suggests Troy.

"You want to cow-pool?" I tease.

"Yeah, that way we can learn about all the different cuts."

My neighbor Troy never does anything halfway. In addition to being one of the country's top lawyers in multi-national business negotiations, he also happens to be a luthier, having worked his way through college making guitars under the tutelage of renowned bass maker Roger Sadowsky. He's also brilliant, charming, and the most grounded and humble person I've ever met. Each day he goes to his office in a suit with a light blue shirt and bow tie. He has so many variations of light blue patterned shirts that his daughter Katia cut squares from his old ones to make him a quilt. A creature of habit, he's been wearing the same round, gold spectacles since the day we met, and most likely years before that. He and Mary, along with Dan and me, are the founding members of *The Best Neighbor's Carnivore Club*, an exclusive meat-eating club that also includes our neighbors Melissa and Amanda, whom we affectionately call *The Melandas*.

"Whose turn is it this week?" Troy asks.

"It's ours," I say. "We're going to do a food and wine pairing dinner featuring Potato Encrusted Beef Tenderloin with a Port Wine Reduction.

"Ooh, sign me up for that!"

Last week, Melissa made a Korean tri-tip dish that was perfectly grilled with a wonderfully tangy marinade of soy, scallions, ginger, and some other ingredients she won't reveal. She has a gift, knowing exactly how to work her Weber, earning her the title of "Grill Queen." She insists upon not completely scraping down her grill, convinced the charred remains add flavor over time.

"You know I love the idea of pooling our money for different cuts of meat, but a whole cow?" Melissa asks. "We live in Brooklyn. Who has freezer space for that?"

I'm glad she stated the obvious, but I hate to burst Troy's bubble. He's been one of my biggest supporters since I've been working at Food Network. There's never a food emergency or experiment that he's not up for. We are eating well on this block, even when things don't go as planned, like the time we almost killed Troy's wife, Mary, one overly indulgent evening.

"So what's on the menu?" Troy asks.

"Check the sheet," I say, as a nod to Nana.

KAREN & DAN'S FIRST ANNUAL FOOD & WINE PAIRING DINNER

Hors D'oeuvres

Smoked Salmon in Puffed Pastry with Caviar, Sour Cream & Dill Sprigs
Baked Brie

Pairing: Champagne, Veuve Clicquot

Amuse-Bouche

Shrimp Ceviche
Pairing: Sauvignon Blanc, Cloudy Bay

A Duo of Appetizers

Ajiaco de Pollo
Pairing: Chardonnay, Rombauer
Pizza Blanco with Shiitake Mushrooms, Smoked Bacon & Truffle Oil
Pairing: Burgundy, Châteauneuf du Pape

Entrée

Potato Encrusted Beef Tenderloin with a Port Wine Reduction
Pairing: Rioja, Marques de Riscal Reserva

Dessert

Dark Chocolate & Orange Tart with Toasted Almonds
Pairing: Sauterne, Château Guiraud

Admittedly, the menu is a bit all over the place, with dishes from Latin America, Italy, and France paired with wines from New Zealand, Spain, and France. We justify that by saying we're going for a *global* experience. The show has been on hiatus for a week, so Dan and I have been preparing the dinner for days.

"Where'd ya put the puffed pastry?" I ask.

"It's in the freezer downstairs," Dan answers.

We're still a little discombobulated in terms of where we're putting everything. We just bought the floor beneath us, doubling our living space. The pathetic thing is that we had so much crap stored in our original space, that we've already filled the new space, only needing to buy a couch and a chair to make it seem homey. Rather than combining the floors, we decided to keep them separate and keep both kitchens. Without consciously realizing it, we've turned them into his and her kitchens, with mine being the savory one and Dan's being the sweet one. If I need a cup of sugar, I have to go downstairs and borrow it from him.

"How's the tart coming?" I ask Dan.

"It tastes good. But it looks a little lopsided, don't you think?"

It actually looks like something you'd get at a French patisserie with his signature web design combining three chocolates, each with different cocoa percentages. He's hypercritical of his desserts, and never seems to be satisfied.

"Are you crazy? It looks gorgeous," I insist. "Stop fussing with it or you'll wreck it."

I'm a little less of a perfectionist when it comes to the savory dishes. I plate with a rustic curbside appeal. I go for flavor over fussy techniques. Now that I've been exposed to so many different styles of cooking, it's as if I've become fluent in the language of recipes. I can now read a recipe and know if I'll like it or not, or what I can tweak to make it more in line with my own palette. I actually cross-reference multiple recipes for the same dish to see which directions make the most sense, or which ingredients I can tailor to my own taste. I've made most of the dishes we're serving before, but the main course, the Beef Tenderloin, is new. Just to be sure, I've read three different ways one can use potatoes to encrust the meat; you can mash them, slice them into chip size, or grate them like latkes.

"Which one are you going to use?" Dan asks. "You know I love mashed."

"I know, but I think it will be too mushy and won't get crispy. And the chip-sized ones might not adhere or will curl out. Besides, latkes have never let us down before."

"True, but you really have to squeeze out the water once you grate the potatoes," Dan says.

Anyone who's made latkes knows the importance of *squeezation*. Watery potatoes in hot oil leave permanent splatter scars.

"Speaking of latkes, I'm going to add some onion to the potatoes for the crust," I add.

"Ooh, nice touch. That should be delicious. Do you think it will go well with the port wine reduction?"

We spend the next few hours rushing around, prepping the rest of the dishes, setting the table, and checking off everything on our list. I have just enough time to quickly shower and dress before our guests start arriving. The house smells like a French bistro as everyone settles in for cocktail hour. Now that we have two floors, we're serving hors d'oeuvres and cocktails downstairs, and then we'll move upstairs for the main meal. Amanda raises her glass for a toast.

"To the Nick and Nora of Brooklyn."

We clink glasses, take a sip, and then continue to prep martinis and open some more champagne, aspiring to be worthy of the title. The entire evening is one big gluttonous event, as we work our way through this five-course feast.

"This tenderloin is unbelievable. It's so tender. What's the crust?" Melissa asks.

"It's onion and potato, sort of like a latke," I say.

"Smart," she says. "Why wait for Hanukkah?"

By the end, we're all sloshing around, after managing to drink every single open bottle and cleaning off each plate. We all know full well that tomorrow morning will be painful, and yet we don't seem to care.

"I think we lost Mary," Troy says. "I'd better take her home."

Mary, the lightweight of the group, might have overindulged just a tad, considering her eyes seem to be going around in circles. The next morning, as my head throbs, and my tongue feels permanently stuck to the roof of my mouth, I wonder how everyone else is doing.

"I just got off the phone with Troy," Dan says. "Mary fainted when they got home."

"What?" I gasp. "Is she okay?"

"Yeah, now she is, but he said it got scary for a few minutes. He suggested we might want to scale things back a bit next time."

Point taken. It's never a good thing to turn a dining event into a medical emergency. A valuable lesson learned just in time for a Fourth of July barbecue I've invited Emeril to with his new girlfriend, Alden. Yes, I've got guts. I am going to cook for America's favorite chef. But I've spent enough time with him to know that he's no food snob, loving a great hamburger as much as a fancy steak au poivre. The guest list is a little tricky, as I wonder who I can invite without them wigging out in front of him. Of course, Mary and Troy are totally cool and would be equally comfortable in the presence of royalty or the owners of our local deli. I want Emeril to feel at ease just to be himself, which is often difficult being so recognizable, so I keep the group small.

"What do you think of this *Matambre*?" I ask Dan, showing him a picture of an Argentinian stuffed flank steak with peppers, cheese, and hard-boiled eggs.

"Really, hard-boiled eggs? You hate them," he says. "Don't you think that's a little weird to make with meat?"

"I don't know. It looks very impressive."

"I think we should stick to classics, like ribs. It's July Fourth."

"That's what he'd expect. I at least have to try something daring."

I do want to impress Emeril. Up until this point, he rarely listens to anything I have to say about food. I know he appreciates my television chops, but whenever I put in my two cents about a recipe or menu, I get the feeling all he hears is that weird teacher squawk from the Charlie Brown animated TV specials. I'm hoping if I pull off a really good meal he might have some more respect for my culinary input. It would be nice to have some say about the food once in a while.

As the day approaches, things start to get tense.

"I don't think the hot weather is going to break by the fourth," Dan worries. "As a matter of fact, they're saying this might be a record heat wave."

Oh, great. We're going to roast. And now, to make matters worse, I just had some emergency hand surgery due to a benign growth under my palm. My left hand is useless for the next two weeks.

"Dan, can you come up here and help me roll this meat?"

"Just a second, I'm on the phone with Mary."

While I wait for Dan, I lay out the flank steak as best I can. I've covered my bad hand with an oven mitt, so I can at least push things around a bit.

"Is Mary okay making the peach cobbler?" I ask.

"She's in the tub with Troy peeling the peaches at this very moment," he laughs.

"Huh?"

"They don't have air-conditioning, so this is the only way they can stay cool."

"Invite them over here."

"I did, but they say they've got it under control, although their fingers are getting pruney."

Somehow, we pull everything together about five minutes before Emeril and Alden arrive. It's just ten feet between the street and our front door and at least five people scream *Bam!* as he steps out of his car to walk into our house. Fortunately, by the time we all get up on the roof, there's at least a breeze and the sun is beginning its descent. I don't know how word spread, but we hear even more *Bams!* coming from our neighboring rooftops.

"Man, you can't go anywhere, can you?" I say. "Isn't it a drag?"

"When they stop noticing, that's when it will be a drag," he says.

"You know, you didn't have to bring anything. You're our guest."

"What? I just threw this together. No biggie."

Emeril has brought two small coolers complete with six racks of pre-grilled ribs and a huge container of his potato salad with bacon and ranch dressing. He must have been cooking all morning. I hope he didn't think he was going to starve.

"Good thing we didn't make the ribs, after all," Dan whispers.

We settle in and it's as if we're all old friends. Alden is quite the charmer. She's a stunning Mississippi blond, with perfectly coiffed hair that wouldn't dare frizz on a day like today, unlike mine, which quickly resembles Harpo Marx. But she's totally approachable with a warm smile and a great sense of humor. She's at ease and has no trouble fitting in. She's a great match for Emeril who tends to keep to himself a bit more in social situations. They're getting serious, and I think they like being around other couples that have some proven longevity.

"How long have y'all been married," she asks Mary.

"What is it now? Twenty years?" she answers, looking at Troy.

"Twenty years of heavenly bliss," Troy nods, placing his arm around Mary and giving her a peck on the cheek.

Alden smiles, appreciating their affection, and then looks over at Emeril who catches her eye with a wink.

After a quick cocktail, Emeril and I go into chef mode maneuvering around each other in my kitchen, as if we've done this a hundred times before.

"KK, where do you keep your tongs?" he asks.

"They're in that blue canister next to the sink."

"Here, let me get that. You're going to get sauce all over your bandages," he scolds. "What the heck did you do to yourself this time? Slice your hand open?"

Emeril has been witness to some of my more klutzy moments. He's seen me trip up the stairs, knock over wineglasses, and fall on my derriere on a slippery floor.

"Believe it or not, it wasn't an accident this time," I explained quickly before changing the subject. TMI with the talent is never a good idea.

He takes a platter upstairs to Dan, who is manning the grill. Emeril vies for space for his ribs, nudging my Matambre to the side.

"I just need to heat up the ribs and hit them with one more shot of sauce," he says to Dan.

Alden and Mary help me bring up some iced tea, black beans, and a salad, as Troy makes sure we have enough beer and wine. We finally settle in for our feast. Of course, Emeril's ribs are off-the-charts delicious. The sweet and tangy sauce gets all over our hands and faces. But no one is touching my Matambre. It smells good, but the meat is a bit gray because it steamed inside of the aluminum foil.

Emeril leans over and whispers, "You should have seared the meat first to get a nice char, then put it in the foil."

I could die a thousand deaths. Now he'll never listen to ANYTHING I have to say about food. At least there's a ton of other chow on the table and nobody seems to care. After we've had our fill of all the savory treats, we dig into Mary's delicious peach cobbler, which has no trace of bathtub water. Before I even get a chance to ask if anyone wants coffee, a barrage of fireworks explodes over the South Street Seaport.

"Wow, you guys have such a great view," Alden says.

"Yeah, and if we walk across our neighboring roofs, we can see the barges all the way up to the 59th Street Bridge," I say. "They're all in sync."

As the green, gold, blue, and red bursts of color rain down, disappearing in a slow-motion sizzle, we hear a cacophony of bangs, pops, and crackles seconds after the final shells leave the sky dark. The neighborhood erupts in cheers and a few more *Bams*.

"KK, now that's a great way to end a dinner party," Emeril declares.

"Well, I know you didn't want a fuss, but I had to do something special."

"Thanks so much for having us," Alden says. "It was so nice to just have a normal night out."

"You can slum with us common folk anytime," Troy teases.

"Dan, you're the man," Emeril says, giving him a hug. "Are you coming down to Philly with us?

"I'm gonna try," he answers. "But I've got to finish up some music for a client."

"Don't take too long. Your wife gets crabby when you're not around."

"Hey! That's not what makes me crabby."

Emeril laughs, knowing full well that the pressures of taking the show on the road does not always bring out my most cheerful side.

"What's in Philly?" Troy asks.

"Oh, I'm really excited," I admit. "We're shooting our Halloween special at the Eastern State Penitentiary."

"The *prison*?"

"It used to be up until the '70s. Now it's a museum, but it's one of the creepiest places I've ever seen. It's a perfect set for Halloween."

"But it's the middle of July."

"I know, but we have to produce it, edit it, and get it out for reviews, so we have to shoot way in advance."

"Leave it up to her to get me to cook in a haunted prison," Emeril teases. "KK, this was great. I'll see you in a couple of days. Make sure to find a good spot for dinner to take the team."

"We have to work, you know," I remind him.

"Yeah, yeah, yeah," he says. "We'll do that too."

This has now become a routine whenever we're away from New York. Regardless of how long our days may be, we always need to end it with a killer meal. Not that I mind. Emeril is a very generous and entertaining dining partner, as are most chefs. Almost everyone I've met since I've been at Food Network has a true passion and love for food and drink. In addition to their gusto for all things savory and sweet, they love to talk about food, figure out the components of what they're eating, and often will regale you with the dreams they've had about food. But their capacity for consumption can be impressive, to say the least.

TOP TEN TIPS FOR HANGING OUT WITH CHEFS

Over the years, I learned the hard way how to hang with the big boys. If you want to live to talk about it the next day, here are my top ten tips:

#10. When meeting at a hotel bar before dinner, come late. That way, you can skip the first two rounds.

#9. Don't bother to order an appetizer. Someone will bring out at least four different munchables on the house to impress the chef.

#8. Do not order a cocktail to start. Multiple bottles of wine will be coming and my advice to you is the same as my father once gave me, "Don't mix the grain and the grape."

#7. The Every Other—For every glass of wine poured, make sure you nurse yours long enough so that the waiters only refill your glass every other time they pour for the chef.

#6. HYDRATE! This is critical. For every glass of wine, drink one glass of water. The water will also help you slow down on the wine and food consumption.

#5. If you are a germaphobe, get over it now. You must be willing to pass plates and share, even soup. Tasting everything is critical.

#4. You do not have to, nor should you, clean your plate. Assume twice as much food will come out of the kitchen because you didn't order what the restaurant chef really wants you to try.

#3. Never put salt on anything you haven't tasted first. It's very bad manners in the chef world. One should assume that the restaurant chef has salted to taste. Besides, your feet will thank you in the morning.

#2. Under no circumstance should you have an after-dinner drink. The sweet liqueurs will wipe out all of the good you did only drinking every other glass of wine. The safest after-dinner choice is chamomile tea.

#1. Never forget: You are not a chef. You are only a mere mortal.

Chapter Ten

OUT-OF-TOWN TRYOUTS

What shall we three eat?
A stew, a roast, or a beast?
Fair is foul, and foul is fair
A steak would work, medium-rare

I'm watching the monitor as Paula Deen's green face makeup is melting into the steaming cauldron she's stirring. Her two weird sisters are cackling away as they add a squiggly eel and floppy octopus into a Sea Creature Stew. All are dressed in homage to Margaret Hamilton's wicked witch, from *The Wizard of Oz*, as they use boat oars to stir their stew.

"Cut," I say. "Makeup, Paula's dripping again."

Our make-up team rushes in, gently wiping down the faces of our three witches, trying not to ruin the green masks that took them hours to create. We're deep in the bowels of the Eastern State Penitentiary in Philadelphia, a made-for-TV Halloween location that on a normal day

115

would give anyone the creeps, with its neo-gothic architecture designed to instill fear into those even thinking about committing a crime. Add in my lighting director's suggestion of bare branches and ever-so-slightly moving skeletons created by long shadows and amber gels, my art director's cob-webs and skulls strewn about, and it's hard not to get the shivers. We all feel like we're making a little horror movie, and it's kicked up everyone's game. But it's been slow going and Emeril is getting antsy.

"Emeril wants to know how much longer before you'll need him on set," Felicia, Emeril's assistant, says. "He's been sitting in that trailer for over an hour. How far behind schedule are you? Does he have time to go out for lunch?"

The last thing I need is for Emeril to take a two-hour lunch.

"We're almost done with this setup and then we'll move on to his Mad Scientist scene," I explain. "Work with me, will ya?"

"I'm trying," Felicia says. "But you know how he gets."

Yeah, I know. He hates waiting for anything. He's so spoiled by how efficient we've become in the studio that he expects everything to just *happen*. But the network wants more and more specials, and each new thing has new challenges. This Halloween special is one of our most ambitious undertakings to date.

The prison, once a temporary home to Al Capone, has its own annual Halloween show called, "Terror Behind the Walls," and since it's off-season, they're happy to help us out. Many of the cells and corridors look like Frankenstein's lair, with cobblestone walkways, mossy stone walls, and a damaged roof that drips rain down into little puddles. The local pigeons have free rein as they play hide-and-seek from the elements, perching on a beam as if they were extras from Hitchcock's *The Birds*, just waiting to attack. The whole place oozes spooky, and I'm convinced it's haunted. I could swear I heard voices in an empty hallway when I took a shortcut to the craft services table for a bagel and schmear, and my third cup of coffee. Even with the natural setting, we still have so much work to do with the lighting and the specific scenes we need to set for cooking.

"Okay, makeup, clear scene please," Mike says. "Roll cameras."

Paula is doing a great job and has embraced her inner witch, even if her Southern drawl might make Shakespeare wince from his grave. She's got a great cackle, and gleefully dangles some live crabs over the cauldron before they meet their untimely death.

"There, there. Put them all in the pot. This will be *spook-tacular*," she says to her sisters.

The network is encouraging us to work with other Food Network talent, particularly for our holiday specials, so not only have I turned Paula into a witch, but Rachael Ray will be creating a Yummy Mummy as a female Indiana Jones, and Marc Summers will be the Bob Vila of candied haunted houses. And how could I resist the urge to turn Emeril into Count Lagasse as our host? In make-up, he's a surprisingly close Bela Lugosi double making Vampire Chicken on a Stake with Roasted Garlic and Braised Sausages. Who says ghosts and zombies can't eat well?

"Hey, Ms. Scorsese. I'm aging here," Emeril nags, as the crew keeps moving lights further and further away for a better effect.

"We're almost there," I assure him.

"You said that five minutes ago."

I pretend not to hear him. Thankfully, Marie steps in to go over some of the details of the recipe with him. Once we're finally set, he's off and running and it only takes a few minutes to actually shoot the scene.

"What's next?" he snaps.

"I need you to change into your mad scientist outfit so we can shoot the cocktail scene."

"And how long from now will that be?"

Man, he's being a pain in the butt today. Can't he see we are all working as fast as we can? I've got poor Marc Summers sweltering down the hall, sticking his hands in gooey, melting bars of chocolate, not knowing until about an hour ago that he has OCD. Rachael Ray has been a champ, not once complaining about the fact that I got her up at 5 a.m. for make-up, and we didn't shoot her scene until 11:00.

"As soon as you're in your costume, we'll be ready," I insist. "The scene is lit and set, so we'll be waiting on you."

Of course, I'm lying. It won't be ready for at least another hour. The art department is having trouble getting all the tubes bubbling in his mad scientist lab, and we still have to break down all the gear and move it down the hall to reset for the next scene. I pull Felicia to the side.

"You know, if he wants to go to lunch, now might be a good time," I suggest. "Just please, don't go too far."

"Give me a realistic time," she demands.

"We'll be ready by four," I guess, hoping it will come true.

As soon as he leaves the set, we all try to get as much done as possible. Without Emeril breathing down our necks, we really are ready by four. Lunch and a couple of glasses of wine have mellowed Emeril, so he comes back on set psyched to pull off the scene. He's wearing a long white doctor's coat with one of those old-fashioned mirrors strapped to his head. All I need him to do is make a cocktail called a *Spellbinder*.

"First, mix some blue Curacao with some yellow Galliano," he instructs, before laughing like a lunatic. "*Bwwwaaaaahhhhaaahhhhaaa!* Now that's a perfect shade of green. Next, add some pineapple juice and then we need some deviled eyeballs to chill. Where are those delectable dollops of disgusting?"

He pulls out a tray of round ice cubes with frozen cherries and chocolate chips, replacing the hole where the pits were extracted. They look like bloodshot eyeballs with some of the cherry juice streaking into the milky ice-like veins. He removes them all from the tray, and some start rolling around the table. He catches three and plunks them into his drink, sneaking in a couple of pieces of dry ice so the drink appears to smoke.

"Cheers, *Bwwwaaaaahhhhaaahhhhaaa!* Now that should put some hair on your chest."

"And cut," Mike shouts.

"Fantastic," I proclaim, "But don't anyone drink that. It's got dry ice in it."

When we shoot without an audience, it's not unusual for the crew to sample the dishes on occasion. But today, I have no time for runs to the emergency room.

"Let's set for the finale."

Thankfully, the kitchen staff has remade all the food so it's fresh and edible. There's a spread laid out on a long antique wooden table, dressed with autumn leaves, cobwebs, skull mugs, and dried corn husks. A steaming small cauldron of Paula's seafood stew sits next to Rachael's Yummy Mummy, basically a meatloaf shaped like a mummy, and Marc's completed haunted candy house is the centerpiece. Emeril has his chicken on a stake in front of him, ready to be carved, and we have a big pitcher of the smoldering Spellbinder on the table. As the cameras roll, the art team hits the floor with a low-hovering blast of smoke, creating an eerie effect of the underworld. On cue, all lift their glasses for a final toast, each taking turns reading the lines on the prompter.

> *Gather ye' round friends and foes*
> *On this special night of wails and woes*
> *We'll lift our glasses to the spirits on high*
> *And toast to those who have passed by*
>
> *Our cries of fear are set aside*
> *As we start to eat and imbibe*
> *Let's drink up, and enjoy this dinner*
> *To all of us, saints and sinners!*

And with that, they all let out crazed laughs and clink glasses.

The camera pulls back, revealing the full scene of them passing platters and chowing down. The crew flickers the lights, creating a lightning effect. *Hold, hold, hold …*

"And cut," Mike says. "That's a wrap!"

The crew lets out a big cheer, as the long day *finally* comes to an end. It's been a seventeen-hour day and the crew still needs a good hour to remove all the cables and equipment from the premises. I feel pretty good about the day until Felicia pulls me aside.

"This can't happen again," she warns.

"What?" I ask.

"Days like this. You're going to have to figure out a better way to schedule his time so that he doesn't have to wait around while you're playing movie mogul. He's got a million other things going on, and he just doesn't have a minute to waste."

Movie mogul? She's got to be kidding me. How do they think this stuff gets done?

"We just busted our behinds to pull this off," I grumble. "I'm sorry the day got away from us at times, but look where we are. This is not a controlled environment, you know."

"Don't shoot the messenger. I'm just saying, you've got to figure out a better way. The network is going to be asking for more and more specials, and you know it's not going to get any easier."

"Yeah, no kidding. How pissed is he?"

"Pretty pissed."

"Crap."

"Just fix it next time and all will be right in the world," she suggests. "Before I forget, we've got dinner reservations at Susanna Foo's in about an hour. They're staying open late for us. She makes the best Peking Duck rolls on the planet. Can you make it?"

One thing I have to say about Emeril and his team, business is business, but eating is like going to confession. All is forgiven when it comes to a good meal. And who doesn't like Chinese?

"For what it's worth," Felicia adds, "I think this was really cool."

Felicia gets it, but she's often in a tough position. She wants to be part of our team but ultimately, she works for Emeril, so there's always just a little distance between us. She doesn't realize how hard it is for me to not take criticism to heart. To be honest, as much as I pretend to have thick skin, I don't. I envy people who can let off steam and then move on as if nothing happened. But when on the receiving end, I absorb the criticism and it can stay with me for days, sometimes weeks. It's funny. It's like reviews—I never remember the good ones, only the bad ones. And the timing of this couldn't be worse. *The New York Times* just reviewed us, and it wasn't pretty.

A few weeks back, Amanda Hesser came to one of our studio shows, the Thanksgiving Leftover episode. She was all sweetness and light, chatting up the crew and the audience. We thought she was doing a profile of Emeril and the show, and then when her article was published, it felt like a hit job. Some of the excerpts stung like a swarm of bees:

> *Emeril Lagasse, more jester than cook, is catering to legions of gleeful fans…. Mr. Lagasse is most widely credited for making sophisticated cooking accessible to mass audiences. But in doing so, he often dumbs recipes down so much that he removes all the intellectual effort that goes into creating subtle flavors in a dish…. Mr. Lagasse captivates his audiences with a loud, high-octane monologue. He works the stove, feeds his clamoring audience like a zookeeper—tossing cubes of salami and bags of potato chips to them—and spouts cooking tips at random.*

The success of Emeril and the show was clearly rattling many in the elite culinary community. Hesser wrote, quoting Michael Batterberry, the founder of *Food Arts* magazine: "A lot of professional foodies are a bit dismayed at the tone of the program. It really smacks a little bit of the wrestling ring or the roller derby."

That one hurt. All we're trying to do is make cooking exciting for people—all people. Not just those with Thermador stoves and Le Creuset Dutch ovens with yearly subscriptions to *Bon Appétit*, but for the lady in Minneapolis who loves her Farberware and only has an hour to put dinner on the table after she picks up her kids from soccer practice. I take exception with Hesser's comment that he *"dumbs recipes down."* I think the success of the show comes from his enthusiasm for good food and his ability to make people realize that you don't need a culinary degree to make it.

"I'm going to write a letter to the editor at the *Times*," I announce to Eileen. "I think she missed the whole point of the show."

"You are absolutely NOT going to write to the *Times*," she insists. "Don't add gas to the fire. If anything, chefs are coming out of the woodwork to defend him. This isn't going to hurt the show one bit. It might even bring in more viewers. How's Emeril taking it?"

"Better than me. He said he sent her flowers."

"Classy," Eileen says. "My advice to you—just let it go. As a matter of fact, I have something to take your mind off it. I want to see how Mary Sue and Susan react in front of an audience."

She explains that she wants me to go to LA and shoot a special with Mary Sue Milliken and Susan Feniger at their restaurant, Border Grill. The two of them are known as the *Two Hot Tamales* on Food Network, and they specialize in Mexican- and Latin-inspired foods.

"Is their restaurant big enough for an audience?" I ask.

"I don't know. You're going to have to go scout it."

Go scout it. To me, these are the three best words in the English language. Scouting is the process of assessing a location to see if it's right for a particular creative concept. We have to check the size of the venue, the height of the ceiling, power resources, access, permits, parking, and a hundred other little details to determine what's possible and what isn't. It's work without pressure, and without our usual entourage of ninety people and truckloads of gear. But it also means a free trip, a nice hotel, and a per diem for me and my department heads, who also happen to be excellent eating and drinking companions. Plus, if I schedule things right, I can leave on a Thursday, scout on Friday, and have the weekend to play.

Border Grill is in Santa Monica, my favorite area to stay around LA, and I'm meeting with Mary Sue and Susan at their restaurant at noon. I've met them in passing a few times back at the N.Y. studios, but I haven't had a chance to really get to know them yet.

"Welcome to LA," Susan says, arms wide open for a hug.

Susan exudes such warmth that it's hard not to like her instantly. She's tiny, with a lean body that is constantly in motion. Her messy salt-and-pepper curls are pulled back by a bandana tied around on her head, and her blue denim chef's jacket is slightly stained from working in the kitchen. Her voice is raspy, like a 1940s femme fatale who doesn't take crap from anyone.

"Did you eat?" She asks, not waiting for me to answer. "Let me have the kitchen send some things out."

We sit down to talk about the show as plate after plate of green corn *tamales*, crispy *taquitos,* and plantain *empanadas* arrive. Her food is nothing like my local Mexican joint. There are no watery salsas and mushy *frijoles* in sight. Every ingredient is fresh and seems to have a purpose in pushing the flavors forward. There's a sweet middle-aged Mexican woman in the corner of the restaurant, quietly making fresh tortillas, one after the other, piling them high before she brings some out to the table. I rip a piece off of one and dip it into a smoky chipotle salsa. Susan doesn't eat, demurring that she's constantly tasting in the kitchen. I feel funny eating while she's not, but it would seem rude not to eat since she's offering. And quite frankly, this food is hard to resist.

"Mary Sue is really sorry she couldn't make it. She had to take one of her kids to the doctor. Some bug is going around his school. But she's super excited about this special. Do you think this space will work?"

"It's much bigger than I thought it would be. It's a great space. And I love the wall murals. Do you think it will be hard to get an audience?"

"Honey, if we offer free food and drink, there will be a line around the block. I wouldn't worry about that."

"You know, I was thinking. Would you have time for some remote shooting outside of the restaurant? I think your fans would love to see you in and about LA, at the beach or a market."

"Sure, we just have to schedule it. Have you ever been to the Grand Central Market downtown? I'm sure we can shoot there. It's the best Mexican market in LA."

"I'm embarrassed to say, I've never been to downtown LA."

"What are you doing tomorrow morning? If you're free, I can show you around. I'll meet you there at ten."

True to her word, the next morning we meet in front of the Belcampo Meat Company. Early as it is, she tells me, "I hope you came hungry. There are a lot of great dishes here to try."

"I'm ready. Lead on."

I have finally learned that whenever you meet with a chef, be prepared to eat.

The market is filled with a noisy mix of people speaking in Spanish and English, both languages flowing into one another with borrowed expressions and common words. As we walk past the many stalls that serve everything from carnitas and tacos to bento boxes, the aromas of roasting pork mix with charring chilis, smoky bacon, and freshly brewed coffee. Although predominantly Mexican, other cultures have glommed onto this space. It is quickly becoming a tourist attraction. Susan seems to know all the vendors, and she steers me toward the more authentic Mexican stalls that serve treats like *sopas, tortas,* and *flautas.*

"Have you ever had a tongue *gordita*?" she asks.

"I love tongue. My grandmother used to serve it all the time."

"Well, I doubt she served it like this," she says, handing me a heavy sandwich. "The dough is made with masa. Gordita means 'little fat one,' and as you can see, it's thicker than a regular tortilla. It's also fried in a skillet, then they split it and stuff it with tongue and *pico de gallo.*"

"Can't go wrong with that," I say, taking a bite. "Wow, it's got a nice crunch. And the tongue takes me back to my grandmother's kitchen."

"That's the best thing food can do, transport you."

Can I just say, I love Susan Feniger. She's the real deal. It's all about the food, always. And anyone who can conjure up memories of Nana for me is going to have a special place in my heart. Although this tongue is cubed, rather than sliced, and served with pico de gallo, not mustard, the pickle flavor and soft texture of the tongue are unmistakable. It doesn't take me long to polish off the gordita, washing it down with some hibiscus juice. We continue eating our way through the market, knocking back a few pork tamales and sopes, and finishing with a fried churro chaser and some Mexican iced coffee.

"Hey, do you need any dried chilis?" she offers. "They have a great selection here."

There's a full aisle of chilis piled into big mounds. In New York, it costs six bucks for a small package of eight chipotles. Here, I can get a full shopping bag for only two dollars. Susan loads me down with *pasillas, guajillos, anchos, chile de arboles, habaneros,* and *mulatos.*

"I'm going to need to check another bag to get these home," I tell her.

"It's worth it. Listen, when you come back here to shoot, I want a full report on what you made with all of these," she insists. "Once you cook with these chilis, you'll never open a can again."

Back at home after the scout, I'm determined to test Susan's theory. I look through her cookbook and decide to make her *Chile de Arbol Salsa.* Dan loves hot, spicy food, so I'm hoping to serve this with some grilled chicken. It calls for thirty to forty chilis, so I carefully count them out. I follow the recipe exactly, pleased that it's so easy. I wait until it comes down to room temperature before I do a taste test. Just as I bring up a full teaspoon and inhale the aroma, I sneeze. I'm not exactly sure why until I put the whole spoon in my mouth. Within seconds, my mouth feels as if a stick of dynamite has just gone off. My face turns beat red, my eyes tear and sweat saturates my shirt. I pull the sour cream out of the fridge and stick my tongue directly into the container, knocking over a few cans that clatter on to the floor.

"Are you okay?" Dan shouts, rushing into the kitchen. "What happened?"

"This is so freakin' hot!" I screech, sour cream spitting out of my mouth.

"Hot temperature or hot spicy?"

"Hot spicy."

He reaches for the spoon.

"I wouldn't do that if I were you. Just take a teeny, tiny drop," I warn.

He sticks his pinky finger into the salsa and tastes it.

"Whoa, you aren't kidding," he hiccups. Super spicy stuff always makes him hiccup. "What chili did you use?"

"This one," I say, holding up the bag.

"The habaneros?"

"These aren't habaneros, those are," I point out, holding up another bag with small skinny red chilis.

"Uh, I don't think so. These must be mislabeled. I know my habaneros. How many did you use?"

"The recipe called for thirty to forty, so I used thirty-five."

"Thirty-five? No wonder this is like rocket fuel. These are four times the size of an arbol and ten times as hot."

He can see that I feel like an idiot.

"I'll tell you what," he softens. "Let's clean this up and order in Chinese. The chicken will keep until tomorrow. You can try again."

The next night, success—the salsa is still pretty hot, but at least this time it's edible. It's got a nice mix of heat from the chilies and tang from the tomatillos, and I love the consistency once it's all pureed. The next time I see Susan, I'll tell her how well it turned out, but maybe I'll just skip the part about my first attempt. Not everyone needs to know I don't know my habaneros from my arboles.

SALSA FOR WIMPS

As much as I love Susan's salsa, I find that using chili de arbol is a bit too hot for me. One thing I've noticed over the years is that my ability to handle the heat has rapidly declined. If you like a nice flavorful salsa without having to reach for TUMS, then try this version using chipotles. It's easy and can be used with chips or as a marinade.

Makes about 2 cups

INGREDIENTS

½ can chipotles in adobo sauce

½ pound Italian Roma tomatoes
½ pound tomatillos, husked and washed
½ bunch cilantro, stemmed and leaves roughly chopped
1 medium sweet onion, chopped
3 cloves garlic, crushed
1 cup water
1 teaspoon salt
½ teaspoon freshly ground black pepper

DIRECTIONS

Preheat the broiler.

Place the tomatoes and tomatillos on a baking sheet. Broil, turning occasionally until charred all over, 10 to 12 minutes. Set aside.

In a medium saucepot, sauté the onion for 4 minutes, until translucent. Add the garlic and cook for 1 minute until fragrant. Add the tomatoes and tomatillos, the chipotles in adobo sauce, and all remaining ingredients. Bring to a boil, and then lower the heat to simmer for 10 minutes.

Transfer to a food processor or blender. Puree until smooth, and strain. Serve at room temperature, or slightly chilled. The salsa can be stored, covered, in the refrigerator for 3 to 5 days, or frozen for two months.

Chapter Eleven

EVEN THE BREAD IS WHITE

"Seymour, Indiana?" I ask. "I have to go where?"

Our brilliant marketing department came up with the idea for a contest, "Emeril Kicks Up Your School Cafeteria," that some kid from somewhere in the middle of nowhere just won.

As much as I love scouting, not every place I'm sent is on my bucket list. I'll admit, as a New Yorker I'm a bit of a snob when it comes to my travel preferences. I tend to be a coastal kind of a gal. To me, the term "fly-over states" seems fitting, as unfair as that might be. But one thing I know by now is, wherever we end up will be an adventure, even in a town that boasts both a Quality Inn and a Holiday Inn Express. Rochelle, one of my producers who can charm anyone into doing anything, is helping me, along with a small crew. We have to hit the ground running and come up with some ideas for an hour special.

Once we arrive in Seymour, Rochelle and I meet with the local sheriff to arrange some logistics for an outside cooking demo.

"Oh, don't worry about that," he assures us. "We can borrow some bleachers from the next town over. There's a Klan rally next month, but they won't need them before that."

Klan rally? Holy crap. Where ARE we?

"Of course, we'd never hold a rally like that here," he says a bit sheepishly, looking over at Rochelle, who happens to be Black.

"Oh, of course you wouldn't," she says, gritting her teeth.

"You know, Indiana is known as the 'Crossroads of America,'" the sheriff says proudly. "It's 'cause of all the intersecting railroads that come in from every direction—north, south, east, and west."

Well, it sure isn't known for that from its monochromatic population. *A Jewish producer and a Black producer walk into a bar in a town next door to Klan country*—but this is no joke. Freaked out after our day of scouting with the local sheriff, Rochelle and I wedge a chair up against the door in our hotel room, just in case *someone* comes looking for us. This very white, small Christian town stuck somewhere in the 1950s is just north of Louisville, Kentucky. There's a bunch of old-time mom-and-pop stores on the main drag, mostly wood-framed one- and two-story buildings, many with crank retractable awnings in need of repair that back in the day probably sold penny candy and allowed you to run a tab. Maybe they still do. Norman Rockwell-looking families walk past us; vanilla ice cream drips down the arms of little kids wearing striped shirts and Levis with the cuffs rolled up. It's hard to tell whose dad might have a white hood or two hidden in his closet and who might be repulsed by the notion.

But we're here to fulfill the contest and we hope we'll be meeting the town's better angels. Our pulling-a-winner-out-of-a-hat method has brought us to this unlikely town, and our lucky pick is a ten-year-old towheaded boy named Andrew, who could be Opie Taylor's twin from the old *Andy Griffith Show*. I am hoping he and his family will be thrilled to see us, but I suspect they don't realize what the consequences of winning will actually mean.

"First, we'd like to set up a scene here in your kitchen and have Emeril and Andrew cook breakfast for you and your family," I say to Andrew's mom.

"You want to shoot in *here*? In my kitchen?" she asks. "We *all* have to be on TV?"

"Well, you don't have to, but it is part of what Andrew won and it would be great to document that. It's only a small crew, just one camera and one sound guy. Think of it as a professional home movie that you'll have forever and ever."

"I guess that would be okay," she says, wondering what she's gotten herself into.

"Mama," Andrew whispers, tugging on her shirt.

"Hush for a minute, can't you see I'm talking to this lady?"

"I don't want the whole school to know about this," he says.

"I know, but it's too late and we talked about this," she says, shooing him away and turning to me. "Don't mind him. He just doesn't like a fuss. He'll be fine."

He's not fine. The poor kid is mortified and hates the attention. He's also painfully shy, and as much as I try to pull some personality out of him, he just doesn't want to be any part of this. I'm not sure why he even entered the contest in the first place. Maybe it's like playing the lottery. You never expect to win, but then you do and you have no idea how to deal with such a huge sum of money, so you blow it all, and end up broke and on some reality show called *Lottery Bites*.

"So, tell me, how does it feel knowing that you won a lunch cooked by Emeril over thousands and thousands of other kids?" I ask, as my cameraman quietly rolls the camera next to me for his interview.

"Fine," Andrew says.

"Can you describe how it feels?"

"It feels fine," he says.

"What do you want Emeril to cook for you?" I ask.

"I don't know."

"If you could have anything you want, what would it be?" I ask.

"I don't know."

"Oh, come on, you must have a favorite food?"

"Nah, not really."

"Pizza? Hot dogs? Hamburgers?"

"Yeah, I guess those," he says.

I have an entire hour special to shoot all about his winning this contest and the only thing I can get out of him are a few grunts. I wrap up the interview, knowing I can't use any of it. I've got to come up with a plan B.

I head back to the hotel and as I walk in, the light bulb in my head comes on.

"Okay, did any of you ever see the movie *Bye, Bye Birdie?*" I ask my team.

They all look at me blankly.

"You know, the musical where Conrad Birdie comes to a small town to kiss a girl before he goes into the Army, and the whole town goes crazy?"

Still more blank stares. Am I that old? I keep going.

"Well, we're gonna turn Emeril into Conrad, and shoot scenes with the whole town going nuts with anticipation, rather than just focusing on Andrew."

"We still have to feature the kid," Rochelle reminds me.

"Yeah, but rather than have him tell us the story, we can have the kids at school tell it. We'll find the chatty ones. They can say how cool it is he won this for them and make him into the town hero. He'll be a celebrity for the day."

"Hmm. That could work," she says.

"No choice, it's gotta work," I insist.

We quickly enlist the help of the school principal, Mrs. Ferguson, who is all in on anything we want to do.

"You're a natural producer," I assert, grateful for her help.

"Well, it's not every day that a TV crew comes to this part of the world. I've got every class working on something related to food; the science class is experimenting with baking soda and various liquids, the math class is working on measurements, and I've even got the English class working on a parody of Hamlet's soliloquy, *To Bam or not to Bam? That is the question."*

"I love it!" I declare. "I also noticed all the 'Welcome Emeril' banners and signs. They look great."

"Oh, we've just gotten started on those. We've got so much more to do before he gets here. The kids are just so excited. Nothing like this has ever happened here before. Whatever you need to do, just let me know."

I can feel the excitement and anticipation running through the halls as the kids gather around our crew, dying to get on camera. We set up a bunch of different scenarios to show Andrew as the town hero, and the kids get into it like seasoned pros.

"Andrew, Andrew, he's our man," the high school cheerleaders chant as Andrew walks by.

"He's so cute, I can't stand it," one girl shrieks as another swoons.

"Andrew, Andrew," a group of boys chants as they lift Andrew on their shoulders and march him around the schoolyard as if he just made the winning touchdown.

Even the local TV news teams are willing to play along as they swarm all around Andrew, sticking microphones near his face. Just like the conquering John Cougar Mellencamp, a homegrown Seymour celebrity, Andrew is big news today. Still not sure what to make of all this, at least he goes along for the ride. I could swear I might have caught him smiling at one point. Hard to tell what he's feeling since he still hasn't uttered a full sentence since we've been here. But we press on.

"What's this kid like?" Emeril asks me. "The schedule says I'm making his family breakfast tomorrow."

"I need a quick scene of you meeting him. It's just one camera, and you and Andrew can make pancakes for the family. The kitchen team is all over it."

"Can the kid cook?" he asks.

"Uh, well, not much. He's pretty shy and quiet actually. But you're great with kids. If anyone can bring him out of his shell, you can."

"So I have to do all the heavy lifting?"

"It's not that bad," I answer. "The family is very sweet and it should only take an hour to shoot the breakfast scene. But wait 'till you see the school. They've gone nuts. It's been totally *Emerilized* for your arrival."

"Okay, okay. Where are we anyway?" Emeril wonders, looking around the barless, well-worn lobby of the local Holiday Inn.

"Don't ask."

The next day, Emeril puts on his charm offensive and sprinkles his Bam dust in every direction. Andrew even warms up as Emeril teaches him how to crack an egg with one hand.

"It's all in the wrist, like this," he demonstrates. "Here, you try it."

Andrew cracks the egg perfectly.

"You see, you got it, buddy. You got potential."

Andrew's face turns fifty shades of red.

By the time we get to the school, even the name has been changed in Emeril's honor. The Emerson, in Emerson Elementary School, has been changed to "Emeril" and there are welcome signs and *Bam!* signs covering every inch of every hall. I don't even have to get the kids to act over-the-top. They *are* over-the-top. The plan is to have Emeril cook lunch with the cafeteria ladies, feed all the kids, and then do a big outdoor demo.

"Hello ladies, you ready to kick up some lunch for these kids?" he bellows. "Ooh, nice hairnet, got one for me?"

Emeril knows a good sight gag when he sees one, so he fumbles his way through opening the hairnet with his big beefy hands, and places it on his head.

"You think it's me?" he asks, as all the lunch ladies squeal like teenagers.

Rolling up his sleeves, he says, "Okay, let's get this show on the road."

And *Bam!* Just like that, he and the cafeteria ladies make a full lunch for the entire school, working with each other as if they've been working in an Army mess for the past twenty years. He brings out a huge vat of Emeril's Kicked Up Mac and Cheese, and serves it to the kids, as I worry needlessly that the kids might not like his spices.

"This is the best thing ever," lisps a sweet girl, back for seconds.

"Glad you like it. Here's an extra BAM, for you."

She shyly runs off, looking back to catch a wink from him.

"Karen, this is really fantastic," Judy enthuses. "The local affiliate is beyond thrilled. The marketing team has been lobbying for an eight-city tour, *Emeril Salutes America,* and I think this will push it over the top."

"Judy, you're killing me."

"Come on, you love it."

She's right. I really do. Where else would I have the freedom to invoke the spirit of Conrad Birdie in a cooking show? But the thing that really gets me is the reach of the show and how it's changed how people think about food, particularly kids.

"Emeril, where can I get truffle oil?" a pudgy boy at the end of the lunch table shouts out.

Emeril has finished serving the kids and now he's sitting down and eating with Andrew and his buddies, just hanging with the boys.

"It's not at the local supermarket, huh?" Emeril asks.

"I don't think so," the boy slowly shakes his head.

"I'll tell you what. I'll send you guys a case. But remember, a little goes a long way."

Truffle Oil. This porky kid from Podunk USA, who has probably grown up eating chicken nuggets and Jell-O, now not only knows from truffle oil, but he wants to cook with it. It's at this moment that I realize that Emeril is the culinary messiah to the masses and I'm just one of his disciples helping to spread his gospel.

TRUFFLE POPCORN

As I was starting to imagine what the kids back in Indiana might actually make with truffle oil, I came up with this simple snack to help get them started.

Makes 1 large bowl

INGREDIENTS

1/3 cup popcorn kernels
3 tablespoons vegetable oil
¼ cup finely grated Parmesan cheese
Drizzle of truffle oil
Truffle salt, to taste

DIRECTIONS

In a medium-sized lidded pot, heat the vegetable oil over medium-high heat. Put three or four kernels in the oil and wait until they start to pop. Then add the rest of the kernels, and cover the pot. Continue to heat until all the kernels have stopped popping, shaking the pot from time to time.

Pour into a large bowl, drizzle with a touch of truffle oil, and sprinkle on the Parmesan cheese. Give it a quick mix and you've got an elegant and delicious treat. Just right for the gang in Seymour, Indiana.

Chapter Twelve

I'LL TAKE THAT TO GO

"I'll have the meat and three with, um, the grilled pork chops, some turnip greens, candied apples, and, um, oh yeah, the mac and cheese. I gotta have the mac and cheese."

I'm staring at the menu wall in Swetts, ordering some southern comfort after a long shoot. Locals and tourists mix in this noisy Nashville treasure that has been clogging people's arteries since 1954, as meals are slopped on plates, then placed on trays before heading to the tables. No need for ambiance or fussy manners, the food transports me to my imaginary Southern mama's kitchen, where she's sure to slap my hands as I lick my fingers savoring every last morsel. I haven't spent much time in the South so, of course, I have to order a side of fried cornbread, and at least try the peach cobbler for dessert. None of it disappoints.

"Glad we have on our eatin' pants," Rochelle jokes.

"Bless the guy who invented elastic waists," I respond.

Rochelle and I are on a mission to find the best bites in America so that we can shoot a series of stories for a special week of shows, *Emeril Salutes America*. It turns out that our trip to Seymour, Indiana, was a huge hit. The local affiliates were so thrilled that Judy asked me to work up a multi-show road trip that has Emeril eating and cooking his way across America

Our first stop is Nashville, but I didn't expect to fall in love with it. Somehow the spirit of the city is seeping into my blood, just like the lard. Some of the highlights from the trip are the crunchy fried pickles I suck down just before getting dragged into a line dance at the Wildhorse Saloon, followed by local craft beer at the Bluebird Cafe. I'm not sure if it is the beer or the music, but I find myself sobbing to a round robin of four acoustic guitar-strumming singers performing *The Chain of Love*. Before we leave town, we stop at the Loveless Cafe for some down-home flaky biscuits and the best peach preserves known to mankind.

"Can I get some of these preserves to take home?" I ask the waitress. "I never want to buy watery jam at the supermarket again."

"Sure honey. We have a shop next door and we can put you on our mailing list. We ship anywhere in the good ol' US of A."

I stuff the jars in my suitcase with all the other yummies I've collected along our trip across America; Goode Company's barbecue sauce from Houston, the chef's secret recipe for handmade pierogies from the Polish Village Cafe in Detroit, and some moon pies from a gas station en route to the Nashville airport. We roll from city to city, shooting stories with local chefs, traveling to markets and popular culinary spots, and gorging ourselves at dinner each night with Emeril, my cheeks getting pudgier by the day. We don't get a break until we get to Boston, and I'm looking forward to a day off where I can just fast for a quick cleanse and sleep.

"Don't we have tomorrow off?" Emeril asks.

"Well, yeah, *you* do. But I've got to put together the schedule for next week," I whine.

"You can do that in your sleep. Let's go to the North End for brunch. I could go for some good Italian."

Because we're only shooting short remotes in each city, there's just a small team with us on the road. Alden is sitting this trip out, and the crew is enjoying the day off. Which makes me Emeril's designated eating buddy. So much for my quick cleanse idea. Boston is my old college stomping grounds, and I love the North End, so frankly, it doesn't take much to twist my arm, even if we're joined by one of Emeril's bodyguards, Frankie.

Now that Emeril is such a big celebrity, Frankie, along with his brother Richie, has become part of Emeril's entourage. It seems that not all fans have good intentions, so he needs protection. If Scorsese made comedies about ex–New York City cops, both would be cast instantly. They're just a step above dee's-dem's-and-don'ts, but not by much, and they always seem to be in the wrong place at the wrong time.

"Frankie! You're in the shot again," I squawk. "Can't you see the camera?"

"Oh, sorry, sorry. When did it move there?"

Oy.

Heading down a quiet cobblestone street, we find an old-school Sicilian restaurant, complete with red and white checkerboard tablecloths. We must seem like an odd group; Frankie with his 1980s NYPD-approved mustache, Emeril in his usual uniform—white T-shirt with black pants and black blazer—and slightly rumpled middle-aged me. But as always, food levels the playing field, and we proceed to have a four-hour lunch complete with a huge antipasti platter, three different pastas we all share, deep-fried calamari, braciole, veal saltimbocca, cannolis, and espresso served with sambuca, three coffee beans, and a twist of lemon. The scent of roasted garlic is wafting its way around the table, lulling us all into a food coma.

"This reminds me of my grandmother's kitchen on a Sunday afternoon," Frankie says after a big belch. "She used to have a huge pot of gravy on the stove, just in case someone should stop by at the last minute."

All I can picture is a six-year-old Frankie by his grandmother's knee, with that goofy mustache.

"For me, my mom always had a pot of caldo verde bubbling away," Emeril remembers.

"We did Chinese take-out on Sundays," I chime in. "My mom loves a good moo goo gai pan."

"Hey, how is Mama Katz? How's the move been?" Emeril asks.

"She loves it out there."

"Wait, I thought your mom lived on Long Island?" Frankie ponders.

"She did, but last year, my brother took a position in Reno. He's a neurologist. I think he wanted to be closer to the slopes, and away from his ex-wife. Mom loved visiting him there so much that she decided to pick up her paintbrushes, pack her bags, and move. She loves the way the light hits the mountains at sunset."

"God bless her," Emeril laughs. "Tell her we miss her."

"Well, you're gonna see her soon. She's coming to our show in San Francisco with my brother Paul."

"We do need her on-site," he jokes. "You know how the weather can be out there."

"Don't worry, she's already communing with her weather gods. She says she'll know more after Thanksgiving weekend. It's too early to tell which way the fronts will be moving right now."

"Your mom's a weatherman?" Frankie asks.

"No, but she has witching powers."

He looks at me skeptically wondering if I'm pulling his leg, but moves off the topic once the tiramisu hits the table.

"Are you having the family over for Thanksgiving?" Emeril asks. "You know I have a killer oyster stuffing recipe you should use."

"Actually, my family is all meeting out in Lake Tahoe. Everyone, except Dan and me, has moved west, so we're renting a big house and having our holiday there with my brothers and cousins."

"That's great. Your mom will love that."

"Yeah, she doesn't have to lift a finger anymore. She says she's retired from cooking."

"Well, you can show everyone what you've learned over the last few years. Make me proud," Emeril says smiling.

After our shoot in Boston, we all go our separate ways. Emeril heads down to New Orleans to be with his family and Dan and I make our way to Lake Tahoe. As soon as we arrive, I go into serious Thanksgiving prep mode.

"You know, you don't have to make everything," my cousin Dave says. "I brought the fixings for a pumpkin pie."

Dave's "fixings" are a pre-baked pie crust and a can of pumpkin pie filling. His sous chef is his four-year-old son, Alex, who is doing a very good job of dripping snot wherever he goes. Both he and his brother Brian are such good germ generators that both Mom and I end up with schnarfy head colds that last for almost a month.

Dave and his family are an interesting group when it comes to food. Dave thinks of food as fuel, not really ever thinking about food as pleasure. His wife Linda is equally uninterested, except that she is a health nut with an aversion to fat. She actually washes the oil off canned oysters before she serves them. Their son, Alex, has a very limited palate, sticking closely to chicken nuggets and Annie's Mac and Cheese. But it's little Brian that has clearly gotten some of my genes. He's a human vacuum cleaner.

"What are you doing?" I snap, slapping Paul's hand away from the timer.

"Things take longer to cook here at high altitudes."

"If that bird comes out dry, don't blame it on me," I say, pulling the turkey out to baste one more time.

"Oy, toots, the way you do things," Paul shrugs, cleaning up the spilled basting juices around me.

Paul and Mom are always on my case because I don't share in their need to be fastidious every second of every day. I may sweat it out in the kitchen for hours, but I always get the sense they're just waiting for me to screw up. Heaven forbid there should be gravy dripping down the side of the boat or my turkey slices aren't fanned out just right or my crust is a tad too brown on the edges. At the end of the day, I really don't care, because my food may not always look picture perfect, but it tastes MUCH better than theirs.

We are hoping for snow, but so far, *not a flake,* as Dad would say. It's hard to believe that he's been gone almost ten years already. I'm still trying to find ways to shake up the family ritual so that Mom doesn't completely fall apart. I don't think she'll ever truly enjoy Thanksgiving again. It was their favorite holiday.

"You know, Daddy and I were married on Thanksgiving Day," Mom announces to anyone who might be listening.

"Yes, Mom, we know," I shout from the kitchen, rolling my eyes at Dan.

"They had to give me a Valium to get down the aisle. Nana says I was white as a sheet."

"Well, you were only nineteen. Probably afraid of the wedding night."

"Oh no, I wasn't a virgin. Your father made sure of that way before the wedding."

"Mom, TMI."

"TM what?"

"Too much information."

"When we were younger, he couldn't keep his hands off me. I would always tease your father that they wouldn't be able to shut the casket when his time comes."

"Mom! There are kids here."

"Don't be such a prude. They can't hear me anyway."

"But I can," Dan teases.

Dan and Mom have developed a very sweet relationship over the years. He has the patience for her that I don't. He's the one she calls when she hears a funny joke, even if she can never remember the punch line, or when she forgets her password and can't start her computer. She finally realizes he's a keeper and treats him like her own son, only without the emotional baggage.

Dad thought Dan was a genius because he managed to connect his four television and audio remotes into one universal remote. He showed his approval every time he pulled out the Macallan.

"Daniel, my boy, get ready to have your world rocked. This is a single malt Scotch, one of the best made. I used to drink Dewars with a twist over ice until a bartender at St. Andrews in Scotland shamed me. He set me straight. No Dewars, no twist, no ice. Just Macallan, neat. Cheers."

I can hear the clink of whiskey glasses in the next room. To this day, my brothers and Dan always toast my father with Macallan.

"To Dad."

"To Bernie."

It's been a long time since we've had the family all gathered like this. I worry that the memories of our childhood Thanksgivings will fade like the black and white photographs from Nana's old basement. But it's times like these that bring back all those memories in full color. At the table, we're all passing around the same food we've been eating for generations. We may be in a different location this year, but the smell of Nana's apple pie still warming in the oven melts the years away.

"Honey, the stuffing tastes just like Nana's," Mom proclaims.

"Can someone pass the cranberry sauce?" Dave asks.

"Paul, the bird's too dry. I told you," I groan.

"It's not too dry. You don't know what you're talking about. Mom, pass the gravy this way, please."

The dinner is a hit, although everyone agrees the apple pie is pretty good, but not great like Nana's. The weekend has been a nice break from our *Emeril Salutes America* tour. But I'm getting anxious about our shoot in San Francisco. It's another big one that we're shooting on Treasure Island, just off the San Francisco-Oakland Bay Bridge. If we build the set in just the right spot, we'll get a gorgeous city skyline as our backdrop. It's the only audience show we're doing on this trip, so it's a full-on multi-camera shoot.

But just as I arrive on site for rehearsal, I realize my cinematic plans may have to change because we can't see a freakin' thing in this pea soup fog. Thankfully Mom has come along to see the show because she has some serious weather work to do now.

"Honey, don't worry about it. I've got it all under control," Mom states. "The fog is just a morning thing. You'll see. It will all burn off by eleven."

Not having any alternative, we move through our set-up as best we can. Mike looks worried.

"We might as well shoot this against a green screen," he says exasperated. "The background is just blown out. I can't do a camera rehearsal. There's nothing to see."

"You'll have to use your imagination," I suggest.

"Your mom must be slipping."

"It's only ten-thirty. She's still got another half hour."

And like magic, at 11 a.m., the clouds part, the skyline comes into view and the sun is so bright we have to put on our sunglasses.

"Okay, this is good," Mike exhales, "But this weather thing with your mom is getting kind of freaky."

"Don't question it. Just go with it."

There is clearly someone from above who looks after this show because, once again, it goes off without a hitch.

"And for my last dish, how about a nice cocktail?" Emeril offers the audience. "It's called a *Fogcutter*."

"What's that under the bridge," I ask, looking at the monitor.

"You won't believe it," Mike says, "but you can actually see the fog rolling back in right on cue."

"You're kidding me?"

"Bucky, get the fog and sweep in to Emeril," Mike calls into his headset.

Bucky's jib camera, which is on a long sweeping arm, zooms in on the bridge as the fog sneaks its way towards us. Who needs Industrial Light and Magic when you have Mom in charge of special effects?

"And then strain it into an ice-filled highball glass and give it a good shot of Amontillado sherry on top as a floater. Garnish it with mint and there you have it—you're very own Fogcutter. And just in time too," Emeril says, looking over his shoulder towards the bridge.

"I want to thank the awesome crew here in San Francisco. You guys have been amazing. Give it up one more time for Doc Gibbs and the *Emeril Live* Band. And a very special thanks to Barbara, for keeping the skies clear once again. See ya' next time."

The band plays out and the fog keeps coming closer and closer. Within five minutes of the show being over, we can no longer see the city skyline.

"Unbelievable. How does she do that?" Mike wonders.

"I've learned not to question it," I reply. "By the way, the show looked great, as always."

"Are you gonna bring your mom to Hawaii with the show?"

"Nah, she's going to have to work long distance."

"Well, that's not much of the Aloha spirit."

"She's got some friends visiting, so she can't make it. I did ask her."

"Ah, too bad. She seems to get a kick out of the attention."

"You can say that again."

That night at the wrap party, almost everyone from the crew stops by our table to thank Mom for keeping the weather at bay. One of the women from the crew squats down to be at eye level with her.

"Mrs. Katz, I'm getting married next month and the wedding is outdoors. Do you think you could put in a good word for me?"

"Oh, I'll do my best, deah. Give me the date and place. I'll see what I can do," she offers.

The next week, we're off to Hawaii and I should have insisted Mom come. It's pouring and almost every shoot is outdoors. We're at the Parker Ranch on the Big Island, and Hugh, our cameraman, and I are chasing cattle in a muddy field, trying to get a good shot before they start stampeding toward our production van. As I try to help him keep the camera dry, I lose my footing and fall right into what I'm hoping is a pile of mud, not cow poop.

"Are you okay?" Nancy shouts, jumping out of the van to help me up. She's the local production coordinator I hired and she's a total pro. The rest of my New York team is just sitting in the van, staying dry, and laughing hysterically. I'm beginning to wonder why I bring them anywhere. They weren't much better at the luau we had to shoot on Maui. Every time I needed someone, they were either lying on benches trying to get a good tan or drinking Mai Tai's. Even Emeril is pissed that he has to work so much. He's made it clear that I'm ruining his golf game.

"Just once, could you guys be on time? Is that too much to ask?" I say to the crew, as we all assemble the next morning to head to our scheduled shoot at a cocoa plantation.

"What's that smell?" Emeril asks.

"What smell?"

"Get in the van and roll down the windows," he orders, motioning for me to drive.

I have no idea where we're going, but like Wimpy in search of his beloved hamburger, Emeril follows the smoky aroma as it lures him closer and closer.

"Turn right," he directs.

We pull into the parking lot of a nearby church. A group of shirtless, sunbaked men are placing a dozen or so chickens on long rotisserie bars, gingerly setting them just above red-hot smoldering chunks of wood. As each drop of fat drips onto the hot coals, a little burst of heaven wafts into the air. Emeril barely waits for the van to stop before he jumps out and approaches one of the men.

"Aloha, how ya doin' this morning?" he asks.

I don't think anyone here recognizes him, but they are a friendly bunch.

"Aloha."

"What are these?"

"Huli-huli chickens. We're roasting them for our church fundraiser," one of the workers says proudly.

"I'd be happy to make a contribution. What kind of wood are you burning?"

"Oh, it's *kiawe*. It's a local wood," he says.

"What a smell. It's like mesquite, but sweeter. Listen, I've got a hungry crew here, can I get two?"

Emeril pulls out a $50 dollar bill and hands it to the guy.

"*Mahalo. Mahalo*! Take three."

The worker wraps three full chickens in thick butcher's paper and Emeril brings them back toward the van.

"Open the back," he commands.

Emeril lays the three birds down in the van and unwraps them, letting the paper soak up the juices. No one says anything as we all lunge for a piece of these mouth-watering brown birds. The first bite makes me reluctant to chew, as I want to savor this moment for as long as possible. The chicken is moist and tender, with the skin not too crisp and not too rubbery.

"I can pick off notes of citrus and salt and a certain umami. Is it fish sauce?" I ask.

"*Umami, schmami*," Emeril says. "It's soy, ginger and I think some brown sugar. But it's the smoke that really sets this apart. I wonder if I can get some of that wood shipped to my restaurants."

It's nine o'clock in the morning and the crew is moaning in ecstasy. As the remnants of the succulent special sauce drip down beyond my elbows and onto my shirt, all is forgiven as we pick every last bone dry.

DAN'S ROTISSERIE HULI-HULI CHICKEN

Huli means turn, and although you can certainly make this dish without a rotisserie, it's well worth the extra effort to use one if you have one. If not, you can cut the chicken into pieces and cook over a charcoal or gas grill. They use kiawe wood in Hawaii and if you can find it, use it. Mesquite is a good substitute.

Although Hawaiian Huli-Huli Chicken is often marinated with brown sugar, ginger, and soy, I like Dan's twist using molasses, orange juice, and chipotles. To me, the test of a good Huli-Huli Chicken is that you can't stop eating it. And there are never any leftovers with Dan's version.

Note: Plan to marinate the chicken for at least eight hours, overnight, or for up to forty-eight hours if you have the time.

Serves 4

INGREDIENTS

For Marinade
1/4 cup orange juice
4 teaspoons sugar
1 teaspoon salt
½ teaspoon ground pepper
1 tablespoon molasses
3 chipotle pepper
1 teaspoon adobo sauce

For Chicken
1 whole chicken, cleaned and patted dry
1 whole orange
1 Ziploc gallon bag
Mesquite wood chips for smoker, or kiawe if you can find it

DIRECTIONS

Mix all of the marinade ingredients together in a bowl. Place the chicken in a large Ziploc bag, pour in the marinade and seal the bag tightly. Massage the chicken making sure the marinade gets distributed evenly. Refrigerate for at least eight hours before grilling, but it's best to let it marinate overnight, or even for 48 hours. Turn the bird every few hours.

The day you want to cook the bird, soak your wood chips for at least 30 minutes. Preheat the grill to 350 degrees F. Place the chips in a smoker box. Be sure to replenish wood chips once they stop smoking.

When you are ready to grill, remove the chicken from the bag and discard the remaining marinade and bag. Stuff one orange into the cavity. Truss the bird making sure the wings and drumsticks don't dangle. Center the bird on the spit running the skewer through the orange in the chicken's cavity. Place the chicken and spit back on grill. Rotate over indirect heat until the juices run clear. Smoke the chicken about 1¼ to 1½ hours, until the internal temperature of the meat is 165 degrees F.

Use oven mitts to remove the spit from the grill. Set aside to rest for 10 minutes, and then slide the bird onto a cutting board. Remove the string and orange. Using poultry shears, cut the legs and wings off, and slice the breast.

Chapter Thirteen

WHAT MOTHER NATURE REALLY INTENDED

"I wouldn't eat that if I were you. That's a poisonous one."

Ed "The Fungi" grabs my arm just before I reach some white mushrooms at the base of an enormous oak tree. They look just like the ones I usually buy at Stop and Shop.

"Those are *Amanita Phalloides*, otherwise known as Death Caps. Nasty suckers."

Contemplating my near demise, I wince as I follow behind him, traipsing my way through this damp northern California forest.

"Did you know there are over 10,000 species of fungi that produce mushrooms? You got your poisonous ones, your edibles, and of course, my favorites, the magic ones."

Ed is a big burly guy with a full beard that seems like it hasn't been trimmed since the summer of Woodstock. He lives in an RV, currently tucked away in the woods, complete with a full kitchen, bathroom, and probably a big bag of weed stashed somewhere behind the driver's seat. He seems to be the point person for a gaggle of mushroom zealots that scour the forest floor in search of these little earthy treasures. I'm scouting this hunt to see if it will make a good segment for our show. Thanks to Ed's enthusiasm, I can tell it will. Lately, we've been doing a lot of segments for our regular cycle of shows that highlight the origins of the food we eat. Emeril has always been interested in supporting local farmers and purveyors.

"Aha! Here they are!" he gleefully announces.

Ed reaches down toward the bottom of a beautiful Douglas fir tree, digging up some glorious golden mushrooms.

"Smell this. It's got an almost fruity aroma," he insists. "It's a chanterelle."

He hands me a delicate, yet cold and firm mushroom that I actually recognize. I've mostly seen it in its dried-out and travel-weary form at Dean and Deluca's for $24 per pound.

"Just inhale. Chanterelles are best cooked. Raw ones might upset the old tum-tum."

Again, here's another warning about the toxins that seem to surround me.

"You're sure smelling it is okay?" I ask to make double sure.

"A good whiff of chanterelle never hurt anybody."

He's right. The mushroom does have a fruity smell—almost like an apricot. I had no idea that this meaty and fragrant fungus was what a chanterelle should really be like.

This isn't the first time my eyes have been opened to the value of eating something fresh from the earth. My television-infused culinary education has not only treated me to a backstage pass into some of the great kitchens in the country, but it has also given me an opportunity to meet some of the most passionate farmers, foragers, and food enthusiasts. It always amazes me how much depth of knowledge they have about a single crop or about the minerals of a certain terroir or where in a vast sea you can find that big tuna that would much prefer to keep on swimming. But more than anything, tasting something in its purest form, the way nature intended it to be, is what makes a food or a fungus truly memorable.

After my shoot with Ed, I head back to New Orleans for another unexpected experience. Emeril has arranged to have a fishing boat take us out to some oyster beds, just off the gulf coast. Having three high-end restaurants in New Orleans, Emeril is a huge customer of not just the local fishermen, but of all the local product in the area. He's always been a passionate proponent of the importance of fresh, local ingredients even before it was politically correct. He's arranged for all of us to go out for the day's catch, so we're all standing by dressed in our yellow boots and life jackets, in search of some oyster reefs. The winds are kicking up and the boat is rocking and rolling.

"Hey, George. You're looking a little green over there," Emeril teases.

George is the cameraman from our local crew and none of them seem too seaworthy. Thankfully, I love the fresh sea air and am enjoying every minute of the adventure.

Eventually, we stop near a reef where the fishermen are able to dredge up enough oysters to satisfy their customer list for that day. The boat captain takes a shucking knife and starts to open a few for us. The briny water filling the shells buoys the plump delicacies as if they are floating in a pool at a luxurious spa. I bring the shell to my mouth, tilting it ever so slightly, not wanting to spill a drop. And then the slippery, unctuous mollusk bursts in my mouth with so much flavor that I wonder why anyone would ever want to drown it in cocktail sauce. The texture is creamy and luxurious, like a perfect custard, and it tastes of the waters below, with a mild hint of minerals and melons. I've had fresh oysters at restaurants before, but nothing can compare to having one that has just been pulled up out of the sea. Although I am sorry that most of our crew has moved to the back of the boat, praying that their stomachs will settle, it does mean more oysters for Emeril and me, as we happily slurp each and every one of them down. We must have eaten five dozen between the two of us. I could have eaten more, but I didn't want to look too greedy.

After that day at sea, I catch a nasty head cold and entirely lose my sense of smell and taste. I haven't been able to enjoy one bite since the oysters, and I've been dragging myself from location to location, counting the minutes until I can get back into bed each night.

Our last shoot is at Frankie and Johnny's, a beloved New Orleans classic seafood joint. It originally opened in 1942 and thrived feeding hungry dock workers and merchantmen that made their livings working on the river. Now, both locals and tourists find their way here to fill their bellies with everything from po-boys to gumbo.

After settling the crew, the manager takes one look at me and shouts toward the kitchen, "One crawfish boil, extra spicy." He turns to me and says, "I'm gonna fix you right up, darlin'."

About fifteen minutes later, an enormous bowl of what seems like bright red bugs comes to the table. I don't know what to do. The manager, seeing my dismay, picks one up and proceeds to show me the proper way to eat a crawfish.

"It's simple, just pinch the tail off like this and separate the meat from the head. Don't toss that head, you gotta first suck out all that yummy goodness. Then peel off the rest of the shell and pop the meat into your mouth." ·

Always willing to try anything, I do as I am told. But as soon as I suck that head, I start choking. The juice is so spicy it nearly blows my head off. Eventually, I get myself back in control and try a few more. It only takes a few minutes for my sinuses to open up and I can actually taste what I am eating. The warmth of the broth and the heat from the spices seem to work like a nasal roto-rooter. This must be the Southern version of Nana's chicken soup.

"You like 'em?" asks the manager. "A local guy brings these in from a nearby swamp each week. You can't get 'em much fresher than that. And man, they sell out fast."

I don't care that it is swamp food. Once I get over the initial shock of the hot spice, I can't stop eating them. They're addictive. It's clearly the secret cure for the common cold, as the spicy broth opens up every nasal passage and awakens my taste buds for the first time in days. And thank goodness I'm feeling better because the crew and I are wrapping up the week with a dinner at Emeril's namesake restaurant in the warehouse district. I'd hate to not be able to taste what's coming my way.

As I walk into Emeril's for the first time, I am impressed by the openness of the room. It's a high-end spot, but it doesn't feel stuffy or pretentious. At the end of the elegant dining room, there's an open kitchen where you can get a bird's eye view of all the kitchen activity while eating at the counter. If you're lucky, Emeril will be in the house and you can watch him do his magic. The kitchen is framed by a series of glass panels filled with different whole spices. The Rockwell Group, an award-winning architecture and design firm, designed it. When we updated our set for the show, I had the great thrill of working with the Rockwell Group's gurus, David Rockwell and David Mexico, to redesign our set to give it the same feel and look of this restaurant.

"I hope you guys came hungry tonight," Emeril says, stopping by our table. "Cause I'm not gonna stop until you say, 'Uncle.' Any allergies?"

We all shake our heads no, as he takes our menus.

"You won't be needing these," he says with a devilish grin.

Dressed in his chef whites and toque, Emeril bounds through the dining room greeting regulars and signing some autographs. He whispers something to his manager, as he points toward our table. The manager nods and smiles.

Knowing that Chef is in the house, the staff is at full attention, moving plates and people in a beautifully choreographed ballet. Emeril's is not only known for its food but for its service as well. If a woman were to ask where the Ladies' Room was, a handsome assistant manager or a waiter would most likely offer his arm to escort her there. If you opened a sugar packet to sweeten your coffee, don't be surprised if someone swoops by to pick up the empty packet within seconds. And if you want to know where each ingredient in your dish was sourced, get ready for a dissertation.

"Here are some appetizers Chef wanted you to try."

Two waiters and the manager are each standing with one plate in each hand. They place them on the table in one perfect, synchronous move.

"Starting at the head of the table and going clockwise, we have some Jumbo Lump Crab Cakes with a Fresh Herb Ravigote and Pickled Sweet Pepper Salad. Next are some of those Louisiana Oysters you and Chef Emeril were kind enough to bring back. He's broiled them with Parmesan and Creole herb butter. For the soup, we have a Bacalao Caldo Verde with kale and fondant potato in a Chorizo broth. At the end of the table, we have a Lavender-Cured King Salmon with *Osetra* Caviar Deviled Eggs followed by some Spanish Octopus *a la Plancha* served with *Aquachile*, cucumber relish, heirloom tomato, Parmesan crisps, and micro cilantro. And last, but not least, you can't leave here without trying Chef's famous New Orleans Barbequed Shrimp served with rosemary biscuits and chives. With this course, we'll be serving a *Soalheiro Alvarinhno*, from Portugal. It's a light-bodied, dry white wine with lovely tart citrus notes."

The manager holds out the bottle for my perusal. I nod my head in approval. The cork is popped, the glasses are filled and the party begins.

Three hours, four courses, and five bottles of wine later, the crew and I still manage to polish off all the desserts including my favorite, the Bananas Foster Bread Pudding. I know I'll probably be in pain tomorrow, but I have to say, every bite was worth it. Emeril doesn't always verbalize his appreciation for his TV family, but he shows it on nights like this, spoiling us with a cascade of heavenly delights. I think he genuinely gets pleasure watching us gorge ourselves. And for all the *bamming* and *kicking it up a notch* he does on the show, I think his soul is truly nourished with the time spent in his restaurant kitchens feeding people.

"So guys, do you have any room for more?" Emeril asks.

"Uncle, uncle," we all say in unison.

We thank him profusely for his generosity.

"You rocked our world," I say.

"That was the goal kiddo. Hey, you guys get home safe, OK? They'll call a cab for you when you're ready. KK—I'll see you back in San Francisco in a few days."

I get up to hug him goodbye and the alcohol rushes to my head. Emeril looks at me all too knowingly.

"You don't need to hug the porcelain bowl again, do you?"

I don't think I'll ever live that down.

"No, I'll be okay. Hopefully, the bread pudding will absorb everything. I just need a good night's sleep."

I was right, I did need a good night's sleep, but I didn't get one. I can never sleep on a full stomach, so I tossed and turned for hours. A long round of tachycardia didn't help either. I think I must have finally fallen asleep around 5 a.m., only to be jarred awake by my alarm going off at 6. I have one more leg of remote shooting for the show, and I have to catch a flight back out to San Francisco in a few hours. I ask the cab driver to stop at *Cafe Du Monde* so I can grab a couple of beignets and a cup of coffee. Nothing like a little fried dough to soak up the previous night's over-indulgence.

As much as I love to travel and all of the food and drink perks that come with this job, it is taking a toll on my body and me. On the road, our shoot days are at least twelve hours long, and then I go back to my hotel room to work for a few more hours, prepping for the next day. I'm not getting enough sleep, which makes me cranky, so my crew is beginning to keep their distance. And the additional inches to my waistline are making me feel dumpy. But I have no time for a pity party because I still have a few more location shoots before I can head home to detox.

On the plane from New Orleans to San Francisco, I map out my next shoot with Steve Sando, the founder of Rancho Gordo, a purveyor of heirloom produce, seeds, and beans.

"When I started out, I couldn't believe that living in Napa I couldn't find a decent tomato," he tells me. "This is supposed to be one of the world's best agricultural regions. All the ones in the market were those hard hothouse tomatoes from Holland. I like to cook. I like fresh ingredients, and I like to eat well. So I started growing my own. And that eventually led me to grow my own heirloom beans. I was attracted to them because they are indigenous to the Americas and I feel it's important to keep that heritage alive."

As he's talking, I'm thinking what's the big deal about a bean? Isn't a bean just a bean? After another hour of my interview with him, I realize—no. A bean is not just a bean. There are hundreds of varieties with different flavor profiles and textures. They are almost as ubiquitous as rice, being a critical crop that offers sustenance and nourishment to most of the world. Think about it; what would chili be without kidney beans? Or cassoulet without flageolets? Or even fava beans without a nice Chianti?

His enthusiasm turns me into an heirloom bean convert. After the shoot with Emeril, he loads us up with a few pounds of his top sellers to bring back to the studio, including my favorite, Christmas Lima Beans. As a kid, I used to gag on the canned lima beans my mom served. They had that pukey green color and were mushy and slimy. But these beans have a gorgeous purple and white swirl and are firm enough to use in a chili or stew. They taste a little nutty, almost like chestnuts—just the right bean to turn a lima bean hater into a lover.

Of course, we didn't come all the way to Napa to just shoot a story about beans. This is wine country and there are well over eight hundred wineries in Napa and Sonoma counties that have a tale to tell. All of the big boys—Stag's Leap, Opus One, Caymus, just to name a few—would make for a good story, but I want to produce something more intimate and unexpected. I remember having met a Napa Valley winemaker, Julie Johnson, through a friend back in Brooklyn at the sushi bar across the street. I was impressed with her passion and knowledge of winemaking, and I loved that she owned a woman-led winery, *Tres Sabores*. She invited me out to her winery the next time I was in Napa and I stored that offer away in my mind. Now that I'm here in Napa, I took her up on that offer and arranged to shoot a short segment at her vineyard.

"*Tres Sabores* translates to three flavors. For me, that means the terroir, the vine, and the spirit. You can taste all of that in a wine, you know. Just look out over the vineyard. It's magical, isn't it? This bountiful piece of land on Napa Valley's Rutherford Bench is the backdrop of every stage of our winemaking process. We worked hard to become a California Certified Organic Farm and that's very important to us. Our pomegranate trees line the vineyard and they attract the bees and hummingbirds. The bees make honey for our farm's hives and the hummingbirds eat insects that would harm the vineyard. We cultivate grapevines, heritage olives, Meyer lemons, pomegranates, and more in our heirloom garden. We're home to an ecosystem that includes bluebirds, red-tail hawks, a herd of sheep, a flock of Guinea fowls, and lots, lots more. So when you taste our wine, you're tasting this environment."

After the interview, Julie walks us around her gardens and vineyard. It's a beautiful day with the Vaca Range in the distance holding off some of the heat coming in from the Central Valley. Her dogs wander up and down the lanes of vineyards, proudly guarding them from any intruders. She points out the different grapes—zinfandel, cabernet sauvignon, and petite sirah varietals—most, just weeks away from being harvested, some already engorged with the nectar of the gods.

We head down into her wine cave, a fairly small one, by Napa standards, that stores about 150 barrels. The cave was dug into a hill with a small excavator as an energy-wise decision. The cover crops and olives that are grown over the roof help to stabilize the temperature and humidity, keeping it cool and wine-friendly. At the entrance to the cave, she has set up a tasting of her most prized wines for me to sample. She begins with a sauvignon blanc.

"When I smell this, it's almost like walking through a farmers' market. I get a whiff of white nectarines, some heirloom cider apples, honeysuckle, and a bit of citrus zest on the nose."

I'm trying to conjure up an olfactory memory of a farmer's market, but my weekend one in Brooklyn often gets contaminated with exhaust and sweaty runners.

"This wine needs no special occasion to open. It's a party in a glass with a fresh aroma of dark fruit, spices, and chocolate, and a robust yet smooth finish. It's a blend with about one-third each of zinfandel, petite sirah, and cabernet sauvignon, and just a touch of petit verdot. I call it ¿Por Qué Non? which means, *why not?*"

I take a sip and notice that it's a bit spicy and jammy at the same time. I can see why she called it ¿Por Qué Non? There's no reason not to drink it.

"This is our *Perspective Cabernet Sauvignon*. We're really excited about this wine. It's one hundred percent cab. This wine really sings of its history here in Rutherford. You get all the classic flavors of this terroir—ribbons of dusty blackberry, deep plums, cherry fruit, cedar, with some sweet spices like star anise on the nose."

As much as I'm enjoying tasting all of her wines, I have to admit that I struggle with the ability to differentiate the aromas and flavors she's talking about. I've hung around winemakers long enough to know the language, but I can never pinpoint the right word when I need it. It's almost like I have palette aphasia. I do smell and taste familiar things, but I can't seem to put them into words. I'm always amazed at how winemakers and sommeliers can taste a wine and rattle off not only what grapes are in it, but where it comes from, what the terroir is like, and what year it was made. There are thousands of wines and I find it difficult to distinguish their subtleties.

For example, some friends of mine in the marketing business were doing a focus group on wines. They invited a few couples over for a blind wine tasting. They had six different bottles in paper bags. We were blindfolded and told to taste each, identifying just the grape varietal, region, and country of origin. Dan and I were definitely game and feeling fully confident that we would be able to at least do that much. Pathetically, none of us could barely tell the difference between the reds and the whites. It was quite the humbling experience.

"I love this wine, Julie," I say, not wanting to commit to the wrong description.

"At the end of the day, that's what a winemaker wants to hear," she says, as she pours a glass for everyone on the crew. "Cheers."

As the crew wraps up for the day, Julie invites me into her kitchen for another glass of wine as she starts prepping dinner for her family. We chat about our mutual friend and catch up on what we've been up to since the last time we saw each other. She's a lovely woman and extremely hospitable. I feel perfectly comfortable sitting back and enjoying the wine, until a full-grown sheep interrupts us, barreling through the door, almost as surprised to see us, as we are to see her. Miraculously, she escapes through the other side of the room and out the back door without breaking a dish. Julie barely flinches.

"Oh, don't worry about her. How's the wine?"

I'm dumbfounded. It happened so fast. If it weren't for the lingering stench it left in its wake, I might have believed I imagined it.

"Does that happen a lot?" I ask.

"Only when someone leaves the gate open. What can I say? It's the life of a farmer.

I suspect Julie and I have very different cocktail party stories to tell, but I'm not sure whose would be more entertaining.

Now that we're wrapping up shooting, Dan has joined me for a few days of fun. Although our fifteenth anniversary is a month away, we decide to celebrate early and splurge for dinner at the French Laundry. Since 2007, Thomas Keller's famous restaurant has held three Michelin stars. Each day they offer a choice between two tasting menus—one meat-and-fish-friendly, and the other vegetarian-centric. Dan and I decide to choose one of each so that we can taste as many dishes as possible.

The build-up for this has been months in the making. Reservations are hard to come by, but thanks to a little nudge from Emeril, we're able to secure a table. We're not quite sure what to expect, but we're pleasantly surprised when we arrive. The building is charming, almost like a country inn, having been constructed of river rock and timbers by a Scottish stonemason. During the 1920s, it was a French steam laundry, hence the name.

Thomas Keller and his staff are passionate about the purity of the ingredients they use and carefully select them, working with suppliers to ensure the highest quality of product. There's also a well-tended garden across the street where they grow many of the vegetables for their dishes. A chicken coop supplies fresh eggs, and the bees do their job of pollinating and producing honey.

Dan and I haven't eaten all day, wanting to be fully prepared for this multi-course experience. We have more than a little sticker shock when we see the wine list, so we decide to share two half-bottles, one riesling and one cabernet sauvignon. Each dish arrives as a piece of art, almost too delicate to eat. At one point the waiter comes out with a piece of raw wagyu beef the size of a piece of toast. We're not sure why, but he shows it to us for our approval, as if it were a bottle of wine. Later, when it arrives cooked, now the size of a piece of bacon, we understand.

"You know there's a one-hundred-dollar supplemental cost for that," I tell Dan.

"There is?"

"It was in the teeny-tiny print at the bottom of the page."

"Well then, I better eat it slowly."

Plate after plate, one more deliciously gorgeous than the next, we try to decide the evening's best dish. Oddly enough, we both agree that it was early on in the meal. Picked just moments before from their garden, two identically shaped spears of Holland white asparagus, sous vide steamed to just this point of perfection, served with a simple sauce, offered the best bite of the night. Simple, fresh, and pure—just as Mother Nature intended. I'm not sure she intended the meal to cost close to $1,000, but over the years, I've learned you just can't mess with her.

LAMB AND SAUSAGE CASSOULET

Although cassoulet is a classic French dish, I have Americanized it as an excuse to use Steve Sando's Rancho Gordo Beans. If I can find it, I like to use a classic French Saucisson, but any garlic sausage will do. This dish is so rich and filling that I only make it once a year. There's a waiting list of who gets to come over to share it and our friends reserve their spots as soon as the autumn leaves start to fall from the trees. It's perfect to serve on a cold, stormy night. Pull out that big cabernet you've been saving for a special meal and enjoy.

Serves 10

INGREDIENTS

Spice Mixture
1 teaspoon salt
1 teaspoon pepper
1 teaspoon onion powder
1 teaspoon garlic powder
1 teaspoon smoked paprika
1 teaspoon fennel seeds
1 teaspoon red pepper flakes

Cassoulet
½ pound dried Rancho Gordo Christmas lima beans
½ pound dried Rancho Gordo flageolet beans
4 strips bacon
2 tablespoons olive oil
1½ pounds lamb shoulder, cubed
½ cup flour
Kosher salt and pepper
1 onion, chopped
3 stalks celery, chopped
2 carrots, sliced
6 cloves garlic, minced
1 stalk rosemary
3 bay leaves
2 tablespoons spice mixture

8 ounces kielbasa, cubed
8 ounces Saucisson de Paris à l'Ail (French garlic sausage), cubed
14 ounces crushed tomatoes
4 cups chicken broth
¼ cup brandy or bourbon
1 cup panko breadcrumbs
½ cup grated Parmesan

DIRECTIONS

Soak both beans overnight in a pot of water. The next morning, drain and rinse them. Add to a stockpot and fill with enough water to cover the beans by 2 inches. Bring to a boil over high heat, and then reduce the heat to low and simmer for 40 minutes to one hour, checking to see when they are al dente. The beans will continue to cook in the cassoulet.

(Note: Christmas Limas Beans cook faster than other big beans. If you use something else, you might want to simmer for 1 hour.)

Preheat the oven to 350 degrees F.

Heat a large Dutch oven over medium-high heat and render the bacon. Remove to drain on a paper towel and set aside. When cool, crumble the bacon into small pieces and set aside.

Add 2 tablespoons oil to the Dutch oven and swirl to coat.

Season the lamb with salt and pepper and dredge in flour. With the Dutch oven over medium-high heat, sear the lamb for 2 minutes on each side, turning until brown. Remove meat and set aside.

Lower the heat to medium and add the onion, carrots, celery, and garlic, stirring frequently, for about 2 minutes. Add a splash of oil if the pot is too dry. Add two tablespoons of the spice mixture and stir for 30 seconds. Add the lamb, bacon, sausages, rosemary, bay leaves, tomatoes, broth, and brandy. Increase the heat to high and bring to a boil, scraping the pan to loosen any browned bits. Add the beans to the pot and stir to combine.

Cover, and place the Dutch oven in the oven, and bake for 1 hour. Then remove the lid, stir, and continue to bake for another hour. Let cool, cover, and refrigerate overnight.

The next day, take the cassoulet from the fridge two hours before you are ready to reheat, so it comes to room temperature.

Preheat the oven to 350 degrees F.

Cover and reheat the cassoulet in the oven for 20 minutes, then remove and stir. Check the seasonings and add any if necessary. Sprinkle the panko and Parmesan on top, and continue to heat, uncovered, for 20 minutes, or until warm.

I like to serve this in warmed bowls with some nice crusty bread on the side. And it's always a good idea to have a little extra Parmesan on the table for a garnish.

Chapter Fourteen

CELEBRITY DUST

"I can't believe I'm sitting here eating with all these great chefs," Rocco confesses. "This is a who's who of culinary giants."

"Rocco, don't forget, you're a great chef too," I remind him.

We're sitting at a long table at Matsuhisa in Aspen. It's closed to the public for the night. Emeril and Mario Batali are holding court on one end, and Rocco DiSpirito and I, and the lesser part of the entourage, are at the other. Bobby Flay, Susan Feniger, and Mary Sue Milliken are at nearby tables. Now that I've been at Food Network for a few years, I've gotten to rub elbows with most of the talent. It's on nights like this that I truly feel like a fly on the wall. It's the inner sanctum of the private chef's club and the goals are good times and serious consumption. As much as I'm trying to play it cool, I actually feel just as dazzled as Rocco does.

The place is buzzing, as never-ending *sake* is poured and delicate Japanese dishes keep coming—*Uni* Shooters, Lobster *Shiitake* Salad with Spicy Lemon Dressing, and Yellowtail *Tataki* with *Yuzu-Miso*—just to whet our

167

appetites. All day long we've been hanging out with renowned chefs like Daniel Boulud, Thomas Keller, and Jacques Pepin. And most are here to pay homage to Nobu himself, who is behind the counter making sushi.

"I can't believe that's really Nobu," Rocco whispers.

"Do you want me to pinch you, because you're not dreaming," I tease.

Rocco's star-struck moment is actually pretty sweet to witness, considering that he's a celebrity in the making himself. Barely out of the pimple stage, he's quite the chef prodigy, enjoying his success at Union Pacific in New York. He's one of *Food and Wine Magazine*'s Best New Chefs this year, along with Suzanne Goin, Paul Kahan, Marc Vetri, John Besh, James Mazzio, James McDevitt, Dale Reitzer, Steve Rosen, and Ron Siegel. Eileen, the network's head of programming, has asked me to helm a documentary special that follows their journeys and it's been challenging because most of them seem overwhelmed by the attention, and are very nervous in front of the cameras. Thankfully, Bobby and Mario are hosting the special, so at least I'll have some pros to help me tell the story.

"Karen, what time do you need me in the morning?" Bobby interrupts.

"I made call time for 10 a.m., assuming you'll have a long night."

"Good thinking," he winks.

Unlike other celebrities, chefs work in the service industry, so having a generous, gregarious spirit is part of the job. And they're magnanimous with each other, offering their best bites at any hour, or pitching in when times get tough. Of course, after too much booze and too late an hour, their bad boy sides can emerge. Their flaws and desires can be all too visible at times. Tonight has the potential of being one of those nights, so not wanting to topple the halo I've bestowed on my favorites, I bail out early.

The next morning, my crew and I are cooling our heels, waiting to shoot the opening introduction to the documentary.

"Have you seen Bobby?" I ask. "I told him to be here by ten."

"No, but let me see if I can find him," Christina says as she picks up her walkie-talkie. "Anyone have a twenty on Bobby Flay?"

Christina is the marketing director at *Food and Wine Magazine,* and she's in charge of this whole event. She's got at least four walkies strapped at various places around her lean body and she's constantly in motion. She deals with everything from wineglass deliveries to chef meltdowns and everything in between.

"Bobby's heading your way, Chris," a voice crackles from the walkie.

Christina is my go-to person for access to anything I need to shoot. She's one of the most competent people I've ever worked with, helping wherever she can with a smile and a mischievous sense of humor.

"Here are some all-access passes so you and your crew can eat and drink your way through the festival during your downtime. But remember, it's high altitude here, so the wine catches up fast."

I instantly love her. She's not just the friend who helps you make a fake ID, but she's a mother hen at the same time. She makes me feel welcome and part of her insider team. We're the muscle behind the chefs, making them look good whether they're doing a demo on stage, or being interviewed on camera.

"This is easily my favorite event of the year," Bobby says in an interview. "The thing I love about Aspen more than anything is that you can actually get drunk on the same bottle of wine twice."

I don't know how he does it, but I could swear his bloodshot eyes twinkle as he laughs at his own joke.

"We are like rock stars," says Jacques Pepin, rolling his *Rs* in his charming French way.

My cameraman and I walk around the huge white tent planted in the middle of Wagner Park in search of chefs to interview. Since this is a documentary, our crew is small—just a camera, a sound person, and me. We also have another small crew covering other simultaneous events like food demos. As the producer, I've got to get as many chefs as possible to talk to me, which isn't easy since most are busy cooking at a station or drinking and carousing with their buddies.

Food and wine stations butt up against each other, serving everything from anchovy *bagna cauda* to yeasty *zeppoles*. Little bites of foie gras on toast points topped with pearls of American harvested caviar beg to be paired with a German riesling or a sparkling wine from Chandon. Martin Yan is stir-frying exotic vegetables as his neighbor encourages us to wash them down with his Willamette Valley Pinot Noir. My favorite is the Spanish Pavilion where the smell of grilled chorizo is luring a huge crowd. Everywhere I turn people are eating, talking, and laughing as the wine continues to pour. And it isn't even noon yet. Although it's a gorgeous, sunny day outside, all are inside this grand tent, sweating and gorging themselves. Don't ever let anyone tell you that hedonists are not a fun bunch.

"Where is your wineglass?" Jacques asks me, as he hands me a clean one. "You can't walk around here without your wineglass. And next time I see you, it had better not be empty." He winks at me and disappears into the crowd.

If I could freeze a moment in time when there is no delineation between work and play, this would be it. I'm standing in the middle of a bacchanalian food orgy, with a wineglass in one hand and my clipboard in the other, talking to some of the most famous chefs on earth. They are a lustful, irresistible bunch, sharing their passions for food and for life with all who make contact, whether the camera is on or not.

"Katz, are you ready?" Diane asks, tearing me away from a station serving baked Brie with fig jam. "We need to get over to the Best Chef ceremony."

Diane is a very talented producer/director who I've brought with me to divvy up the work on this special. She's also an old friend, and we've had a blast spending the last few days here, even if last night is kind of fuzzy. It's great to be able to bring someone like her in to help me because Eileen has been throwing a ton of work my way. With the success of *Emeril Live,* and specials like this, I've become the "it-girl" food producer. I even have an agent now. Other chefs want to work with me and some of their celebrity dust is starting to sprinkle on me too. I'm trying to not let it go to my head, which is easier said than done.

Even back home, when Dan and I go out on our own, we get the VIP treatment. My business card goes a long way in terms of opening doors. I know I have arrived when Dan and I have the pleasure of dining at Jean-Georges in New York, and the red carpet is rolled out for us.

"Welcome, I hope you enjoy this. It's my *oeufs au caviar*."

Jean-Georges, in his crisp white, spotless chef's coat, has brought out the dish himself. He's a classically handsome Frenchman, his features all perfectly proportioned, with salt and pepper hair that seems as if he just stepped out of a men's salon, ready for a photo shoot with *GQ*. As his welcoming gaze meets mine, I melt like a half-eaten profiterole. He's brought out an egg with the top fifth of its shell removed in a perfectly level cut. It stands tall in a ceramic eggcup—the same type of cup Mom used to use for Dad's soft-boiled eggs. But the eggcup is the only thing similar about this dish. Inside the shell is a delicate whipped egg mixture that's luxuriousness is only surpassed by the extravagant tablespoon of caviar that rests on top.

"It's too beautiful to eat," I say.

"Thank you, thank you. Please, enjoy," Jean-Georges says. "Tell me. How's my friend Emeril?"

"Oh, he's great. We just finished a week of shows, so he's back in New Orleans."

"Please send him my best. I'm so glad you could join us tonight. *Bon Appétit.*"

Jean-Georges makes a tiny bow, and then he's off to say hello to Howard Stern and his wife, who are at a nearby table. Dan and I take a bite of the dish and it is spectacular. The caviar just bursts in our mouths. It's a study in contrasts; the texture is hot and cold and creamy, and the flavors are both sweet and salty. We notice the couple next to us staring at our dish and then at us.

"Excuse me," the man says, "but who are you guys?"

"Oh, my wife is an executive producer at Food Network," Dan says proudly.

"Really? I love that network. We watch it all the time," the man's wife says. "You must get great perks."

"Obviously," I say, pointing to the eggs. "Wanna taste it?"

The woman is a bit hesitant to eat off a stranger's plate, but her husband isn't.

"Whoa, that is off the charts," he says to his wife. "We should order it."

"I wonder if I could make this at home?" I say to Dan.

"How do you think they cut the top off the shell so perfectly?" he asks.

"I have no idea, but it's worth a few dozen eggs to try."

"You know, this dish has to go on our 'Best Bites' list."

"Totally," I agree.

I think Dan loves my job even more than I do. He's an all-cuisine-loving kind of guy who is happy sampling the delicacy of two perfectly sous-vide asparagus spears from a Michelin three-star restaurant, as well as the sticky, honey-barbeque sauced Korean chicken wings from the joint down the street. An equal opportunity eater, he is always at the ready to try something new. Dan has also become the king of desserts, always bringing his addictive chocolate treats to the set when he visits. They don't last long. Emeril even made one of his desserts on the show, *My Buddy Dan's Mile High Parfait Pie*. It's a decadent combination of chocolate ganache, chocolate pudding, butterscotch pudding, and whipped cream layered in a graham cracker crust. When the recipe went up on the website, some of the viewers gave it high marks.

"Awesome! I made it for my family on Christmas day. They all raved about how good it was. They fought for the last piece and asked for the recipe," wrote Daisy from Miami.

Jewell from Greensburg, Louisiana, raved, *"A holiday hit! I made and used everything in the recipe but the graham cracker crust. Instead of making a pie, I layered the parts of the pie in pre-made chocolate cups and plastic cups for individual servings of dessert. I didn't find the recipe too difficult, which is great since I'm NOT a cook. It was delicious and a big hit at our holiday gathering!"*

Dan couldn't believe the response, and the positive feedback has only encouraged him, which is not good for my ever-expanding waistline. Neither are our frequent binges at the latest up-and-coming restaurants in New York. We recently took our friends Roni and Stuart to Tao, an ultrahip Asian-fusion restaurant near the Plaza, where an enormous thirty-foot Buddha hovers above the crowds. I have become friendly with the chef, Sam Hazen, who's a big teddy bear of a guy, with a salt-and-pepper goatee like Dan's. He's warm and generous, sending out dish after dish of complimentary appetizers and dishes that he thinks we should try. The appetizer plate is almost as long as the table with a tasting of *gyozas* with chili garlic sauce, Peking duck spring rolls with hoisin sauce, *satay* chicken with peanut sauce, rock shrimp lettuce cups, and a salmon, tuna, and albacore *tataki* with a trio of seaweed.

"This is all incredibly delicious, but how are we going to have any room for our main courses?" Stu asks.

"We have to taste everything. I don't want to insult Sam," I say.

"Do you guys eat like this all the time?" Roni asks.

"Yes, but we try to pace ourselves," I say. "It never works."

We're honestly stuffed after the appetizers, and we decide to take home half of the main courses because I know that a dessert platter the length of a canoe oar will appear before we leave. We pick at each delightful morsel, making sure to open our oversized fortune cookies for some kitschy predictions. Once outside, we all groan, our bellies extended beyond their natural state.

"That was the most gluttonous meal I've ever had," Stu says. "But next time, can we go somewhere where no one knows you?"

I laugh, realizing how spoiled we've become. It's hard not to take advantage of the perks that come along with a hit show. It's a little glimpse into the world of VIPs, and I won't pretend that it's not fun and exciting. TV can put chefs on the map, and producers have become almost as important as they are. *Almost.*

Back at work in the studio, it's tuna salad and Diet Coke for lunch as we head into another week of shows. There is little time for indulgence and self-importance, especially when we've booked a very important guest.

"Karen, let me introduce you," says Geoffrey. "This is Julia Child. Julia, Karen is Emeril's executive producer."

"It's such an honor to meet…" I start to say.

"Yes, dear," Julia interrupts. "Where's the kitchen? I'd like to meet the cooks."

Geoffrey Drummond is Julia's long-time producer, and he gives me a look, implying I shouldn't take offense, then whispers, "She really likes to meet the cooks."

Even at the age of eighty-eight, with her shoulders hunched and her gait slow, Julia towers over me. Her mere presence reminds me of the time I saw Katharine Hepburn on Broadway. As soon as she walked on stage, you could feel the electricity in the theater. It's the same with Julia. I, and everyone around me, know we are in the presence of a national treasure. And that voice. That delightful voice is still high and lurching, with just a slight hint of breathlessness due to age.

Her dismissiveness certainly knocks me down a couple of pegs, putting things back in a more realistic perspective, but I try to take the blow gracefully. We've had many guests on *Emeril Live*—Willie Nelson, Aretha Franklin, Patti LaBelle, Al Jarreau, Chick Corea, even Elmo—but no one has had us on our toes as much as Julia Child. It's as if royalty has graced us. It's near heartbreaking that she has so little interest in any of us production people, but she makes up for it as she waltzes into our kitchen to talk to each and every chef, sous chef, cook, and bottle washer.

"Tell me, where did you go to culinary school?" she asks one of our sous chefs, genuinely wanting to know her background and aspirations.

"The Culinary Institute."

"That's a wonderful school," Julia says. "You keep at it, but you might want to turn that chicken before it burns, dear."

"Oh! Thank you," the sous chef says, quickly returning to her station to flip her bird.

Usually, Marie or someone from the kitchen would prep our culinary guests before the show, but Julia seems to just want to talk to Emeril about what they'll be making. Emeril is on his best behavior, having a deep respect for Julia. She recognized his talent at a young age and had him on one of her shows where he ably and amusingly showed her how to suck the heads and pinch the tails off crawfish. He gently walks her through the recipes, showing her how things are placed on the set. I have never seen him do that with any other chef who visited the show. But he did it for Julia.

We've kept the surprise from the audience, so when Emeril introduces Julia, the place goes nuts. I'm not sure she was expecting such a rowdy bunch, but she certainly plays along and has no problem correcting or questioning Emeril.

"That's a pretty scrawny chicken, don't you think?" she asks.

Emeril laughs, surprised by her chiding.

"Well Julia, it's the end of the week and the kitchen probably blew their budget," he jokes.

I know Geoffrey is a bit overprotective of her, but I can see him relax once he sees she's having a good time. When the show is over, rather than leaving through our main door where her car is waiting, Julia walks back into the kitchen, stops to sign some autographs, and thanks the staff, leaving through the back kitchen door. An appropriate exit for the woman who once said, "People who love to eat are always the best people."

FRENCH HARVEST SOUP

The first thing I ever cooked out of Julia Child's *Mastering the Art of French Cooking* was her recipe for *Soupe à l'Oignon*. If you're true to the recipe, it requires you to hover over your onions for an hour. I've changed it up a bit and turned it into a roasted vegetable soup so I can shove the veggies in the oven and walk away for an hour. I'm proud to say this was my first televised recipe. We did a

"Crew Favorites" episode on *Emeril Live*, and this recipe was my contribution. One fan from California gave me this rave review on the website: *"Her current employer may have to make space for her at the counter to showcase her cooking expertise! This recipe is WONDERFUL and easy! It's a hearty soup to enjoy on a cold day. I'm glad we had leftovers—we couldn't get enough of this wonderful soup!"*

Serves 4

INGREDIENTS

1 large yellow onion, skinned and quartered
1 large sweet pepper
1 large bell pepper
1 head garlic, cut in half
3 ears corn
1 large tomato
2 Yukon gold potatoes, halved
¼ cup olive oil
3 cups chicken stock or bone broth
Salt and pepper
1 tablespoon adobo sauce (chipotle)
1 baguette (for croutons)
2 tablespoons olive oil
½ pound Gruyere cheese, thickly grated

DIRECTIONS

Preheat oven to 375 degrees F.

Place the onion, peppers, garlic, corn, tomato, and potatoes on a baking sheet, and generously brush with the ¼ cup of olive oil.

Roast for approximately 45 minutes. The skin on the peppers, tomatoes, and garlic should be broken. Allow to cool, and then peel off the skin. Scrape the kernels off of the corn cobs and set aside.

Chop all the other vegetables into large chunks. Place in stockpot with corn and enough chicken stock to almost cover the vegetables. Add the adobo sauce, and season to taste with salt and pepper. Bring to boil over high heat, and then reduce the heat to low and simmer for 20 minutes.

Slice the baguette into ½-inch rings and brush each piece with olive oil. Place separately on a large baking sheet, and place under the broiler for about thirty seconds until they start to brown. Flip over and broil for another thirty seconds, making sure not to burn them.

Strain the vegetables, saving the broth. Divide the veggies among the soup crocks. Add enough broth to fill the crocks within ½-inch of the lip of the bowl. Place the croutons on top, and cover with grated cheese. Place the crocks on a pan and broil for thirty seconds to melt the cheese. Serve hot.

Chapter Fifteen

EVENTUALLY, THE SOUFFLÉ FALLS

"So, tell me about Emeril?" Brooke asks me.

"What's to know? He's pretty much the same guy you see on camera, just a lot quieter."

Brooke is the new president of Food Network, the third one since I started here nine years ago. She's got a reputation for no-nonsense and she's certainly not new to the power seat. Unafraid of making big changes, she launched the Biography Channel during her time at A&E and proposed the concept for the History Channel. I hear she does what needs to be done, even if that means there may be some collateral damage like firing staff or cutting budgets.

She's asked me to lunch and I'm a little unsure about what to say and what not to say. She's not particularly warm and fuzzy. I suspect she's more like a very good poker player who keeps her cards close to her chest. I attempt to be charming and witty although her angular, humorless face distracts me. Studying me, she takes a sip from her second glass of wine. I don't even touch my first, wanting to stay sharp.

"Well, I know *Emeril Live* has been a tent pole for the network for a long time, but it's also our most expensive show," she estimates. "I'm not sure we're getting the bang for our buck, taking the show on the road. And the specials aren't really bumping the ratings that much either."

"But we're still the number one show," I state.

"For now," she conjectures.

I don't think she means that as a threat, more like a prediction. It dawns on me that I've been cruising along a paved highway for the last few years, with one hand on the wheel and the other holding a map to wherever I feel like going. But now I've got a sinking feeling that the road ahead is going to be filled with potholes, and maybe this old jalopy ain't gonna make it. If I'm being completely honest, I've pretty much milked as much out of this format as I possibly can.

What's more, the landscape around me is changing fast. Food competition shows like *Iron Chef* and *Top Chef* are quickly gaining obsessed followings, and our audience is aging out of the demo. I should have left the show a couple of years ago to explore new opportunities, but I couldn't bear the thought of someone else producing it. I've stayed out of loyalty, pride, and fear; only one of which is a good enough reason. It's like I'm the old wife trying to hold on to a marriage that is about to fall apart over the young secretary. For the first time in years, our trajectory is not going in the right direction, and it feels too late to save it.

If Emeril sees the handwriting on the wall, he's not showing it. His empire is bigger and more successful than ever, with over twelve restaurants, ten cookbooks in print, with more on the way, as well as a line of cookware, and a deal with B&G for spices and other food products. I can't even go shopping without seeing his face plastered all over the soup section. He is the captain of a big ship that doesn't turn easily or quickly.

When I was back in the studio, I told Emeril about my lunch with Brooke. "You know, Brooke doesn't want to put much extra money into production this year. We're going to be stuck in the studio most of the time."

"Yeah, she mentioned something like that," Emeril shrugged. "Look, it's business. Besides, my schedule is nuts the next few months. I don't think I could find time to travel with the show, anyway. But you'll think of something."

"Funny you should say that. I've been doing some counting, and I don't think you realize it, but you're about to do your 1,500ᵗʰ show on this network."

"1,500? You're kidding me?"

"Nope. Going back to *How to Boil Water, Emeril and Friends,* and the *Essence of Emeril,* not to mention *Emeril Live,* you've got a whole freakin' library in the can."

"So, what are you thinking? An anniversary special?"

"Exactly. We'll get a bunch of celebrities to send videotaped messages, book some special guests, and roll in some fun old clips. We can even get some of the other network chefs to cook with you. And it won't cost much, which Brooke will love."

"Don't let her rattle you," he assures me. "We're not going anywhere."

For years, Emeril has been in the good graces of the muckety-mucks high up at Scripps, Food Network's parent company. The network was practically built on his shoulders, and his value is immeasurable to them. I think he thinks Brooke is just another network president that he'll survive, having seen so many others come and go. I hope he's right.

About a month later, I'm sitting in my office reviewing the ratings, and I can't believe what I'm reading.

"How did we go from the number one show to number eight overnight?" I scream into the phone at someone from the sales department.

"Don't shoot the messenger," the sales secretary responds. "We're no longer selling on just households. Our key demo is now women eighteen to thirty-five. Your audience is more male and older, so it's slipped down in the list."

"Can you move the goalposts just like that?" I ask.

"Well, yeah, we can," she says. "It's a done deal."

This is bad. This is really bad. If Emeril thinks that there's loyalty here at the network, then he has forgotten his own words—*it is just business.* From a purely mathematical perspective, there comes a point where the risk outweighs the reward, and we're getting dangerously close to that point. If our numbers are down, ad sales can't charge as much for the time, the marketing department won't put as much effort into promoting us, and before we know it, we'll be yesterday's leftovers.

"Karen, what's your schedule like?" Nancy, Brooke's secretary asks. "Can you meet with Brooke tomorrow at four? She wants to see you."

"Yeah, of course. Do you know what this is about?"

"You know I can't say anything," she says, not looking me in the eye.

Nancy has been here even longer than I have. She was the previous network president's trusted secretary, and she holds the keys to every secret door. She's loyal and good at what she does, having no desire to climb the corporate ladder. She keeps the trains on the tracks. And, if you get on her good side, she'll make sure you get all the good swag. But today, from the look of her body language, I don't think she has anything good to offer.

As I go home, my head starts swimming with the possibilities, all of them bad. By the time I get there, I am in one huge foul mood.

"Why do you always go to the negative?" Dan asks. "Maybe she wants you to do another show?"

"No. No way."

"You don't know what this is about. Why get all upset?"

"Upset, who's upset? Do I seem upset just because the last nine years of my life are about to go down the tubes?"

"Don't you think you're being a little extreme?"

"What's wrong with being extreme? I like being extreme."

"I see where this is going. Why don't we go to Geido, have a couple of sakes and maybe Osamu-san will make you your favorite—uni and quail egg?"

"I'm in no mood to be social. You go."

"No, I'm not going to leave you like this."

"For your own safety, I think you should go."

Dan knows better than to argue with me at this point. He knows that sometimes I just need to stew by myself. He hightails it to Geido, and I go in search of something for dinner. Rummaging through the fridge, I spy some leftover wonton soup, a half-eaten takeout barbeque chicken, and some cheese.

CHEESE! When I find myself in times of trouble, I melt cheese. I make myself an insanely naughty grilled cheese sandwich with caramelized onions, two thick slices from a brioche I was planning to use for French toast in the morning, and way too much Brie. Now all I need are some potato chips and a good tearjerker chick-flick.

I settle on *The Way We Were,* because I have to have my Barbra in times of crisis. And right on cue, with the flick of Hubbell's hair at that last scene by the Plaza, the waterworks open. I love a good movie cry. Afterward, I feel relieved and refreshed, and after inhaling four of Dan's diabolically delicious chocolate chip cookies, I am ready to face whatever lies ahead.

"Hi Brooke," I say, tapping on her door the next day. "You wanted to see me?"

"Yeah, thanks, come on in. Shut the door, please."

Oh, this can't be good.

"How long have you been here at Food Network?" she asks.

"Oh, about nine years now," I say, trying not to sweat.

"And you not only produce *Emeril Live,* but *Essence of Emeril* and a few specials each year, right?"

"That's right."

"And you've been on contract all that time, not staff, getting paid for each show you produce?"

"Yeah, well, I have a good agent."

"Yes, you do. Too good. I've just been talking to him."

She talked to him, and he didn't call me?

"As you've probably heard, we just canceled Sara's show," she states matter-of-factly.

Sara Moulton's *Cooking Live* has been on Food Network's air since the early days. Every day at five, Sara stands ready for calls from cooks around the country, trying to figure out how to tie up a roast, or how to make jam from scratch. She doesn't flinch when the random prank caller gets through, or when her soufflé falls. She's been a pro from day one, and I can't imagine how she'll take this news.

"Some of the staff have been with the network for years," Brooke continues. "And I want to have the other shows absorb as many of them as possible."

"I'm sure they'll be happy to hear that," I respond.

"I'm glad you feel that way because I want Georgia to take over *Essence of Emeril* from you."

She should have just taken a meat cleaver and stabbed me through my stomach. I am dumbstruck; I don't know what to say. I have been Emeril's executive producer on all things Emeril since I got here. Granted, *Essence* is a simple dump-and-stir show that any of the producers at the network can handle, but it's been my baby for years, along with *Emeril Live*. I'm going to take a serious financial hit without both shows, but I'm even more upset that someone else will be producing him. But what can I do? I don't want to be the reason someone might lose a job. I'm friendly with some of Sara's staff, and I know they've all been freaking out.

"Does Emeril know?" I ask.

"Yes, we discussed it," she says. "But he understands the position I'm in."

Did he at least fight for me for one freakin' second? I want to ask her, but I know I have to keep my cool. I can't tell if she's enjoying this or not, but she does have a very satisfied look on her face. Or maybe it's the look of power—something she has at the moment, and I don't.

My anxiety level rising, I retreat to my office, close the door, and call my agent, Jon. "Did you know about this?" I ask.

"I just got off the phone with her. There wasn't time to give you a heads-up. I'm so sorry, but there's nothing in your contract that guarantees you both shows indefinitely."

"She hates me."

"She doesn't hate you, but she made it clear she doesn't like the deal I made for you."

I'm one of Jon's first clients. He was just beginning his climb up the William Morris ladder when we met, and he's taken very good care of me ever since. But now, a few years later, he's representing on-air talent like Rachael Ray and Bobby Flay, both of whom will make far more money than I ever will, so I realize I'm not his first priority, although he does still try to make me feel that way.

"Listen, you're doing great with *Emeril Live*," he says.

"She's taken away our budgets for road shows, you know."

"Not to defend her, but look at it this way: from her perspective, she needs a new hit, not one coming up on ten years. She's got to put money into something new."

"I know," I whine. "But I can't help but feel like we're being cast aside, like an old shoe."

"You're not an old shoe," he assures me.

"Not me, the show."

"You know what I mean. *Emeril Live* still has a lot of life left in it. Just find a way to keep it going."

Nine years, almost 1,500 shows, 10,000 *BAMS!* and enough garlic to stuff an elephant, and I've got to smile and keep it going, pretending all is right with the world. I know my staff will hear about this before I even open my door. This place is a gossip mill. You can't even overcook a steak without everyone hearing about it. I'm sure with the sledgehammer going out to Sara's show, my guys are going to be worried too. I have got to keep it together, so I put on my best Andy Hardy face, open the door, and walk to the center of our production pit.

"Okay, guys. Where's that case of Cabo Wabo tequila that Sammy Hagar's people sent? Get some paper cups and meet me in my office. We've got some brainstorming to do."

FEELING SORRY FOR MYSELF GRILLED CHEESE SANDWICH

When life starts to go to the dark side, I can always cheer myself up with a good old-fashioned grilled cheese sandwich served with a side of potato chips. I'm sure, given enough cheese, it will cheer you up too.

Makes 1 sandwich

INGREDIENTS

3 tablespoons butter, divided
1 small onion, thinly sliced
2 slices brioche
¼ wheel of Brie or cheese of your choice, sliced
¼ apple, thinly sliced
Fig jam, your favorite brand
Potato chips (optional)
1 or more cocktails (optional)
1 pint ice cream (optional)

DIRECTIONS

Melt 1 tablespoon butter in a skillet of medium heat. Add the onion and cook for 8 minutes until browned and caramelized, set aside.

In the same skillet, melt 1 tablespoon butter and brown one side of each piece of bread. Remove from skillet and place one slice on a cutting board with the brown side facing up. Slather on fig jam. Top with sliced Brie, apples, and a heaping spoonful of onions.

Top with the other slice of bread, brown side touching the onions. You now have a sandwich with the two uncooked sides facing out.

Melt the remaining tablespoon of butter in the skillet over medium heat, and carefully place the sandwich back in the pan. When the bottom has browned, carefully flip the sandwich over and brown the last remaining side. This way, all sides of the bread are toasty and buttery. It adds to the crunch factor—a very important element when one is feeling blue.

Serve immediately with a side of potato chips, your choice of alcoholic beverage, and a pint of your favorite ice cream.

Chapter Sixteen

SPACE: THE FINAL FRONTIER

"Karen, there's a woman from NASA who's trying to reach you," says one of our press assistants.

"NASA? Like space NASA?" I ask.

I'm used to getting calls from lots of high-profile people and companies. Everyone wants a seat at our bar. I figure a retired astronaut is probably coming to town, and he wants tickets to the show.

"Hi, I'm Nicole from NASA's PR department. Is this Karen Katz, Emeril's executive producer? I've been trying to track Emeril down, and I was hoping you could help."

"If I can."

"This might sound a bit out of left field, but I've got a request from our food lab that I was hoping Emeril could help us with. I'm not sure you're aware of this, but when astronauts are in space for a long period of time, their ability to taste gets diminished. They've been requesting food with more flavor and spice, and we were hoping Emeril could make some suggestions, you know, help us kick things up a notch or two."

"I'm sure he'd be honored to."

"Fantastic. What's the best way to reach him?"

Holy crap. I've got NASA on the phone. My head is spinning. I can already see the headlines—*Emeril Spices Up Space, One Giant BAM for Mankind.* This is what the show needs to keep us relevant. It's been a few months since Brooke made it clear we were no longer a network priority and unfortunately, none of our programming stunts have gotten much attention.

"This might sound crazy," I suggest, "but could he send up a care package to the crew on the International Space Station?"

"Well," she pauses, as any good PR person would at an intriguing idea, "I don't think something like that has been done before, and I can't authorize it, but it's an interesting idea. Let me talk to the powers that be."

This simple phone call begins an eighteen-month process. Nicole and I are both "idea people," but we don't have the authority to make this happen on our own. Our jobs are to convince our bosses that our idea is worth the time and money to pursue. We both have to get buy-in from a lot of people, but we're determined, so we start cutting through the red tape. And there is a lot of tape to unravel.

Nicole has to move mountains on her side, going up the chain of command at NASA, level by level. At Food Network, suddenly no one seems to take me seriously. Even with my excitement, Brooke is neither impressed nor confident that my idea will ever happen, but she doesn't stop me from pursuing it either. Emeril thinks it's cool, but doesn't have the patience to get into the weeds with me. His branding and culinary teams are a little nervous allowing his food to be freeze-dried. Emeril is a serious chef and after taking those hits from the food glitterati about what they perceived to be a "dumbing down" of food on our show, they don't want this to add fuel to the fire. But eventually the coolness of working with NASA tips the scales and they agree to help.

Before we even get started, I have to relearn how NASA actually gets food into space. I do have a leg up, having done a show at one of their test kitchens a few years back. It's a fascinating process. The simplified version is they make a variety of dishes and then freeze-dry them. But not everything freeze-dries well, so there's a lot of experimentation and testing that goes on. And you have to watch out for crumbs. Crumbs in space are bad. They can float into places where they have no business being. There are also other things to consider, like the crunch factor. A good crunch can make an astronaut's day. A lot of planning and thought has to go into it because you don't want to have a group of "hangry" astronauts cursing your culinary team from 254 miles in the outer atmosphere. Food is one of the few pleasures they get up in space, so the goal is to make something nourishing and satisfying.

"I've got some specifications that just came in from NASA," I share with the kitchen staff. "You guys should review it. They've had a lot of experience with what works and what doesn't, so I think this might save you a lot of time."

Susan and her awesome culinary team are game to work on this with me. They start coordinating with Emeril's camp and after much discussion, everyone agrees to Emeril's Mardi Gras Jambalaya, green beans with garlic, kicked-up mashed potatoes with bacon, and rice pudding. After months of back-and-forth between our kitchen and NASA's, we receive some samples of his food in NASA freeze-dried bags. They look like hospital IV bags, just with all the liquid sucked out. We need to rehydrate them and taste for approval.

"What do you think?" I ask Susan.

"There *is* a kick and the flavors are coming through. It tastes like his food. I think we're finally good to go."

"Houston, we have liftoff," I say.

She rolls her eyes at me.

"Sorry, I couldn't help myself."

Now that the food is settled, we have to wait to get approval for transport. That's the really hard part. There's a lot of stuff that has to go up to resupply the International Space Station, and every ounce is scrutinized and prioritized. But the astronauts do have to eat, so we're hopeful Emeril's food will be added on. About a month later, I get a call from Nicole.

"Hey, Karen. Good news. We're a go for July Fourth on the STS-121."

"STS?"

"Oh sorry, that's short for Space Transportation System," she explains. "The Space Shuttle Discovery is the next one flying. Its mission is to test new safety equipment and deliver supplies. You should come down for the launch. Have you ever been to one?"

"No—I'd love that! You know, now that this is real, it would be great to feature this on one of our shows. Don't you do ship-to-shore video calls or whatever you call them?" I ask.

"All the time."

"It would really bring the story full circle if we could have the astronauts taste Emeril's food and talk to him about it, don't you think? We'd feature it and promote it on one of our shows."

"Well, it's not that easy to pull off," she balks. "The astronauts' schedules are fully booked, but let me see what I can do. You'll need a satellite hook-up on your end."

"We can make that happen. I'll talk to my tech guys."

"Why don't you do that first, and if it's a go on your end, I'll pitch it on mine."

We're two weeks out from launch. Nicole and I have worked out all the details and now that this scheme is finally real, suddenly everyone at the network wants in on it. The press department connects with Kim Severson over at the *New York Times*, and she does a feature story on us. I'm interviewed, along with Brooke, so that helps bring my stock up a bit. Our operations department really steps up and arranges the satellite hook-up. And I'm feeling like the Cheshire Cat, knowing that I pulled this off. Just try to kill my show, just try.

July Fourth arrives and I'm really nervous about the launch. I couldn't make it down to Florida for this one, due to our shooting schedule, but I'll take Nicole up on her offer for the next one. My fingers are crossed as she assures me the lift-off was perfect and Emeril's food made it onboard. It takes another week before we can schedule a video visit with the astronauts, but the day finally arrives for the satellite hook-up, and thanks to the entire team, it comes together perfectly. Our slot is scheduled for 1:30, and on the dot, the image comes on our monitor. Floating in front of us from the ISS are NASA astronaut Jeff Williams, Russian cosmonaut Pavel Vinogradov, and European Space Agency astronaut Thomas Reiter, all of whom have sampled Emeril's food. It takes a moment before Emeril gets used to the time delay, but eventually, he and the astronauts get into a rhythm.

"Hey guys, can you hear me?" Emeril asks.

"We hear you loud and clear," Jeff says. "Thanks for sending up your food. I didn't even need to take out my trusty Tabasco sauce to spice it up. It's great."

"Well, it was a team effort between our awesome kitchen staff, your folks at NASA, and my producer, Karen Katz."

He said my name … in space! MY NAME IS IN SPACE. It's out there, in the atmosphere, floating along in zero gravity. Who knows where it will travel next? Will it skip off the moon and head towards Mars, and then through the rings of Saturn, only to eventually rush into some wormhole that will take it to the other side of the universe? Will some unknown alien pick up the radio wave in four billion years, wondering who I am, and what on earth is jambalaya? I know. I've watched the movie *Contact* way too many times, but it could happen.

"Well guys, enjoy the food and thanks for taking the time to talk with us today," Emeril says.

"You can send us your food anytime, Emeril. Thanks so much."

And within five seconds, the screen goes dark, the slated time over exactly as planned. Everyone in the studio is as excited as I am, and a lot of the other staff has come down to watch. This is the Food Network, and it's not every day we go into space. This is cool. Way cool.

But that was so yesterday. It doesn't take long before everyone moves on to the next big thing, so I don't get to bask in the glory for very long.

After the *Times* story comes out, we're back to being the old dog sniffing around for crumbs, while the cute new puppies are dashing about, getting cuddled by everyone. Competition shows like *The Next Food Network Star* and *Chopped* have all the attention now.

Within a year, *Emeril Live* will have run its course, and no one is really surprised when the show is canceled, but that doesn't mean it doesn't hurt. Brooke calls me into her office to tell me the bad news a few days before the announcement goes out to the press. Although I'm fully aware of what's coming, I am surprised to find myself choked up and speechless as I listen to the words come out of her mouth.

"You all had a great run. You should be proud of what you and your team have done. But it's time for the network to focus its energies and money on new formats and new talent."

Carrie, our network publicist, tries to put a good spin on it by releasing a statement.

"The only reason to end the show would be that it hit a ton of television milestones and, you know, all good things come to an end."

Brooke spoke to the *Times* saying, "All good things come to an end, and it was time to do something new." Nothing like coordinating your responses.

I know that Emeril feels betrayed and is taking it hard, but he doesn't leave empty-handed. Grandfathered into his contract is ownership of most of his shows. He eventually parlays that into a multi-million-dollar deal with Martha Stewart. That should soften the blow for him.

As for me, I get to keep the 500 cookbooks that publicists have sent over the years, a case of Cabo Wabo tequila, and a beat-up blue oval 8-quart Le Creuset Dutch oven. On our last day, Susan throws a small goodbye party in the Food Network kitchen for my staff and me, and I uncharacteristically burst into tears. I even surprise myself. Until this moment, I had no idea how much this show has defined me. Who am I if I'm not Emeril's producer?

Later that night, I call Mom to tell her about my last day and ask her the same question.

"You're a Katz," Mom says. "That's who you are, and don't ever forget it. There will be other shows and other Emerils. We always land on our feet. Ten years ago you didn't even know who Emeril was. Who knows what the next ten years will bring? Life will throw you many curveballs and hand you unexpected surprises. Trust me, I know. Now, can we talk about something important? Do you want me to bring Nana's noodle pudding or her cranberry sauce mold for Thanksgiving?"

KARENALAYA

Emeril's Mardi Gras Jambalaya might be great for space food, but I've created my own version that's a little lighter and spiced to my liking. It's a great one-pot dish that can feed an army—or a group of astronauts.

NOTE: The stock and tomato products are the liquid sources for the rice. If two cups of rice require 4 cups of water, then make sure your stock and tomato liquid combined equals 4 cups.

Serves 6

INGREDIENTS

2 tablespoons canola oil
1 red onion, chopped
4 stalks celery, chopped
1 green pepper, chopped
1 pound turkey meat leftovers, chopped
4 links lean sausage (pre-cooked), sliced
4 cloves garlic, minced
1 (14-ounce) can diced tomatoes
1 (14-ounce) can tomato puree

2 whole chipotle peppers, with two tablespoons of adobe sauce from can
¼ teaspoon cayenne
2 cups turkey or chicken stock
2 cups rice
Salt and pepper, to taste

DIRECTIONS

Heat the canola oil in a large skillet over medium heat. Sauté the onions, celery, pepper for 6 minutes until the onions are translucent. Season with salt and pepper. Add the turkey, sausage, and garlic and cook for 4 minutes.

Add diced tomato, tomato puree, the chipotle peppers with sauce, and the cayenne. Cook for another 2 minutes. Add the stock and rice and test the seasoning.

Increase the heat to high and bring to a boil, then cover, reduce the heat to low, and let simmer for 20 minutes, or whatever time the rice instructions suggest.

Serve in warmed bowls with a side of cornbread or your favorite crusty bread.

Chapter Seventeen
IS THERE LIFE AFTER EMERIL?

The morning light streams through our bedroom window, gently warming my face before waking me. Lying in bed, stunned, mourning the loss of my show and possibly my career, I can hear the sounds of the world outside my bedroom. The peaceful coo of a pigeon is drowned out by a chattering jackhammer that is shredding pavement like a Stratocaster guitar. The street rumbles as the garbage trucks go by, shaking out its kinks like a timpani being tuned. Horns honk themselves into a crescendo as the traffic cop raises his arms so all can settle and begin their day—all but me. I've been doing a pretty good job of attending my own little pity party. Convinced that I will never work again, I've been taking my time sorting through all those hundreds of cookbooks I took from the office.

"Should I alphabetize them by author or by cuisine?" I ask Dan.

"Where are we gonna put them all? The shelves are already bulging," he says.

I'm not sure Dan is exactly thrilled about having me around all day. He's used to working from home and having the place to himself. He's well aware of my moods, and I can sense that he's tiptoeing around, trying not to make me feel worse than I already do. He's had twenty years of practice, and he's gotten pretty good at it.

At least I wasn't escorted out of the building when *Emeril Live* was canceled. My team and I had ample time to wrap out ten years of shows, and we used the time wisely, editing our resumes and networking. My agent is encouraging me to pitch show ideas to other networks—my least favorite thing in the world to do. I've never been good at pitching. To be good at it, you have to be willing to be rejected 95 percent of the time. Make that 98 percent of the time. Good ideas are constantly rejected and bad ideas get green lit. Sometimes, there's no sense to the process—just timing, politics, luck, and good relationships. But he's set up some meetings for me, so I've got to rally and make a good impression.

It's not long before I find myself in the lobby of Discovery down in Silver Spring, Maryland, waiting to pitch the head of development for TLC. He keeps me waiting a good thirty minutes past our appointment, but eventually, his secretary comes to fetch me. I am brought to a tiny, windowless conference room that has a table too big for the space and only one chair. I sit and wait another ten minutes. Eventually, Howard bursts into the room, as if he's been running a marathon and is just stopping for a quick sip of water. He's a skinny, hyper guy who could be either nerdy or trendy, depending on the situation, seeming to survive only on Diet Coke and an occasional cookie.

"I'm sorry I'm so late, but it's been quite a morning. Ugh, she didn't bring in another chair. I'll be right back."

And off he goes, returning after another ten minutes with a rolling chair.

"So, your agent is Jon Rosen? He loves you, you know. I've never heard him talk up a producer like you."

"Oh, I'm glad that 10 percent is working for me."

He laughs, and asks, "So Emeril was canceled after all these years. You must be devastated. What happened?"

He seems genuinely interested, not in a sympathetic way, but in a gossipy kind of way. I can tell he wants to hear the dish.

"Well, you know, all good things come to an end. We had ten great years and I guess the network felt it was just time."

"Uh-huh," he says, not buying it. "So tell me, what's your next move?"

I proceed to tell Howard that I have my own production company, and I've brought some shows to pitch. He politely listens to me rattle off my new ideas; his eyes glazing over as they probably do with most producers that stop by.

"TLC is a lot different than Food Network. We're always looking for stories about unique people and families," he says. "We're much more talent-centric than process-driven. If you have interesting people attached, I'd be happy to take a look at them."

I knew I was bombing. They've had tremendous hits with shows like *Jon & Kate Plus 8* and *Little People.* But the talent I've been working with just aren't eccentric enough. They are just charming cooks, none of whom have twenty kids or live in a trailer park or weigh 600 pounds. We chat for a few more minutes as Howard tries to pull more dirt out of me, but eventually, he needs to whisk his way to his next meeting, and I head down to the lobby. I know I have to do this kind of thing, but to be honest, my heart isn't in it. I'd much prefer to be making the widgets, not selling them. Dejected, I think about lunch as I ride down the elevator. Maybe a nice croque monsieur with a glass of chablis will cheer me up. Just as I'm about to reach the exit in search of a nice bistro, I hear, "Karen! Karen!" It's Howard, running after me.

"I'm sorry, but I just thought of something that you'd be perfect for. We're starting a new channel called *Planet Green*, and our CEO wants us to have an environmentally conscious cooking show. Do you think you could work up some ideas?"

Could I work up some ideas? "I'd be happy to," I say.

"I want to introduce you to our head of production, Chris Weber. She's spearheading the project. Can you wait a few more minutes? I'll see if she can meet with you while you're down here."

"You mean now?"

"Yeah. Why schlep back down from New York again?"

About ten minutes pass and Howard's assistant comes back to tell me that Chris can meet with me in about twenty minutes. I was so looking forward to that croque monsieur, but a tuna sandwich from a deli down the street will just have to do.

"This must be fate," Chris says, as she welcomes me into her office with a disarming smile. "We're launching this new channel in just a few months, and I've been pulling out my hair trying to get enough programming going in time."

Chris is a rarity in the business. She's smart, direct, honest, funny, and reasonable. After a few minutes, she's already won my favorite executive award.

"I've gotta be honest. I don't know the first thing about food," she says.

"Believe it or not, I didn't either when I started with Emeril. But now I feel as if I've gotten a full culinary degree."

"Thank goodness, because I need someone who can just take over this project and deliver eighty episodes in the first year. You're the only producer I've met that has experience with that kind of volume in the food space."

She's right. Most series run in ten to thirteen episode cycles. But *Emeril Live* was run more like a daily talk show. We produced ninety shows each year, so eighty are not daunting to me. I guess being the ex-executive producer of a hit show still has some street cred.

"But we don't want a studio show," she continues. "We're working with Whole Foods as our main sponsor, so we're going to use a local one in Fairfax, Virginia, for the shoot."

"You want to shoot in a supermarket?" I ask. "During the day?"

"That's the plan," she says.

"Locations can be tough to control," I say.

"Tell me about it," she agrees. It's clear she's no novice to production, but if the powers that be want a show in a supermarket, that's what she's going to deliver.

"Here's the deal. *Planet Green's* focus is on environmentalism and sustainable living. And food is obviously a big part of that. Whole Foods is a natural partner for this, and the only stipulation is that some cooking and shopping has to happen in the store. But there can be remote pieces too. As a matter of fact, we'd prefer that. Other than that, the creative is wide open."

Now this sounds like a cool challenge. Starting a new show from scratch, having a commitment of eighty episodes, and trying to make the world a better place through food doesn't sound too bad. Cue the Hallelujah Chorus.

"I'd love to take a shot at it. When do you need a proposal?"

"Yesterday to tell you the truth, but could you get me something by next week? I'll need a schedule and budget with that as well. You'll have to back time from early June—that's when we launch."

Whoa. That's six months from now. How am I going to pull this off?

"Sure, no problem," I say confidently. "How's by next Wednesday?"

And just like that, I'm back in business. To be clear, things like this *never* happen so easily or so quickly. But obviously, they're in a bind, and I just happened to be in the right place at the right time. Wouldn't you know it—just as I was getting comfortable in my slovenly morning ritual of doing nothing—I actually have to get my mojo back and get to work even if it kills me, which it might.

Over the next week, I research everything from sustainable farming and the slow-food movement to snout-to-tail eating. Offal has become my new fascination. There are so many directions this show could go, and I love pulling all the pieces together. I decide on a format that introduces the people who passionately care about the food we eat—the organic farmers, the fishermen who focus on sustainability, the ranchers raising grass-fed, free-roaming animals. Each episode will open with a documentary-style piece on one of these purveyors, and then we will bring their product into Whole Foods and our TV chef will cook with it. I write up a list of known health-conscious chefs to pitch, and I work up the schedule and budget.

It's so nice to be doing something new. For the last ten years, I've been in my own little Emeril bubble. Cushy as that was, it really wasn't that stimulating once Brooke and the budget police put the kibosh on producing anything new and fun. Chris, on the other hand, is a dream to work with and we move quickly to get the concept green-lit. Before I know it, I'm in LA casting for a chef and I'm feeling totally back in the game.

"Hi Karen, it's Chris." Her voice sounds funny.

"Everything okay?" I ask.

"Well, that depends on your point of view. Everyone is really happy with having you on board and we know you're going to make a great show, but our CEO wants to have a big name as host."

Oh, no. I've just wasted the last two weeks setting up all this casting.

"I can understand that," I say, trying to be a good sport. "I get it. I can put together a list of possibilities and …"

"He actually has someone in mind. He wants," she pauses. "Are you sitting down?"

"Yeah?"

"He wants Emeril to host."

You have *got* to be kidding me.

"Emeril? He wants Emeril?" I ask as my voice raises a few octaves.

"You should know better than anyone how popular he is. It would bring instant attention to the show and to the network."

I can't even think of anything to say.

"Karen, you still there?" Chris asks.

"Sorry, yeah, you're right. I know."

"Listen, I know this wasn't what you had in mind, but I really think it's going to be for the best. Take some time to get used to the idea and let's talk tomorrow. Okay?"

Gut-punched, I hang up. I don't even know what to think. Just when I thought I was starting fresh on my own terms, it feels like a massive step backward. Are people going to think I only got the gig because Emeril was involved? Am I doomed to always be known as "Emeril's producer?" He's such a creature of habit; I don't know how he's going to adapt to this new format. And knowing his schedule, I'm going to have to shoot everything out of sequence to get him in and out of our location as fast as possible. Then there are the fans. How are we going to keep them away as we shoot?

I spend the next few days piling on problems that haven't even happened yet. Now that we're shooting this through my company and not the network, I'm responsible for all costs and overruns. There are so many "extras" that are associated with a big name that I have to jack up the budget by ten percent. Chris seems to understand, but before the contracts are officially signed, she wants me to talk to Emeril to make sure we're both on the same page. I haven't spoken to him since we taped our last show a few months ago, but I'm determined not to fall back into old bad habits. I make a list of things I want him to understand and I anxiously wait for his call.

"K.K., how ya' doing? Can you believe this?"

"I know. It's crazy."

"I read your treatment for the show. I like it. I like it a lot," he assures me.

"You do know you're going to have to cook a vegetarian dish on occasion, maybe use tofu," I tease.

"Hey—you know me. I'm all about good, fresh, local ingredients. Seriously, there's a ton of local food stories you could do all around that area. I don't think you're going to have a problem."

"You're right. I've been doing some research and we've got some great resources nearby. But you know, we have to shoot in Virginia, right? At a Whole Foods?"

"I know, I heard. We'll make it work. As long as I have security, we'll be fine."

"I wanted to talk to you about that," I say, gathering my courage. "I totally get the need for security, but I can't travel Frankie and the whole entourage back and forth from New York. The budget can't handle it."

"Listen. I get it. It's your company. You do what you have to do. There are just two things I want from you—a good security guy and Sal."

Thank the heavens for Sal. Sal was Emeril's right-hand chef on *Emeril Live*. Although we had a ton of people in the Food Network kitchen that worked on the show, Sal was Emeril's go-to guy, probably because he's such a talented chef as well. He has a fantastic Italian restaurant, *Dimaio's Cucina* in Berkeley Heights, New Jersey, where I know he has spoiled Emeril on many occasions. On set, they communicated on some other-worldly level, often changing recipes with a point of a finger or a tilt of the head. Sal didn't need to work on our show, but he always showed up for Emeril. They're like brothers, and I have no problem bringing him along, assuming he'll make the crew his famous artisanal pizza from time to time.

"Sal? Of course, you got it," I promise. "I'll give him a call."

"Oh, and find some good restaurants in the area. You know I'll want a good dinner after we shoot."

"I know, I know, I know."

Well, that went a lot smoother than I imagined. I thought for sure he'd insist upon bringing some of the old crew known for buzzing in his ear about all the backstage gossip he doesn't need to know. Actually, I suppose I shouldn't be that surprised. He can be relatively low maintenance when he wants to be. When I think back, he and I never really had any direct issues; it was always those crew members who liked to stir the pot that made life difficult. And as long as I can keep them to a minimum, maybe we can make this work.

I gather my dream team together. I've got my Marie back. She left me to get married a few years ago and moved down to Potomac to be with her new husband. She lives not far from Whole Foods and jumped at the chance to be onboard. I've also got Charissa, the culinary producer who replaced Marie, who certainly is free since we all got the axe. Both have Emeril's trust and mine, so, thanks to them, with Sal on board too, the last thing I'll have to worry about is the food. Dominique and Elina are two talented producers that I put in charge of our remotes, knowing they'll be able to charm anyone into filming with us. And lastly, Charissa convinces me to hire her friend, Jed, a nasal, wiry, big-eyed character, who was one of Wendy's prop assistants. I figure if he could survive Wendy, our eccentric art director on *Emeril Live*, he'd have to be good. Charissa swears by his talent and promises me he'll work his butt off. I can't really afford to bring down any more people from New York, so I round out the technical team with a great local crew out of Baltimore and DC.

Chris has set up a meeting with Rick, the manager of Whole Foods, so that we can work out some of the logistics. Walking into the store is like walking into a foodie's paradise. I swear I can hear angels singing as I march through the door. In New York City, we're not known for our sprawling supermarkets, like the rest of the country. I'm used to walking down an aisle and having to back up my cart because someone needs to reach the peanut butter. Here, you could drive a Buick down each aisle.

There is a pasta bar, a salad bar, a sushi bar, a vegan section, a fresh fish counter, a butcher's counter, and even an *enoteca* where you can buy a prepaid card, stick it in a dispenser, and pour yourself any of 100 different glasses of wine—totally my kind of store. And yet, it's pretty much empty. There are only a handful of customers walking around, mostly tasting free samples. When Whole Foods opened in New York, there were lines around the block for weeks. Maybe this is just the lull before the storm.

"No, this is pretty much how it's been," the manager tells me. "We're hoping the show will bring some business our way. We only opened a few weeks ago, so it's taking a while for people in the area to check us out."

This is actually good news for me. The fewer people, the less noise, and the easier it is to shoot. I feel bad wanting the business to remain slow, but truth be told, I secretly hope that it does. We negotiate a schedule, and I arrange to have the manager close his side café so we can use that area to stage all of our props and feed the crew. My list of to-dos is starting to have a lot of checkmarks.

Back in New York, I've sublet 5,000 square feet of office space to house our editing systems and pre-production offices. As expected, Emeril can only shoot one week each month, so we have the other three weeks to prep and edit each ten-episode cycle of shows. By the time we're ready to shoot, I've got fifty people on payroll and a truck full of Le Creuset cookware under guard behind the store.

As the New York team arrives down in Fairfax, I notice Charissa seems a bit off and is busy schlepping pots and pans to the set, which isn't really her job. She keeps looking at me and then looking away.

"What's wrong?" I ask, knowing her too well.

"I don't know how to tell you this," she fumbles.

"What? What? Just spit it out."

She summons her courage and says, "Jed's in jail."

"Come again?"

"Jed's in jail. He was working on a video project with some friends in an abandoned building, or so they thought, and they got busted for trespassing."

"You mean good old dependable Jed? The guy you swore would come through for us and would work his tush off? That Jed? Your liege?"

"Listen, I know this looks bad, but he's really dedicated and talented. He was just trying to help out a friend. I think that shows character."

"Uh huh, character."

"Don't worry, we're all covering for him and his friend will be posting his bail any minute now. She just called me and told me he'll be here first thing in the morning. I promise."

I don't know whether I should laugh or cry, but it is heartening to see everyone pull together to cover for him.

"Okay, but just remember," I warn, not being able to help myself. "He's *your* responsibility."

As the blood drains from her face, I try not to crack a smile, realizing the absurdity of the situation. I've been around long enough to realize that Murphy's Law always applies to production. Let's hope that this will be our only hiccup.

Thankfully, the charges were dropped, and as promised, the next morning Jailbird Jed arrives to much fanfare and teasing. With his lean 120-pound frame and quiet demeanor, he's the least likely person you'd expect to spend the night in a cold cell with tattooed junkies and petty larcenists. Clearly mortified and aching to forget the last twenty-four hours, he digs in and gets to work. I have to say, I admire his resilience. Finally, now that things are settling in, I can concentrate on the shoot itself rather than the day's drama. Emeril arrives tonight, shooting starts tomorrow, and I've got to review the scripts, rundowns, and schedule.

On set in the morning, Emeril arrives ready to roll. He makes it feel like a reunion, like the band is getting back together. After a few hugs for the old gang and some introductions to the new crew, Emeril huddles with Sal and the culinary team to make sure all is well in their world. Surprisingly, he actually looks relaxed. I thought he'd have those first-day-of-school jitters. Maybe it's just me. There's a big difference being in a controlled studio environment where the network takes all the risks, versus being on-location where I'm the fall guy should anything bad happen. And it's only a matter of days before it does, again.

———————

It's 6 a.m. The phone rings in my hotel room.

"Karen, it's Jed. We've got a big problem and Rick is freaking out. You'd better get down here."

Of course it's Jed. He's been trying so hard to expunge his jail experience from my memory that I think he actually sleeps on set to make sure everything is perfect for the next day.

"What happened?" I ask when I arrive in a panic.

"I'm not sure, but I think the sound guy must have unplugged the refrigerated cheese case yesterday to get the buzzing to stop and he forgot to plug it back in. Rick says he can't sell the cheese now."

I know that cheese case. It's at least twenty-five feet long with a delicious assortment of stinky and runny French cheeses, local artisanal herb blends, and great big wheels of aged Parmigiano-Reggiano. By the time I get to the store, Rick has one of his workers ringing up each individual piece of cheese at retail prices so he can charge me for it. He's so mad, I can see the veins on his neck pulsing. Without missing a beat, I take full responsibility.

"Rick, I'm so, so sorry. This is totally our fault."

"You bet it is!" he barks. "What am I supposed to do with all of this? I knew we'd have to make some adjustments, but you guys can't just come in here and destroy everything."

"Rick, calm down. This was obviously an accident. We haven't destroyed everything. The crew has worked really hard to keep a low profile."

"You call this a low profile?"

"You know what I mean. Just tell me, what's the damage?"

He hands me the bill. It's $5,483.50. I swallow hard.

"Don't worry, I'll cover it," I say, my voice cracking, not even trying to negotiate for cost.

He softens slightly, knowing full well he's overcharging me. But I can't afford to piss him off. If we get kicked out of this location, we're screwed on so many levels. Once he calms down, I realize that had we been in Europe, most of these cheeses would never need to be refrigerated. Hard cheeses can stay out for hours, and I know he knows that. I'd guess 80 percent of this is still perfectly good to eat. Most of the crew agree and fill bags with as much as they can grab to take home. The only thing that really pisses me off is that the soundman barely apologizes, causing Jed to give him the evil eye. I'm starting to like that Jeddie.

"He totally ripped you off," Emeril protests.

"No kidding," I agree. "But what am I supposed to do? It was our fault."

Being a businessman, I think he's impressed that I sucked this one up. I'm sure he can feel my pain.

"So, what's for lunch? Fondue anyone?" asks one of the cameramen to lighten the mood. It takes a while before I find this even remotely funny.

Surprisingly, Emeril seems at ease with the new format. I didn't even have to tweak the concept too much now that he's on board. We're still focusing on a single topic like heirloom tomatoes or farm-raised salmon.

We'll either do a remote where we meet the farmer or fishermen or butcher to learn about their process, and how it is better for the environment than traditional mass-produced methods, or we'll invite an expert to join Emeril as he cooks. He loves talking about food and he's naturally curious about anything related to it, so we barely have to prep him about anything. By the end of the half-hour, we hope the viewer will not only learn about healthier and more sustainable alternatives but will walk away with a few yummy recipes. It's a simple premise, and it doesn't take long before the team jells and everyone is in sync.

One week a month, we form our own little bubble in this small suburban town and get into a rhythm. There's a nearby Hyatt where I've made a deal for Emeril and the team to stay. I would have put Emeril up in a much fancier hotel like the Ritz, but to his credit, he wanted to stay with the rest of us. He likes company for dinner, and Sal is his designated drinking buddy for nightcaps at the bar.

There's something inherently discombobulating about shooting on location. It's sort of like living a double life. The responsibilities of spouses and kids and leaky faucets go right out the window, as your colleagues become your new family. It is a little like camp with adults. There are flirtations that go a bit too far, one too many vodka tonics, and the women all get on the same menstrual cycle. The work is intense, but there's no escape at the end of the day. You're stuck with the same people 24/7, whether you like it or not.

As the boss, I have no choice but to play the "mom," a role everyone knows I hate. I force myself to look the other way as long as no one is going to lose a finger or any other important limb. But I do have to step in when things go too far. I have no choice but to set an example by firing someone for driving home after drinking too many beers at the end of the day. Or making sure that Sal keeps an eye on Emeril, cutting him off after his third Grand Marnier. How that man can drink something that sweet before bed, I will never understand.

But there is something to look forward to each day. Emeril likes a decent meal, so most nights, our New York gang gathers in search of new culinary treats. You'd think in Fairfax, Virginia, that it would be challenging, but my ace culinary team never disappoints. They swing a wide net, checking out everything from strip mall Pho to high-end dining in DC.

One of our standbys becomes Captain Pell's, home to the infamous steamed blue crab. One phone call guarantees they'll hold all of those delectable jumbos for Emeril and our group. To whet our appetites, we munch on fried oysters, steamed clams, baskets of hush puppies, multiple sides of fries, and, of course, at least a case of beer to wash it all down before we get to the main event. With bibs around our necks and wooden mallets in hand, we smash those perfectly steamed, spicy jumbos, picking out every last millimeter of meat, leaving only the shells as our witness. If gluttony is a sin, we're all going to be sharing a big table in hell one day.

I'm beginning to think Emeril is actually enjoying this show. He is as happy as I am to be without his entourage. He also doesn't have to be "on" every second of the day. Since there's no audience, no VIPs to entertain, no energy to ramp up in front of a crowd, and no "suits" from the network, he can relax and do what he likes best: cook. We do have an executive from Planet Green assigned to the show, but she's happy to stop by for a good lunch and a hang with the crew. Lisa is actually very supportive of the show and has become a good filter between our team and the network.

"We've got a lot of shows in the can now to satisfy our commitment to Whole Foods. What do you think about taking the show on the road?" Lisa suggests. "Can the budget handle it?"

"I'll look into it," I answer, intrigued.

I'm always up for a good road trip. I crunch some numbers, and it looks doable if we can stay within driving distance. Dominique starts researching and finds a unique town in Vermont that strives to be a completely sustainable community.

"Check this out," she says. "There's this little town, Hardwick, Vermont. It's got a population of only about 3,000. It seems to be the center of a small sustainable food movement. The *Times* did this big article on them. It's got a bunch of young entrepreneurs from even smaller surrounding towns helping one another create a cyclical farm-to-table community."

Dominique goes on to explain that at its most simplistic level, the farmers grow the produce that services the restaurants. The restaurants use the food waste to create compost, which then goes back to the farmers for use in their fields. This creates a low environmental impact, with the benefit of enjoying fresh food that hasn't lost its taste due to over-packaging and shipping. One of the local farms, Pete's Greens, is committed to supplying delicious, organically certified vegetables to the local community, with hopes that the more awareness consumers have regarding the importance of eating local, the healthier the benefits and the more support food producers have throughout the region. Jasper Hills Farms is a nearby working dairy farm with an impressive underground cheese cave that is used by the farm and other local producers. Their cheese-aging vaults are neatly lined with wheels of pungent and creamy cheeses just waiting to ripen. Here, bacteria and mold are their friends. And of course, they use the whey from the cheese-making process to feed the roaming heritage-bred pigs. Why waste?

There are so many stories we can cover that we decide to do a week of shows plus a one-hour special there. Since the town is so small, there's no hotel nearby that can house the crew, so I rent an adorable country inn that we take over as our home base. Within moments of our arrival, the entire town is abuzz with our presence. After all, it is a small town and everyone knows everyone else's business.

The community is very professional and extremely cooperative in helping us understand the importance of what they're trying to do. Tom Stearns, owner and farm manager of High Mowing Seeds is the David to Monsanto's Goliath.

"We're committed to high-quality organic seed production," Tom says proudly. "That's our philosophy. We want to offer a deeper understanding of how re-built food systems can support health on all levels—healthy environments, healthy economies, healthy communities, and healthy bodies. We're not like GMO producers that manufacture seeds that can withstand toxic pesticides, allowing farmers to spray gallons of it on their crops without killing them. We believe there's a better way without poisoning the food we eat."

He becomes our main point person and introduces us to other committed farmers and artisanal food producers who share his philosophy. At first glance, the entire community seems like one utopian environmentalist dream—farmer helping farmer—all committed to a healthy, economically sound food system. It's all for one and one for all—very Woodstock 1969. But as we get to know them, it becomes clear that they expect us to embrace their philosophy as well. Which probably explains why a bunch of townies start hanging around the inn, expecting us to feed them and party until dawn. They're not getting the hint that we all want to call home and check in with our loved ones and then go to bed. Our mornings start early.

It's day three of a monster head cold and I've decided to stay in and have some chicken soup while most of the crew goes skinny-dipping with the locals. As a city girl, I get pretty spooked in the country at night, particularly when alone, convinced that the woods are filled with hatchet murderers. So when there's a knock at the door, my anxiety level skyrockets.

"Is Elina here?"

A twenty-something, sweet-looking blond farmhand is standing at the door, trying to peek past me to see who's around.

"No, she's in town with some of the crew," I say, making sure to block his unwanted entrance.

"Do you mind if I wait for her?" he asks.

"To tell you the truth, it's not a good time," I say. "But I'm happy to tell her you stopped by. What's your name?"

"Just tell her Gary stopped by. And could you give her this?"

He hands me a jar of dirt.

"It's compost from our farm. I thought she'd like it."

How cute—he came courting with compost. That's a new one. Should I tell him she's more of a flowers-and-chocolate kind of gal or just let it go?

"I'll be happy to tell her. I'm sure she'll love this."

"You're sure I can't wait for her?" he asks, incredulous that I won't let him in, not because he's aggressive, but because it's not the answer he'd ever expect from someone in this town.

"Yes, I'm sure," I say firmly.

"Thank you, ma'am," he says, slightly embarrassed, bowing his head.

"You have a good night," I say, forcing a smile as I shut the door.

I wait to hear his footsteps as he walks away, hoping he's not going to stake out a spot on our porch, but eventually, he's gone from sight. For the next few hours, it's just me, the jar of compost, and the creaks from this old inn to keep me company. As I stare at the compost, I can see there is a purity and richness to the dirt. I slowly twist it open and inhale the earthy scent of a summer afternoon after a light rain. This is so much more than just a jar of dirt. It's a new beginning, a start to create something nourishing, not just for the body, but also for the soul. In this one small gesture, this young man is boldly taking a chance that Elina will see the potential of a relationship that can grow into something that has meaning and purpose.

Okay, clearly the Nyquil is kicking in. Perhaps I'm reading too much into this. Maybe the kid just wants to get laid. But being in this town gets under your skin, just like the dirt under the local farmers' fingernails. I promise myself that from now on, I will consciously buy local as often as possible; I'll save my food scraps and deliver them to the greenmarket every Saturday for composting; I'll start buying things in bulk; I'll cut back on red meat; and I'll try to get Dan to eat seitan. No, for real, I will. Really.

Back home after production, the hippie dust doesn't totally disappear. I begin to read labels more thoroughly, opting for pasture-raised chickens and grass-fed cow's milk. I buy all of my produce from our weekly green-market that only carries vegetables grown within a 100-mile radius. I get myself one of those eco-friendly bags that I can fold up into a four by four-inch wad and stuff in the bottom of my purse so I have it at the ready. Of course, I'm no saint. I still won't give up a good gooey Camembert, given the chance. But it's a start.

I finally feel good working on a show that might actually have an impact on how well people eat. That's not to belittle all the years we spent entertaining people on *Emeril Live*—but to be honest, we were promoting an awful lot of pork fat and overindulgence. The extra twenty pounds I packed on during those years prove my point. At this moment, everything seems to be moving in the right direction. I'm eating better, I feel better, the team is solid, Emeril is happy, and my company is even profitable by midway through our second season. As much as I try to hit the pause button and savor this moment, I know nothing lasts forever—although another week would have been nice.

While we are filming, a new sheriff has come to town at Planet Green. Not surprisingly, once the network launched, there were bound to be adjustments and changes. And, after two years and 160 episodes of *Emeril Green*, the new network president feels like she has enough episodes for repeats and wants to spend her money elsewhere. Although we aren't canceled, we aren't renewed either. The team takes it pretty well. We still have a few months of work to finish up our edits, so the staff has time to look for work. Emeril takes it all in stride. He's so busy with his new deal with Martha Stewart's company that he doesn't mind having his schedule open up a bit. I guess after *Emeril Live* we all learned not to get too invested in any show. Or at least we've learned how to pretend we're not invested. I suppose I'll just have to go back to sorting through my cookbooks as I wait for my next show.

"Honey," Dan shouts from across the room. "Where do you want me to put all of these vegetarian books?"

"There should be room somewhere between Ukrainian Cuisine and Vietnamese Street Food," I yell back.

"I think we've jammed as many as we can onto these shelves. Maybe we should start cooking our way through them one by one."

Well, I've certainly got the time now.

KOHLRABI SLAW

After working on *Emeril Green*, I became inspired to cook with fresh local ingredients. One of my favorite things to do is wander through our weekend greenmarket. I like to pick up unusual vegetables and figure out what to do with them. Kohlrabi, with its weird tentacles, is one of those challenging vegetables that I just can't resist. It's part of the cabbage family, so it's perfect for grating, and it remains fairly crunchy once dressed. I've given this a bit of an Asian twist with the addition of wasabi mayonnaise. It gives it a good kick.

Serves 6

INGREDIENTS

1 large kohlrabi, peeled, stemmed, and grated
½ head Napa cabbage, shredded
2 carrots, peeled and grated
½ red onion, thinly sliced
3 scallions, sliced into 1-inch lengths
¼ cup wasabi mayonnaise
1 tablespoon vinegar
1 tablespoon honey
1 teaspoon salt
Freshly ground pepper

DIRECTIONS

Combine kohlrabi, cabbage, carrots, onion, and scallions in a large bowl. Mix with your hands to combine.

In a small bowl, whisk together the wasabi mayonnaise, vinegar, honey, salt, and pepper.

Pour the dressing over the salad and gently toss, fully coating the salad.

Refrigerate, covered, for at least 2 hours before serving.

Chapter Eighteen

WHY LEFTOVERS ARE NEVER AS GOOD AS FRESH FROM THE OVEN

Now that I'm home after the show wraps, I force Dan to watch the movie *Julie and Julia* for the fifth time. He suggests I cook my way through all of our cookbooks and blog about it—in alphabetical order no less. Since I have time on my hands, and I am clearly starting to drive him crazy by being home, he thinks it is a practical solution to get me out of my funk. But before I can even reach for my book on Afghan cuisine, I am pulled back into Emeril's world once again. With his new Martha Stewart deal, Emeril needs to keep his face out there in public, promote his brand, and ensure that the engines of high commerce are profitable. His deal gave Martha the rights to all of his media and products, while he kept his restaurant business to himself. ION, a syndicated network, is interested in having Emeril host a new show, and Emeril has asked me to come up with some new ideas.

Ironically, the highest-rated food shows are no longer on Food Network. Bravo's *Top Chef*, Fox's *Master Chef*, and Travel Channel's *No Reservations* with Anthony Bourdain have ushered in a more entertaining and reality-based food culture. Classic format cooking shows have been relegated to non-primetime hours, while shows with a hook, or competitive angle, are gaining avid viewers. Having spent so many years in Emeril's orbit, I think it's time he steps up his game and opens up his restaurant world a bit more on TV. And it wouldn't kill him to open himself up too.

There's another side to Emeril that most people don't see. He's not just a celebrity food icon; he's also an accomplished chef and businessman, and more importantly, an inspiring mentor to many young chefs. Within his organization, there are a number of people who have risen within the ranks and stayed by his side for twenty years and counting. They remain out of loyalty. And Emeril has earned their loyalty by being dedicated to his craft and sharing his full-throated enthusiasm and passion for food with all who enter his world. He's the real deal. His organization is run like a tight ship. There is one philosophy, and you either get with the program or you get out. They even have a word that they use for new employees—*Emerilized*—which means to follow Emeril's ideals about how food should be prepared and served. For those who join the organization, it's not just a philosophy; it's a way of life.

Emeril is a big believer in growing talent from within. People who were once busboys and dishwashers are now general managers and chefs de cuisine. Emeril doesn't care where you come from as long as you're hard working, willing to learn, and able to keep up with him. For an aspiring chef, what better opportunity is there than to train under the watchful eye of the master himself?

To me, this is the most interesting and unseen part of Emeril's world, and I think people would want to see what happens in the back of the house. So I come up with a primetime reality-competition show idea called *Being Emerilized*. The concept is simple. Take twelve culinary students, throw them into the fast-paced kitchen of one of Emeril's restaurants, and create challenges to test their mettle. They each get to vie for a one-year contract to work as a *commis* chef, or sous chef, in one of Emeril's restaurant kitchens. Who will win the opportunity, and how they get there, is where we'll have all the sturm and drang that viewers have come to expect in reality competition shows.

I'm super excited about the show, and present the concept to Emeril and his team, where it is an immediate no-go before I can even finish explaining the idea. Emeril's restaurant business is sacred ground and he doesn't want to reveal the man behind the Garland stove.

"And besides, KK," Emeril says. "I think all they really want is an updated *Emeril Live*. Let's meet with them, and then we can go from there."

Crap. I can't. I just can't. But for old times' sake, I agree to take a meeting.

I walk into the Martha Stewart Living Omnimedia offices on West 26th Street for a meeting with Emeril and the head of ION. I've never been inside Martha's world. Unsurprisingly, the offices are quite tasteful. There is a lot of light and glass and humane, neatly organized cubicles. But there's also a coldness to the space. It's eerily quiet as people work silently at their computers. The floors are concrete, so I step lightly for fear of breaking the silence with the clickety-clack of my uncomfortable new high heels. The only sign of life is the luscious smell of French pastries wafting out of the test kitchen, nearly leading me in the wrong direction.

I'm guided past Martha's corner office with its breathtaking view of the Hudson, into a small conference room to meet with Emeril and the team from ION. After small talk and pleasantries, a no-nonsense high-powered executive in a very expensive suit, asks me a surprisingly familiar question.

"So, do you think of this as a cooking show with entertainment or an entertainment show with cooking?"

I'm struck by how it's the exact question I was asked by Felicia almost thirteen years ago. As I try to read the room, I see Emeril is uncomfortable, fidgeting with his hands and looking down, rather than at me. Times have changed. No one wants *just* a cooking show anymore. They want something sexed up a bit, and both Emeril and I know it.

I grit my teeth, put on my most enthusiastic smile, and say, "Oh, it's definitely an entertainment show with cooking, no question."

And with that answer, I get the go-ahead for ten episodes. There are moments in life when you know you're making a big mistake, but you make it anyway. Every cell in my body knows this is one of those moments. I'm justifying it because I don't want to let Emeril down, I want to keep my staff working, and maybe, just maybe, we can make this work one more time. How hard could it be to sex up the old format?

This time, I don't have the luxury of Food Network's facility and support, so I'm on my own. I make a deal with Penn Studios in midtown, a relic from the glory days of NYC production. Just a block down from Penn Station, it must be the bleakest stretch of Manhattan, with the exception of Macy's, of course. The buildings are the same as those seen in old black-and-white movies from the '40s, when women wore hats and gloves and Gimbels still existed. By now, years of soot and grime have leeched into the brick mortar, and the whole neighborhood looks like it could use a good power wash. The studio itself fits right in. It's dirty, dingy, and depressing, the ghosts of canceled shows whisper in the dark. But it's all I can afford. I have always trusted my gut, so why am I ignoring daily bouts of nausea?

Studios are windowless, cavernous spaces. Without a set or lighting in place, there's nothing inviting or interesting about them. Our production offices aren't much better, although mine at least is a decent size. My desk is dusty—and not with recent dust either, but with dust ground in from the days of Edward R. Murrow. There are random packets of ketchup and Sweet and Low stuck to the bottom of my top left-hand drawer. The phone smells like rancid French fries, and the couch has cracks in the leather. I send a production assistant out for some Handi Wipes and Fantastic and spend my first afternoon disinfecting everything within reach.

Thankfully, it's not hard for me to pull together a team for the daily grind of shows. Much of the infrastructure is just like *Emeril Live,* and I bring back some of the key department heads to help me launch it. The tricky parts are the entertainment aspects. What exactly does that look like, and how can I incorporate it into the show, while still allowing Emeril time to cook a few dishes? This will put Emeril in the role of host, not just chef. He's got to interview celebrities, which means he has to probe and listen and engage, not his strongest suit. I bring in two game show/comedy writers to help come up with some fun segments like they have on *Ellen* and other daytime shows. The team is fully capable and everyone goes in full steam to make this work.

The folks from ION are nice enough, but there is one key element they neglected to mention from the onset. This show is heavily sponsored, which means we have to figure out ways to integrate their clients' products into some of our segments. It doesn't help that most of the products have nothing to do with food, or Emeril's world. For example, one product is a printer. What am I supposed to do with that? Should we make a menu up and use fancy fonts? That's entertainment?

Another problem is time. Emeril is only giving me a week to shoot all ten contracted episodes. We don't get time to make a pilot, to review and tweak it, or to give it room to breathe. We have to hit the ground running and get it right from the start. On paper and in prep, things seem like they're coming together. I hire Dave Koz as our bandleader. He's an accomplished saxophonist with his own following, making many of his fans swoon from his adorable sweet smile, big brown eyes, and perfectly coiffed hair. He puts together an amazing team of musicians, causing us all to stop and listen as they rehearse.

And now that the set has gone in, the joint is coming alive. It's gorgeous with some of the walls gelled with different colors so that the lighting department can change it based on mood. There's a kicked-up cooking space where Emeril can make his magic with full state-of-the-art LG equipment, thanks to our main sponsor. There's also an audience box, almost like at the opera but on the floor, that makes no sense to me, but I don't have time to adjust for it. We've put in a chat area, a performance stage, and a 'front door' for our guests' entrances. I'm a little nervous about the audience. At *Emeril Live,* tickets were a hot commodity. People would come from all over the country, and we always had more than we could seat. But now that three years have passed, people have moved on, and it's hard to get the word out to fans without Food Network's email lists. We bring on some professional audience wranglers that somehow get groups of Westchester ladies who lunch to come down by bus. They don't really feel like Emeril's people, but we have no choice. We're used to having firefighters and big guys from Jersey who tailgate with homemade portable grills that fill the room. This doesn't feel right. As a matter of fact, it feels very wrong.

Martha is helping us kick off our premiere as our first guest, so everyone is on his or her best behavior. My culinary team has been working with hers for the past two weeks to get Martha's mother's pierogi recipe just right. Lisa, one of our show chefs, has been testing pierogies for days, laying her latest batch out on French linen with hopes of impressing Martha. When Martha arrives, I can swear a cold wind precedes her entrance. In person, she's quite a formidable figure, standing straight up at almost six feet in heels, while her minions follow closely behind. She is clearly on a tight schedule and has no time for pleasantries. Lisa and my team are all huddled around a sheet pan filled with the unboiled pierogies. Martha's producer seems relieved, as she glances over at them. But not Martha. She lifts up one of the linen sheets, touching the side of one of the pierogies.

"These are too dry," she says dismissively. "They won't do."

There's a long pause as she glares at us.

"Whose idea was this?"

Everyone is silent. Lisa is devastated, this being the sixth batch she's made. Martha's producer looks terrified since she's the one that suggested this recipe.

"It was my idea," I say, taking the bullet.

"Hmmm," says Martha, as she looks me up and down, her left eyebrow rising ever so slightly. And then she just walks off into the dressing room.

"What should we do?" Lisa asks.

"No, it's okay. She didn't insist on any changes," says Martha's producer. She turns to me and says, "Thanks, I'm sorry about that," knowing full well I just saved her butt.

"No worries. I can see you have your hands full."

As soon as the segment is over, Martha and her entourage are on to the next thing, and we press on. Emeril's interview segments are awkward, the cooking segments are rushed, and I'm worrying about some of the segments the comedy guys have written. They've come up with audience participation games and, on paper, I don't find them funny.

"I'm calling this game 'Appetizer Annihilation,'" pitches Kevin, one of the comedy guys that I think has been sleeping here. "It's a race with three challenges. First, our contestants must use the bicycle pumps to burst their balloons. Next, they must find the hard-boiled egg hidden in the bowl of raw eggs by smashing the eggs against their foreheads. Then they have to find a chicken wing in the kiddy pool of blue cheese dressing without using their hands. First to finish is our winner."

Not only is it not funny on paper, it's a freaking mess in real life. By the end of the game, our contestants are covered head-to-toe in the sticky and stinky blue cheese dressing, and I can see Emeril is so mortified that he doesn't know what to say. We break for commercial, and at this moment, I know it's over. I broke the cardinal rule—never play with your food.

This show is a bomb. It's not just bad, it's painful. And I'd love to make up excuses and blame someone else, but if I'm really being honest, it's totally my fault. I didn't follow my gut, and I pretended that I agreed with something that I knew could never work. Emeril's appeal as an entertainer comes from his passion for food and cooking. Taking away that passion and repackaging him into something else won't work. Deep down, I knew that from the beginning. But Emeril wanted it, ION wanted it, and I fooled myself into thinking that I wanted it.

There is no way to stop it now. We only have a few more days of production and the segments have all been prepped. If I could only hit the pause button and reassess our game plan, we might be able to salvage it, but there's no time. All I can do is try to edit out the worst moments in post to make the shows watchable.

Fortunately, the end comes fast, and the show airs to little fanfare. If you blinked, you'd miss it, which is a blessing. At least the failure was relatively quick and quiet. ION doesn't have a huge viewership yet and thankfully, critics didn't screen it. Emeril seems to have taken it all in stride, putting one foot in front of the other and moving on to the next thing. For me, it's not that simple. I have spent the last thirteen years of my life working on shows for this man. We've had such tremendous successes and having it end like this is soul-crushing. In the beginning, there was a blank slate, a feeling that anything was possible. But now I feel like an old bottle of Cabernet in the back of my wine cooler. It got great reviews from *Wine Spectator* when it hit the market, but when you pop the cork, you realize it hasn't aged very well.

PIEROGIES: THE CHEATER'S WAY

As much as I hate to admit it, the pierogies that our kitchen staff made from Martha's recipe were outstanding. But having looked at the recipe, I needed a nap just thinking about how long these would take to make from scratch. My advice is to go to your neighborhood freezer section and buy some quality frozen pierogies. Then dress them up as follows:

INGREDIENTS

4 tablespoons butter, divided
1 teaspoon salt
1 package frozen pierogies
2 large Vidalia onions, chopped
Chopped chives, for garnish
Sour cream, for garnish

DIRECTIONS

Melt 2 tablespoons butter in a large skillet over medium heat. Add the onions and cook 8 minutes, until brown and caramelized. Remove the onions to a bowl and keep warm.

In a large pasta pot over high heat, bring 4 quarts water to a boil. Add 1 teaspoon salt and the frozen pierogies. Cook the pierogies as per the package instructions.

Melt the remaining butter in the skillet over medium-high heat. Drain the pierogies, and add them to skillet, browning them for 1 to 2 minutes on each side.

Place the pierogies on serving dish. Cover with the onions, and garnish with chives. Pass a bowl of sour cream around the table.

Chapter Nineteen

THE JERSEY BOYS

"So, what do you want to do next?" Bradley asks.

I'm out to lunch with Josh and Bradley, both young agents who used to be assistants to my first agent, Jon Rosen. Once Jon became successful, he passed me down to Josh, who is now passing me down to Bradley. I suppose in a couple of years I'll have someone old enough to be my grandson as my agent.

"Even though I've been doing food for the last thirteen years or so," I begin, "don't forget, that I've done everything from documentaries to variety shows to kids shows. I'd love not to be pigeonholed. I'd even love to do international work."

"Really? I had no idea you would be willing to travel," says Bradley. "We have offices worldwide. Let me put the word out."

Agents are great when it comes to negotiating. I've never begrudged them their 10 percent. They've always gotten me better deals than I ever would have gotten on my own. But in terms of actually landing you work, there is never a guarantee that they'll ever really get you a job. They make a few phone calls on your behalf, but if they don't get any bites fairly quickly, you go down to the bottom of their call sheets. I can't rely on them to land me my next gig, so I put the word out that I'm available, and Howard, the head of programming at TLC, comes through again.

"You know Buddy Valastro, the Cake Boss, right?" he asks.

"Sure. He's been a big hit for you guys."

"Well, we're doing a cooking show with him, and you'd be perfect to produce it."

"A baking show?"

"No, actually. Not cakes, but a more traditional cooking show, mostly Italian food from his family recipes. It's called *Kitchen Boss*."

"Really? I'm surprised. Is this a new direction for TLC? I thought you guys didn't do straightforward cooking shows."

"I know, we don't. But *Cake Boss* is such a hit we want to capitalize on it. And who doesn't love Italian food?"

He has a good point. Fortunately, William Morris manages Buddy too, so Bradley puts in a good word for me from their end. But I've got to get Buddy's blessing, so I head out to his headquarters in Hoboken, New Jersey. It's not the family bakery featured on the show, which is a tiny shop on the main drag, Washington Street. It's amazing they can fit a crew in there with all the customers waiting impatiently for cannolis and *sfogliatelle*. His offices and warehouse are actually about a mile away, just off the Jersey side of the Holland Tunnel. He's built quite an impressive facility that houses an enormous baking factory to fulfill online orders, supplement his shop in Hoboken, and create all those crazy cakes. He also just built a production studio for his competition show, *Next Great Baker*, that doubles for some of the *Cake Boss* scenes. I have to give him props for realizing the value in keeping everything in-house. Not only does it make it more convenient for him, but also I'm sure he must charge back to the network for its use, as any smart businessperson would.

"So, you were Emeril's producer, I hear," he says, sizing me up.

"Yeah, for years. We had a good run."

"I'd say so. He's built quite an empire," he says admiringly.

I'm struck by how much alike he and Emeril are at first glance. Both seem like those guys who got put into vocational school in their senior year because they were screwing around during their academic classes, only to have the last laugh as they became gazillionaires from their trade. Although neither is classically handsome, both are manly men with the type of confidence that comes from knowing you earned all you have by putting in the time and hard work. Neither of them suffers fools or bull. And they don't need their egos stroked.

"I'm not a formally trained chef like Emeril, but I know my way around a kitchen."

"Not to worry. We'll have an army behind you. And clearly, you're used to having television cameras in your face."

"No kidding, I barely know what to do with myself when they're not around," he jokes.

He walks me around the facility and it's clear, he really is "the boss" to an eclectic mix of misfit bakers and a family that all work for him, although they all like to say they work for the family business. And they are *exactly* as they appear on camera, in all their Jersey glory.

The next day, Bradley calls to tell me I got the blessing from the boss and I should start to put together the team. Since Buddy really has little formal training, I bring on Marie to head up the culinary team. I know she'll be able to make him comfortable and prop up the content we'll need. Buddy is used to reality-style shooting. I'm not sure how he's going to do looking straight down the barrel of a lens all by himself. It's not as easy as it looks. As a matter of fact, it's hard to cook and talk and follow a recipe at the same time. By the end of our run, Emeril and I had developed such a shorthand that we only had to look at each other to know what needed to be done. With Buddy, I've got to figure out what works best for him.

Fortunately, we have some rehearsal time to work out the kinks. Although we've given Buddy a ton of research that fits with the dishes he's making, he doesn't seem very comfortable playing "teacher."

"Buddy, I'll be right in your ear," I say. "If you forget something, don't worry, I'll be there for you."

An IFB earpiece is a producer's power and an on-air talent's security blanket. It's the strings to the puppet. It's the voice from on high. It's the brains behind the beauty. And in Buddy's case, it's sometimes the voice in his head.

"So today, I'm going to make you one of my favorites, Veal Osso Buco," Buddy reads off the prompter and then just stands there.

"Osso Buco is Italian for "bone with a hole," a reference to the marrow hole at the center of the cross-cut veal shank," I explain in his ear.

"You're hazing me, right?" he continues, talking to me, not the camera.

"Keep taping, I can edit this out," I say to our director. "Buddy, I was just feeding you some info from the research. Just put it into your own words."

"Oh, I get it," he says, still talking to me before looking back at the camera. "Osso Buco. It means bone with a hole. Don't ask me why. Look it up."

"Stop tape!" I shout.

It takes us a few hours before we find a way to communicate with each other, but eventually, we figure out a better way. Fun food facts and historical context aren't going to fly with him, so the best thing to do is to personalize the dish. He needs to talk about its relevance to him or his family. He's a good storyteller and his family certainly doesn't lack for characters, so it's a natural fit. I can continue to try to sprinkle in some useful information for the folks at home when he gets off-track, but this feels like it will work.

After a few days, we get into a rhythm and once he feels comfortable, we decide to bring on some family members as guests. No one really likes to pick favorites, but in truth, his sister Maddalena and her husband Mauro are mine. They are both warm and loving and welcoming. That's not to say the other sisters aren't, but they are tougher nuts to crack and don't trust easily. Each is proud of the recipes they share, and all reveal the perfect amount of familial ribbing that makes good TV. Hands down, the best recipe of the season came in with Buddy's Aunt Anna and her Ultimate Mac and Cheese. In addition to its classic béchamel sauce, it's got browned, crumbled sausage, and three cheeses—Fontina, Gruyere, and Parmesan. Buddy never had a chance to bring any home that night. The crew devoured it and I did a good share of the damage myself.

Now that I'm in Buddy's good graces, what I really want is the chance to work on his competition series, *Next Great Baker*. Although *Kitchen Boss* is exactly what TLC wants, in truth, cooking shows like this one are becoming dinosaurs. Competition is what's hot and I need to make the jump into it to stay current. But at my level, it's hard to transition to new formats without having experience in it. I need someone who knows me and is willing to give me a chance. Buddy's shows are produced by High Noon, a production company out of Denver, and I've made some good contacts there. Now that I've worked with them, I'm starting to nudge my way over to their competition team with hopes they'll give me a shot.

Art, Buddy's original executive producer, is the lead on the show, and he is tied to him like I was to Emeril. Between *Cake Boss,* the competition show, and other projects, Art is stretched thin and needs a showrunner to deal with the day-to-day on *Next Great Baker.* Art comes from the world of reality, having cut his teeth on shows like *The Bachelor,* and I can tell he's hesitant to bring me on board, knowing that I haven't done this type of show before. But I've got a lot of support from the home office and Buddy, so he reluctantly hires me.

Fortunately, some of the crew is from *Kitchen Boss* and they want me to succeed, so I'm stepping into a friendly environment. Michael Pearlman, our director, is a talented, funny, energetic, curly-haired nice Jewish boy who is more than willing to fill in the blanks with some of the details needed to run the show. After all, the better I do at the job, the easier it is for him, and so it's a win-win. Filling out the triumvirate is Marcus Anthony, our no-nonsense associate director, who keeps everyone in line and on time, thanks to his military training and professionalism. But I also have a secret weapon, someone who has no official role on the show, but who proves to be one of our biggest assets—Buddy's cousin Frankie.

Frankie is a big guy with a big mouth and big ideas. He has picked up a lot about television production during the *Cake Boss* years, and in another life, he'd have been a great producer. One of the toughest things about the show is coming up with fresh ideas for cake challenges, but that doesn't daunt Frankie. He's always got something up his sleeve, whether you've asked him or not.

"You know, we could blow up the cakes from the losing teams, leaving only the winning cake intact," he says. "I know a guy."

Frankie knows lots of guys. You need a fire truck standing by? No problem. Explosives? He'll have them for you in an hour. You need a cake to swim with the fishes? He knows a guy with a boat and a lift. He's very resourceful and the ultimate go-to guy. He makes me believe the possibilities are limitless. So does the rest of Buddy's team. There's a lot more going on here than just mixing flour and butter. In addition to having a state-of-the-art kitchen that can pound out hundreds of cakes a day, they have an enormous workshop complete with drills, woodworking tools, and a multitude of motors and other gadgets that can be used to make cakes spin, move, or light up like a Macy's Fourth of July fireworks barge. It's the ultimate Santa's workshop for cakes.

I never realized how much engineering and art goes into building these enormous cakes. It's hard to believe how far the dessert world has come. This is a long way from Nana's apple pie. Of course, now the artistry behind the cakes makes sense when I stop to think about it. Each cake needs structure, and sponge cake can only take so much weight on its own. There needs to be some type of skeletal frame so that the cake can be supported. This is where Buddy's team is so ingenious, as they help the contestants bring their wild creations to life, hoping no one loses a finger in the workshop.

Once an infrastructure is complete, layers of vanilla sheet cake, or some Rice Krispie concoction, are used like modeling clay to create the outline or general shape of the cake. Next, the bakers literally sculpt the specific shape they want by using a serrated knife to cut away the part of the cake not needed. After that, they can roll out different shapes and colors of fondant to form the skin of their masterpieces. And then with the tools of Michelangelo, they can create the details that will make or break a winning cake.

Now that I understand the capabilities of the bakery, it's a slightly easier process to come up with challenge ideas, particularly with Frankie in my ear. So, why not make a superhero-themed cake, or a Sunday Italian supper-themed cake, or a fashion-themed cake, complete with stilettos and a Gucci purse?

As the creative process continues, we also need to finalize our picks for the cast. This is the part of the process that I will never understand. Why would people want to sequester themselves away for weeks only to expose their deepest vulnerabilities for all of America to see? That's basically what every contestant agrees to on a reality competition show. They think they understand how challenging it will be, but they really don't. Some come for the chance at the grand prize money, some want their fifteen minutes of fame, and some really haven't thought it through. It's the producer's job to select a cast with the skills needed as a baker, but who also have big personalities with the potential to crack. The more bravado someone has, the better. Eventually, we settle on a baker's dozen of wannabees and start production.

It takes a few episodes of tearful eliminations to whittle down the group so that the most dramatic and talented bakers emerge. By the sixth week in the competition, they have been totally sucked into this insular world we've created, and they're already exhausted from eighteen-hour days with little sleep. All who weren't taking the competition seriously have been squeezed out like the last remnants of icing in a pastry bag. The only ones that remain are those bakers who are desperate for the win.

While we're in the midst of the grind of our endless workdays, which includes tossing the losing cakes off of roofs or smashing them in the back seat of a van doing donuts in our parking lot, I'm also supposed to be focusing on putting our grand finale together. We're taking the whole cast and crew out to Las Vegas to shoot at the Venetian Hotel. The idea is supposed to be a surprise for the finalists. If they make it to the finale, they get to go to Vegas—all expenses paid—to compete in the final challenge—a Venetian-themed cake to be created in twenty-four non-stop hours. The winner will receive the $100,000 grand prize and an apprenticeship with Buddy. All of the work and craziness they've struggled through in the last couple of months will culminate here.

A road show with the size of this team is a huge undertaking and, as expected, once in Vegas, I'm locked inside our production offices 24/7. No late-night gambling, no buffet breakfasts, no smoky lounge singers for me. Just round-the-clock headaches and arguments with the union security guys, and attempts to babysit our cast, who like to sneak out of their rooms and drink away their stress when they should be sleeping. Wrangling everyone is nearly impossible, and after hearing some bad reports about the late-night shenanigans of some on the team, I give up trying. But my awesome production management team is faithfully by my side and we get done what needs to be done. We spend countless hours behind those "Employee Only" doors, trying helplessly to find our way around the labyrinth of concrete hallways to the loading docks and stainless steel kitchens. The internal industrial workings are the yin to the glamorous external Disneyfied Venetian yang.

After a week of planning, negotiating, and set-up, it's time to start this sucker. The contestants are on edge, but ready to go. Our plan is to shoot all the way through the challenge, so we've prepped everything we'll need, although an intravenous coffee line wouldn't be a bad idea. As exciting as the challenge may seem once edited, in real life, it will take twenty-four hours to build these cakes. It's almost as exciting as watching paint dry. But leave it to our cunning contestants to add some drama. One of them gets caught turning down the oven temp of her rival.

Eventually, we get to that final moment when Buddy will reveal the winner. We've set up bleachers for an audience just outside the entrance to the hotel. It's a gorgeous night and the lights of Vegas are a perfect backdrop, twinkling on cue. There's always a great rush when we get to a moment like this. It's the culmination of so much work by so many people, often against challenging odds. And as the winner is announced and the confetti flies, it's just as much a celebration for us as it is for them.

I realize that it's been over one week since I stepped outside the Venetian during daylight, so the next morning, after sleeping in, I decide to treat myself to a cocktail poolside. When I pull open the doors, the noonday sun stabs me like a chef's knife, nearly blinding me for a few seconds. As my eyes refocus, I see rich men with pot bellies bulging out over their Speedos dancing to club music with beautifully tanned women in their perfectly fitting string bikinis. Something tells me these women are not their wives. I suppose this is what they mean by "what happens in Vegas stays in Vegas."

Still dressed in my jeans and T-shirt, I commandeer one of those private canvas cabanas and order myself a nice cold Margarita, no salt. For the first time since I started this job, I finally have nothing to do but relax. It doesn't take long before the Margarita takes the edge off my constant state of anxiety, and my mind drifts between pride in what we pulled off and exhaustion from wondering why I put myself through this.

Breaking my reverie, my phone rings. It's Bradley, my agent.

"Hey, how's it going?" he asks.

"Great, we literally just wrapped last night."

"Perfect timing. Listen, I just got a call. Are you still interested in international work?"

"Yeah, of course."

"Well, what do you think about Singapore? There's a production company looking for a showrunner for a new competition show. They've seen your credits and they're interested."

"Singapore, huh? Can you tell me more about the show?"

"I don't know a ton. I just know it's a competition show, something to do with fitness and fashion."

"No food?"

"I don't think so. Call me when you get home and we'll hook up a Skype call with the production company guys."

"Wow. This could be just what I need. Keep me posted. Thanks."

As I sip on my Margarita, my mind wanders back to those early days sitting in front of my beloved black and white TV in my childhood bedroom. Who knew that wanting to be a producer like Mary Richards could take me all over the world—from Hoboken to Singapore? And that I'd learn how to make everything from lobster risotto to a six-foot cake that looks like Wonder Woman. I've got to say, the work may be hard, but it's never boring. I might never know where the next gig will take me, but I like the idea that I may have to cross an ocean to get there.

Once I'm home, and after a few intense conversations with the production team, I land the job. To be honest, I had to look up where Singapore is on a map. Based on its latitude, 1.35 degrees north of the equator, it seems that I won't need any sweaters. Luckily, the main language spoken is English and from what I've read, Singapore seems to be a food paradise with a mix of every type of Asian cuisine one can imagine and a thriving international haute cuisine scene. I've got my Pepto Bismol at the ready and I am looking forward to tasting my way through the country.

Everything happens so quickly that I don't have much time to think it through, which is probably a good thing. Before I can say *char kway teow*, I am on the way to the airport for who knows what kind of adventure. While we've never been apart for this long, Dan is excited for me and promises to come out towards the end of the shoot. When it's over, we'll travel around Southeast Asia together.

As I sit in my very cozy business class seat, trying to keep down the three gin and tonics I foolishly chased with a Grand Marnier on ice, thinking it would put me to sleep, I marvel at the insane nature of this business. I've barely had time to blow the dust off my passport and pack my panties; yet, here I am, off on an eight-month adventure I know very little about. But I need this. Sometimes, opportunities come up that are so out of your comfort zone that you have no choice but to go for it. I just spent the last fifteen years of my life producing food television, and at the beginning of that, I could not have predicted how my life and career would change.

Now it's time once again to do something more challenging and hopefully less fattening.

The sun is starting to rise from the east like a big fireball inching its way through streaks of magenta clouds. I can see the coastline of the city as an endless stream of tankers head for the harbor. The plane will soon touch down. A new day is dawning in Singapore. It's a new day for me too.

I'll let you know how it goes.

Conclusion

It's been almost twenty-five years since I walked onto my first TV kitchen set. Those small counters with fake slop sinks surrounded by a handful of cameras have been replaced by stadium-sized gladiator sets fit for ninja chefs to create dishes of flavor-defying gastronomic wonder. Shows like *Chopped* seem to have their own channel as they are on an endless broadcast loop. The challenges are harder, the ingredients are more exotic, and the chefs are far more inventive. Who knew you could pair kumquats with chocolate and Brussels sprouts and make them taste good?

But the real evolution in food television is that it has become an art form. Some might call it food porn, but to me, watching an extreme close-up of glistening ganache gently poured on top of a mound of perfectly ripe strawberries is a thing of beauty. The seduction is no less appealing than one's first look at Cézanne's *Le Panier de Pommes* or Renoir's *Still Life with Fruit*.

Today there are cameramen and lighting designers that specialize in the shooting of food. Special rigs have been developed that allow a plate to spin at specific speeds so you can see a 360-degree view of undulating meringue. The old days of shooting three one-hour shows in one day are long gone. A simple recipe of Giada making pasta puttanesca could take up to eight hours to film, mostly to capture each individual ingredient being poured, chopped, or minced in tantalizing slow-motion and at multiple angles.

Our obsessions with all things food are not even limited to our own borders anymore. Thanks to food explorers—ranging from the late, acerbic Anthony Bourdain to the *Salt Fat Acid Heat* queen Samin Nosrat, and even to the hilarious and adorable Phil Rosenthal—a world of deliciousness has been brought into our living rooms. Taking us on journeys down the Mekong River for our first taste of duck and banana blossom soup, to the Tsukiji fish market in Tokyo for an auction of a million-dollar tuna, around the alleys of the brilliantly colored Spice Bazaar in Istanbul, and up to the high-end kitchen of Massimo Bottura in Modena, Italy, we can now taste the world with our eyes while lying in the comfort of our own La-Z-Boy. If you're so inclined, a whole new industry of culinary tourism has been created to allow YOU to roam these exotic markets and cook with local chefs. You can go to any city and find a culinary tour guide to take you to places where the locals eat. Want someone to introduce you to duck egg embryos or cockroach-infused soup in Hanoi? I know a guy.

The chefs made famous on Food Network, *Top Chef,* and *Masterchef* are known worldwide. You can have pasta from Jamie Oliver's *Jamie's Italian* in Singapore, or stop by Gordan Ramsey's *Hell's Kitchen* in Dubai, or even try a plate of sushi at *Morimoto* in Mexico City. And don't worry about missing your favorite shows, because whether you're visiting Portugal or Paraguay, you can watch the local version of *Masterchef.* There are over forty countries that have purchased the format and produce their own shows with local chefs.

As we move away from our television sets and become more glued to our devices, there is an ever-evolving place for food there as well. Whether watching the mesmerizing YouTube videos of bread baking or simply sharing a dinner selfie on Instagram, everyone seems to want to know what everyone else is eating. Ambitious Gen Z cooks have flocked to Tik-Tok to become tomorrow's food stars, creating videos that show viewers how to make almost anything in shorthand. With jump cuts of ingredients, sped-up cooking processes, and a myriad of hacks, I now know not only eight different ways to decorate my pie crusts, but I can also make a no-knead bread in a Dutch oven in less than three hours, dirtying only one bowl. If you can imagine it, there's a video and a recipe just waiting for you at the touch of your fingertips. How do you get the conch out of its shell? There's a video for that. Interested in a miso-glazed Chilean sea bass? Well, you can choose from over one hundred different recipes with a simple Google search.

Even during the pandemic, as the restaurant community was reeling from its devastating losses, food television found a way to survive and thrive. Thanks to technology, celebrity chefs can now shoot from their home kitchens with an iPhone, ring light, and a decent mic. Personal assistants have become cameramen and the show goes on. Even Amy Schumer learned how to cook from her chef husband while in quarantine and her show was an instant hit on Food Network. Networks saved millions of dollars while loyal production crews worked on shoestring budgets trying to figure out how to handle onerous safety protocols. Stuck at home, we were baking banana bread and making our own sourdough starters, waiting for a new normal to begin.

Food TV has been our collective salvation. It has offered comfort during a difficult time. It has allowed us to vicariously travel in search of gluttonous fantasies. Now that time has passed, we can once again visit those lands we've only seen through sweeping wide shots, and we can taste those sumptuous dishes experienced in slow-motion close-ups.

What food and travel will look like in the future is still unknown. I can only imagine how it will transform through AI. But I can guarantee that the depiction of food through television—or whatever new device may come—will evolve into something deliciously inspiring.

As I sit here now, home after the three seasons of shows I ended up producing in Singapore, bingeing my way through all fourteen seasons of *The Great British Baking Show*, I find myself pondering whether I should attempt a hot-water-crust-pastry meat pie, or a sticky toffee pudding. I wonder how long it will take me if I cook one dish from each of the cookbooks on my shelves. I worry that the local supermarket will run out of yeast and bread flour again. There's always so much to think about when it comes to food. For now, I think I'll just order take-out.

—*Karen Katz, October 2023*

Acknowledgments

It was a tradition at the end of each production cycle of *Emeril Live* for me to thank the entire crew in what sometimes became an emotional and lengthy speech. At the time, Food Network did not allow for end credits and I felt it was important to acknowledge all the hard work that everyone put into the show. Television production is a team sport and the long hours and challenges we experience are all too often overlooked.

The same could be said about writing this book. As lonely as the process was at times, I have so many people who generously encouraged me and helped to fill in the blanks of my faulty memory. Speaking about memory, as it turns out, it is a cagey thing. While writing this book, I went back to many of the people involved in my story to make sure that I was remembering events correctly. What I found was, if you ask five people about the same incident, you'll get five different versions and perspectives. I did my best to present these stories as truthfully as I experienced them, but I'm sure there are details others might have wished I included—or excluded. In a handful of instances, names have been changed for the sake of privacy, but by and large, a huge thank you to all those mentioned who made these wonderful memories with me.

It takes hundreds of people to make a TV show, and I thank each and every crew member, network colleague, chef, and office husband who stuck with me in the trenches through the years. I wish I could have included all of you in this book, but your omission does not diminish my appreciation for you or your value to me.

To my family, friends, and colleagues who read various drafts of this book, jolted my memory bank, or were cheerleaders throughout this journey, I thank you. I'm sure I left a few people out, so for those, please forgive me. Big hugs to Ellen Abrams and Kevin Baker, Mary and Troy Alexander, Katia Alexander, Harriet Bell, Josh Bider, Petey Brown, Betty and Tom Cammisa, Grayson and Ryan Clapp, Melissa Cook and Amanda Smith, Genie Davis, Heidi Diamond, Cortney Donelson, George Duran, Debra Englander, Susan Feniger, Tyler Florence, Janis Fox and Ric Corn, Dave Garten and Linda Bonder, Alex and Brian Garten, Sue Garten, Christina Grdovic, Christopher and Willa Hallowell, Maddy Jacobs, Barry and Marcie Katz, Paul and Linda Katz, Penelope Koechl, Diane Kolyer, Emeril Lagasse, Daniel Leeds, Jake Levy, Mark Mandelbaum and Desi Minchillo, Charissa Melnik, Sara Moulton, Catherine Mullally, Sarah Moore and Martin Frické, Marie Ostrosky, Chris Patt and Grace Kao, Violet Patt, Scott Preston, Susan Ring, Louise Roe, Jon Rosen, Alison Schary, Martin Schweizer and Setsuko Maruhashi, Mika Schweizer, Mike Schear, Roni and Stuart Selig, Korky Shklair, Bradley Singer, Vicki Steffani and David Brand, JM Stifle, Marc Summers, Linda and Peter Tazzia, Jennifer Todd, Ellen Tomlinson, Gary Ventimiglia, Gabriella and Francesca Verdugo, Vicky and Jackson Wiedmeyer, Carol Yohanan, Joni and Richard Zlotowitz, and all the ladies from La Cañada, Mexico, especially Miriam Garcia who always laughed at my jokes and had a tissue on hand for my tears.

Many heartfelt thanks to Elizabeth Cohen, my book coach in the early days of this project, who was the first to convince me that I had a story to tell. And to Susan Leon, who guided me through the later drafts and convinced me that I might have a story to sell. Mariana Alexander and Alex Laing unknowingly came up with the title, *Getting Sauced*, when they presented me with a handmade birthday card featuring Mariana's dad and me toiling away on our mother sauces. Once I saw it, I knew I had the title for the book. Then the ubertalented Debbie Berne turned it into a wonderful cover design.

Without the help and patience of my agent, Janice Shay, I'm not sure whether this book would have ever been published. My gratitude on so many levels is immeasurable. A million thanks to David Hancock, Addy Normann and the whole team at Morgan James Publishing for taking such good care of this book. And to my publicist, Andrea Burnett, thank you for being such a great champion of this book and helping to get the word out.

A special shout out to my mom, Barbara Katz, who was a great sport as I ripped her cooking skills—or lack thereof—to shreds. She has been a fierce and loyal champion my entire life, and I know she is *kvelling* as she reads this. And for reluctantly allowing me to tell our story, a very big I love you and all that other mushy stuff to my husband, Dan.

About the Author

For the past thirty years, Karen Katz has been a multi-award-winning television executive producer, showrunner, and writer, with over 1,500 hours of programming under her belt. Her work has appeared on Food Network, Discovery Networks, HBO Family, WETA, BBC, NHK, Nickelodeon, Lifetime, PBS, and Fox International. From behind the camera, she has witnessed and taste-tested the delectable creations of some of the world's most beloved  chefs. Her work has taken her from the comfort of her Brooklyn home, which she shares with her husband, to the far reaches of Europe and Asia where she spent her downtime discovering all the culinary delights available. She is a passionate home cook and very proud of her lobster risotto.

For more information, travel stories, and great recipe ideas, visit her website at thekatztales.com or follow her on Instagram @thekatztales or on Facebook at The Katz Tales.

A free ebook edition is available with the purchase of this book.

To claim your free ebook edition:

1. Visit MorganJamesBOGO.com
2. Sign your name CLEARLY in the space
3. Complete the form and submit a photo of the entire copyright page
4. You or your friend can download the ebook to your preferred device

Morgan James
BOGO™

A **FREE** ebook edition is available for you
or a friend with the purchase of this print book.

CLEARLY SIGN YOUR NAME ABOVE

Instructions to claim your free ebook edition:
1. Visit MorganJamesBOGO.com
2. Sign your name CLEARLY in the space above
3. Complete the form and submit a photo
   of this entire page
4. You or your friend can download the ebook
   to your preferred device

Print & Digital Together Forever.

Snap a photo

Free ebook

Read anywhere